The Emergence of a
Euro-American Radical Right

The Emergence of a Euro-American Radical Right

JEFFREY KAPLAN
LEONARD WEINBERG

RUTGERS UNIVERSITY PRESS
New Brunswick, New Jersey, and London

Library of Congress Cataloging-in-Publication Data

Kaplan, Jeffrey, 1954–
    The emergence of a Euro-American radical right / by Jeffrey Kaplan
and Leonard Weinberg.
        p.   cm.
    Includes bibliographical references and index.
    ISBN 0-8135-2563-2 (cloth : alk. paper). — ISBN 0-8135-2564-0
(pbk. : alk. paper)
    1. Right-wing extremists—United States.   2. Right-wing
extremists—Europe, Western.   I. Weinberg, Leonard, 1939– .
II. Title.
HN90.R3K54 1999
303.48'4'094—dc21   98-23536
                                                                                        CIP

British Cataloging-in-Publication data for this book is available from the British Library

Manufactured in the United States of America

Contents

Preface

As with the credits at the end of a motion picture, it is a tradition for academic authors to take a moment to attempt to thank everyone who contributed to the successful completion of a manuscript. Invariably, more names are omitted than included, lest the sheer number of credits become an epic in itself. This is particularly so with a collaborative volume such as this. So, although we will mention but a few to whom the authors owe particular debts of gratitude, we would like to note that there are a considerable number of people who generously shared their time and their ideas and without whom this work would have been impossible. We have in mind the activists, scholars, and observers on both sides of the Atlantic who were interviewed or who contributed ideas and materials after the initial research had been completed. Many of them will be found in the pages that follow, and to all we would like to express our thanks.

We must thank first and foremost the Harry Frank Guggenheim Foundation whose generous award of a 1995 Research Grant to the authors, and whose sponsorship of an academic conference the following year in New Orleans, allowed for a valuable exchange of ideas among a group of American and European scholars specializing in the radical right wing. Additional funding was supplied by a University of Nevada Foundation International Activities Grant awarded to Leonard Weinberg.

We are grateful as well to Professor David Rapoport, Dr. Tore Bjørgo, Frank Cass, and the Norwegian government for their sponsorship of a conference in Berlin in 1995 that served as the true genesis of this project. In the formative period of this research, we owe much to Dr. Heléne Lööw of Stockholm University, without whose forbearance and assistance this project would not have been possible.

It would be an understatement to say that this volume could not have been produced without the guidance of a patient editor, and in this respect, we are indeed fortunate that Martha Heller of Rutgers University Press was an active participant at every stage of the book. We would like to thank as well Dr. Bron Taylor of the University of Wisconsin, Oshkosh for his reading of the manuscript and his sage advice. Finally, our thanks go to Beverly Adams, the secretary of the University of Nevada Reno Political Science Department.

The Emergence of a
Euro-American Radical Right

Introduction

WE HAVE WRITTEN this book from two perspectives but with one purpose. Our purpose is to provide readers with an account of the emergence of a Euro-American radical right movement at the end of the twentieth century. The perspectives or points of view naturally reflect differences in the two writers' disciplines (cultural history and political science) and ways of grappling with racism, anti-Semitism, and right-wing extremism, in general.

Until recently most studies of right-wing extremism in Western Europe and North America have tended to stop at the water's edge.[1] Few studies paid attention to developments on the other side of the Atlantic. For the most part, European analyses have been preoccupied with the problem of fascism, especially its origins, postwar legacy, and contemporary relevance.[2] The study of the American radical right, much like other accounts of the country's political and social life, has tended to stress American exceptionalism. Here studies have paid particular attention to the consequences of slavery, the country's profusion of religious denominations, and immigration experience. If fascism emerged from a peculiar "distortion" of European history brought about by World War I, then the Ku Klux Klan and the Christian Anti-Communist Crusade, for example, reflected things distinctive to America's historical record.[3] To the extent observers perceived transatlantic influences to be at work, the trajectory they detected was always from the "Old World" to the New, as illustrated by the fact that both Hitler and Mussolini won some admirers in the United States during the 1930s.

Another tendency we detect in the study of radical right-wing politics has to do with the fact that few of its journalistic or scholarly analysts have been sympathetic observers. Far from it: given the Holocaust, the legacy of National

Socialism, and so on, many observers, for perfectly normal reasons, have tended to demonize the individuals and movements involved. This outlook has been reinforced by the role of such watchdog organizations as SOS Racisme, the Simon Wiesenthal Center, the Anti-Defamation League, and Klanwatch whose goal is to have members of the public regard the racist and anti-Semitic right with the same affection they would the AIDS epidemic or the outbreak of ebola fever.

In terms of the racist and anti-Semitic right's overall contribution to national or international enmity, the various watchdog organizations' characterization may very well have a point. However, in our view there is a price to be paid for reducing the groups and individuals involved to screen villains straight out of Central Casting. The price is that these efforts distort the reality. The groups and individuals who make up the radical right movement may have embarked on a destructive path, but they are often more complicated, considerably more personable, and far more nuanced than is suggested by the caricatures.

Against this background, the goals we hope to achieve in this volume are as follows. First, we intend to subject contemporary radical right groups active in the wealthy industrialized countries of the Western world, the United States, and Western Europe, to comparative analysis. Accordingly, we point to a variety of transatlantic similarities and differences. Next, we take into consideration forces at work promoting the emergence of a Euro-American radical right, a movement that cuts across national boundaries. Here it seems to us that in an era of "globalization," when, for example, American and European leaders of various political movements, including environmental protection and women's rights, meet with one another on a regular basis, it should not be astonishing that their counterparts on the far right have begun to do likewise. We also note that in an era when computer technology and the social consequences of the Internet have become subjects of intense discussion, that a "cyber-community" of European and American right-wing extremists seems to be developing. We also take note of the fact that at present such American radical right entrepreneurs as William Pierce (author of *The Turner Diaries*) and Gary Rex Lauck exert at least as much influence on their European counterparts as the other way around.

Last, we want the reader to develop a clear understanding of those individuals and groups from which the Euro-American radical right movement is emerging. To do this we introduce some of the key figures by, to a significant extent, letting them speak for themselves. Not only do we introduce some of their major statements taken from the home pages of such web sites as Storm Front and Zundelsite (along with some of their important hard copy documents), but we also report the results of extended interviews one of the writers (Kaplan) had with movement leaders in the United States, Norway, Sweden, and Finland.

In order to achieve our goals, we have divided the book into two parts. Part

One, for which Leonard Weinberg is largely responsible, views the radical right through a wide-angle lens. The point of view of the observer is largely that of an outsider looking in and seeking to report what he has observed. The focus is more on the forest than the trees. Consequently, chapter 1, the "Overview," introduces the reader to the broad social and economic forces at work on both sides of the Atlantic that are promoting the formation of the Euro-American radical right. The second chapter offers a history of earlier attempts, during the 1920s and 1930s for the most part, made by radical right entrepreneurs and fascist movements to promote transatlantic bonding.

Chapter 3 is devoted to a comparative analysis of right-wing extremist activity in Western Europe and North America with a particular emphasis on the current situation. It reviews the major groups and political parties involved along with an account of who their leaders are and what they seem to believe about the world. It also reports biographical data concerning the kinds of people who are attracted to or vote for these groups and parties both in the countries of Western Europe and the United States. Chapter 4, "The Ties that Bind," investigates the evolving transatlantic linkages between the European and American right-wing extremism. Emphasis is placed on the fact that the United States has now become a locale from which racist and anti-Semitic ideas, conveyed in various forms, are sent to European destinations.

Part Two of the book, most of which was written by Jeffrey Kaplan, provides the reader with a close-up view of the Euro-American right. In chapter 5 through 8 the reader will become acquainted with a cast of characters (few of whom are household names), from James Madole, a streetcorner agitator active in the Yorkville section of New York in the years following World War II, to Tommy Rydén, a contemporary Swedish National Socialist, whose political views have led him to promote a Euro-American network of right-wing extremists—a network that is evolving as these words are written.

In addition to Madole, chapter 5 discusses the careers of George Lincoln Rockwell, founder of the American Nazi party; Francis Parker Yockey, founder of the European Liberation Front; and the neo-Nazi Europeans Bruno Ludke, Einar Åberg, and Colin Jordan, who played important roles in the formation of the World Union of National Socialists (WUNS) during the early 1960s. Chapters 6 and 7 are devoted to what might be termed "the ideology of race and place today," that is, they report the efforts, both individual and communal, of anti-Semitic and race-conscious figures on both sides of the Atlantic to establish a new cross-national identity for themselves and their "kinsmen" based on race rather than, or in some cases in addition to, national attachments.

Chapter 8 consists of an extended interview with Tommy Rydén, the young Swedish racial supremacist. With some prompting, Rydén describes his life and how at an early age he came to make contact with American leaders of the

Ku Klux Klan and similar groups. He also reports the price he has had to pay for devoting much of his life to the promotion of the cause.

Throughout these chapters the reader will get some sense of the ideas, some religious others secular, that are driving the formation of a Euro-American radical right. The overall obsession is with the role of Jews in the Western world in general and in the United States in particular. The rhetoric typically abounds with references to the fantasy concept of ZOG (the Zionist Occupation Government), an Israel-centered Jewish conspiracy now in effective control of governments in Scandinavia and the United States. Holocaust denial serves as another important transatlantic discourse. As the reader will see, the overriding anti-Semitism is often accompanied by a veneration of Nazi Germany and a profound fear that the race it sought to champion is in imminent danger of extinction.

Part One   The Forest

Chapter 1   Overview

THE COUNTRIES OF Western Europe and the United States are experiencing a
new and potentially important cultural and political development: the appearance of a right-wing extremist movement that transcends national boundaries
and, indeed, crosses the Atlantic with as much ease as do E-mail messages on
the Internet. At first glance such a development seems very unlikely. Unlike
the now largely defunct communist movement with its appeal to "proletarian
internationalism," we normally associate right-wing politics, and radical right-
wing politics especially, with intense nationalism and, not uncommonly, xenophobia. If Marx and Engels appealed to "workers of the world," Mussolini asserted
that Fascism was not for export. This may be true, but consider the following.

In Sweden there is presently the White Aryan Resistance, known by its
Swedish acronym VAM (Vitt Arikst Motstånd), a group named after Tom
Metzger's California-based racial supremacist organization. Their enemies are also
identical. As in the United States so too in Sweden, leaders of VAM see a Jewish conspiracy, the Zionist Occupation Government (ZOG), manipulating events
in Washington and Stockholm. Sweden is hardly alone. Thanks to well-wishers
in the United States, the Federal Republic of Germany now has some Ku
Klux Klan groups,[1] a development it shares with Great Britain and other members of the European Union. In a widely read article in *The New Yorker*, Ingo
Hasselbach, a former German neo-Nazi, describes how he and his associates were
supplied with propaganda by Gary Rex Lauck, of Lincoln, Nebraska, and the
Canadian, Ernst Zundel. While the latter individuals have smuggled "hard copy"
neo-Nazi material into Germany (where its publication is illegal), there is now
a growing "cyber-community" of right-wing radicals that links Europe and
America. As Les Back of the University of London reports, computer bulletin

boards and World Wide Web sites located in the United States are now used by Europeans.[2]

There are also examples of right-wing influences crossing the Atlantic from east to west. The racist skinhead scene, a conspicuous but not numerous one in the United States,[3] is of British origin. *White Patriot* ("Worldwide Voice of the Aryan People"), published by the Arkansas Klansman Thom Robb, uses a Celtic cross on its masthead. The *National Socialist Vanguard Report* of The Dalles, Oregon, offers its readers a "Hail Victory!" salutation as it chronicles white racist activities in various parts of the world. Likewise, *Calling Our Nation*, the Aryan Nation's periodical, appeals for "Teutonic Unity" and includes among its staff members Tim Bishop, "Col-Gruppenführer" and C. W. Nelson, "Maj-Sturmbann-fuhrer." This is to say that the use of symbols and slogans drawn from the European Nazi experience are quite common among radical right groups presently operating in the United States.[4] There are also personal interactions to report. Manfred Roeder, the long-time German neo-Nazi leader, has not only contributed a number of articles over the years to *Calling Our Nation* ("The Greatest Revolutionary of All Time"—devoted to Hitler), but attended various Aryan Nations meetings. Comparing Hitler's mission to that of Christ, Roeder states:

> Hitler had solved all of the pressing problems of our time. He and his work were destroyed because his opponents did not want to accept that some of his ideas were universal and valid for every man. He was destroyed because his enemies succeeded in the use of the superpower USA for their purposes, just like the Pharisees succeeded in using the superpower Rome to crush the idea of Jesus 2000 years ago.[5]

In yet another illustration, the Institute for Historical Review, a Los Angeles-area organization committed to denying the reality of the Holocaust, routinely attracts "revisionist" Europeans to its meetings in the United States.

Our purpose in using these examples is not to generalize based upon a handful of illustrations, but to call the reader's attention to what we regard as a significant trend in contemporary extreme right-wing politics. However, before we can hope to analyze this trend and the various developments associated with it, we need to clarify our terms. We need to define what we have in mind when employing such terms as right-wing radicalism and right-wing extremism. This task is particularly important given the transatlantic nature of our inquiry and the difficulties associated with "stretching" social and political concepts from one context to another.

What Is Right?

A case could be made for using such terms as "neo-Nazi" or "neo-fascist" in seeking to identify the phenomenon in which we are interested. The concepts are vivid, calling to mind the German and Italian dictatorships of the interwar period, and are of some relevance. There are, after all, some groups and a handful of minor political parties in Western Europe that wish to put an end to their countries' democratic institutions and re-create dictatorships from the earlier era. On the other hand, there is the tendency for the terms neo-Nazi and neo-fascist to be used indiscriminately, often as epithets, by political observers intent on delegitimating the views of those to whom they apply the terms. Even or perhaps especially for scholars these terms cause problems. Thus, the Italian writer Umberto Eco has recently written a description of "Ur-Fascism" or "Eternal Fascism," the enduring relevance of fascist values in societies over the decades; while Piero Ignazi, another contemporary Italian scholar, who, like Eco, teaches at the University of Bologna, argues that the Nazi and fascist movements were really products of the stresses of industrial-era Europe, movements largely out of place in a postindustrial or postmodern landscape.[6]

There is also the problem that many of the right-wing groups and organizations active today are not opposed in principle to constitutional democracy and do not always support the idea of a strong state with which Nazism and fascism are routinely associated. Instead some, particularly ones active in the United States, wish to virtually dismantle the state and replace it with local-level institutions believed to be both less threatening to their values and more in the letter and spirit of the Constitution and of the early American Republic. So, despite the occasional use of Nazi paraphernalia and laudatory references to the achievements of the Third Reich expressed by some of the groups involved, we think the terms neo-Nazi and neo-fascist are at once too emotion-laden and too narrow to capture the collection of individuals, groups, and organizations with which we are concerned.

In the United States such watchdog organizations as the Anti-Defamation League and Klanwatch use the term "hate group" in identifying many of the organizations under discussion.[7] As with neo-Nazi and neo-fascist so too in this instance the term is typically used sententiously by observers who wish to attack rather than analyze the groups involved. If we wished to study the operations of groups much of whose time is given over to the expression of hatred we would have to investigate various groups on the far left as well as ones on the right.

An alternative approach to the problem of definition would be to rely upon those involved to identify themselves. The virtue of relying on self-definition is that those involved may have a better sense of what they are about than their, not uncommonly, hostile observers. Accordingly, if we follow this strategy the term "the movement" seems to enjoy widespread use at least in the United States.[8] In this country members of various KKK, Christian Identity, and neo-Nazi groups tend to refer to the movement when talking about all organizations committed to the causes of anti-Semitism and white racial supremacy. The term has the additional benefit of conveying some sense of community, of individuals who self-consciously share a common outlook on the world. In fact, the movement may refer to a common subculture, a collectivity of individuals who are drawn to the same books, magazines, movies, music, symbols, historical experiences, religious and political figures, and who view the present and future with a single, often millennial, perspective.

We do not wish to discard the movement, but we see it as having certain limitations. For one, not all the groups and organizations with which we are concerned are devoted to the cause of racial supremacy, at least not in a narrow sense. And for another, while the movement is often used by European activists, it is often prefaced by such adjectives as nationalist, white nationalist, or racial. For purposes of analysis, we prefer to think of the movement as more a question than an answer. In effect this book is devoted to answering the question of whether or not or the extent to which just such a Euro-American entity is now emerging. For example, as national identities in Western Europe erode as the result of European integration or the changing ethnic composition of the countries involved, are certain segments of the population now susceptible to the creation of a new form of identity that cuts across national boundaries and indeed spans the Atlantic?

But in order to address the question we first need to define the characteristics that such a movement might exhibit. Here we think it is essential to discuss the radical right and right-wing extremism.

The term radical right is of American origin having come into use during the 1950s as part of an effort by scholars to understand the McCarthy experience and the anticommunist crusades of the postwar era.[9] The concept crossed the Atlantic, via the social sciences, and has come to enjoy wide usage in various Western European countries. Illustratively, by the 1980s the sociologist Franco Ferraresi published *La destra radicale*, a collection of essays about strongly anticommunist right-wing groups in Italy seeking to topple that country's democracy by paramilitary and conspiratorial means.[10] And more recently the English scholar Geoffrey Roberts has written about "Right-wing Radicalism in the New Germany."[11] "Right-wing extremism," on the other hand, is European in origin. This concept must also be seen in the context of the postwar era. In the immediate aftermath of the war, the inclination of scholars was to apply the labels "neo-fascist" and, less commonly, "neo-Nazi" to groups and parties whose memberships and world-views could be traced to the interwar dictatorships. As these nostalgic organizations came to be superseded by newer postwar ones, such as the antitax Poujadists in France and Alfred Von Thadden's National Democratic party in West Germany, observers, particularly German scholars, became inclined to replace the old terms with the more generic concept of right-wing extremism.[12] As with right-wing radicalism so too in this case, the concept has been able to cross the Atlantic. Thus the prize-winning American volume by Seymour Martin Lipset and Earl Raab, *The Politics of Unreason*, is subtitled *Right-Wing Extremism in America, 1790–1970*. In terms of frequency of usage, the latter term seems to have triumphed over the former. No matter their origins, we are still left with the problem of indicating what we mean when we refer to right-wing radicalism and right-wing extremism. The best way of solving the problem is to distinguish between style and substance; in other words, we think it best to treat radicalism and extremism as an approach, a way of acting, while applying the term right wing to a particular content.

Lipset and Raab identify extremism with an outlook, one that is built around "monism" and "moralism."[13] Extremists are people who reject ambiguity, who believe there is only one right answer to any question, which they possess, and believe, further, that those expressing various "wrong" answers are not merely misguided but evil in some sense. Accordingly, extremists tend to reject ambiguity, the world is black and white with no shades of gray. Given this view, they identify compromise not as a necessary part of life in complex situations, but as betrayal and a sign of moral weakness. It follows, given the nature of democratic politics in pluralist societies, that almost all politicians will be thought cowardly and treasonous. Extremists also have a tendency to display what the American historian Richard Hofstadter referred to as a "paranoid style."[14] Hofstadter did not believe such people were paranoid in a clinical sense; rather he thought extremists had a general tendency to view the world in conspiratorial terms. Negative events do not simply happen as the result of accident or incompetence. Rather, they are the consequence of some comprehensive conspiracy. Indeed extremists tend to explain most phenomena by reference to conspiracy. For example, in the United States there is apparently widespread belief in a "New World Order" conspiracy, one designed to turn the country over to the United Nations or international bankers or both.[15]

In addition to outlook there is also the matter of behavior. Given the view of the world described above it is hardly surprising that extremists or radicals in the political realm should not feel themselves bound by the democratic rules of the game. This is not to say that groups or political parties may not operate under such rules when it appears expedient or convenient. But their adherence to those rules is usually based on a judgment of tactical advantage more than principle. Since they regard those with whom they disagree as enemies, extremists operating in democratic and constitutional settings will not feel constrained from using violence and various types of extralegal "dirty tricks" directed against both the state and private groups in order to achieve their objectives. If public life is defined as a fundamental conflict between good and evil, then any actions taken in the name of "goodness" are by definition, good.

If this is the style, what is the substance? Or, what do we mean by the term right wing or rightist in the 1990s?

In earlier times, rightism tended to be defined in terms of a defense of the social and political status quo against groups seeking to transform it. In nineteenth-century Europe the right typically defended monarchy against those forces seeking to create a republic. During the first decades of the twentieth century the right was identified with the defense of the state, republic or otherwise, against those out to achieve some form of socialist order. An alternative, though not entirely separable, version of right wing involves social class. That is, since the French Revolution right wing came to be associated with the interests of the upper classes, based on birth or wealth, as against the left-wing advocates of the lower classes.[16] Whatever their virtues in an earlier time, these conceptions of right seem much less appropriate for the 1990s. After all, many of the groups and organizations with which this book is concerned are composed or supported by individuals drawn from the lower strata of society and their goals often encompass more an attack on than a defense of the status quo. For these reasons we think it makes sense to define right wing in terms of a particular set of beliefs.

Foremost among these is a belief in inequality. Either at the individual or collective level, rightists believe that humans not only differ from one another in very important ways, but these differences may be ranked from high to low. Subsidiary beliefs follow from this fundamental perception.[17] Racism defined either in biological or cultural terms, is a widely articulated right-wing understanding. Another belief common to the contemporary right-wing perspective is a particular form of nationalism, one that "strives for internal homogenization: only people belonging to the X-nation have the right to live within the borders of state X. . . . On the other hand, there is the drive for external exclusiveness: that is, state X needs to have all people belonging to the X-nation within its borders."[18] Xenophobia is commonly related to this form of integral nationalism. The fear of and hostility toward foreigners (Foreigners Out!) is obviously a common focus of current right-wing activity in Western Europe and the United States.[19]

In addition to these core beliefs, observers in various countries have linked the contemporary right with a number of negative or "anti" viewpoints. Until the collapse of the Soviet Union in 1991, anticommunism and anti-Marxism were essential components of the rightist world-view. Anti-Semitism (a special form of racism), including Holocaust denial, continues as a widespread theme.[20] And for some, though not all, of the groups and organizations with which we are concerned there is another belief of extreme importance. We refer to the view that the world, as it approaches the year 2000, is on the verge of a catastrophe of biblical significance. This millennial view is especially important for those rightists whose social and political understandings have been shaped by certain religious texts; the Book of Revelation seems to be of particular importance.

We will assume from this point that the right-wing extremism or right-wing radicalism prevalent in the Western world consists of the procedural and substantive beliefs and traits outlined above. The next question with which we are concerned involves their location or setting in a social and political sense. At this point it makes sense to turn our attention, once again, to the concept of movement and ask ourselves questions about the characteristics of the radical right movement.

New Movements

Apparently unknown to right-wing extremists, even those who think of themselves as belonging to the movement, there is a substantial body of social science literature devoted to the nature of social and political movements. We do not propose to review this massive body of writing.[21] Rather, we want to use some of it in order to provide a framework for our discussion of an emerging Euro-American radical right movement.

First, movements, according to Sidney Tarrow, are "collective challenges by people with common purposes and solidarity in sustained interaction with elites, opponents and authorities."[22] What Tarrow is telling us is, approximately, as follows. Social and political movements represent a form of collective action stimulated by a combination of grievance and opportunity. Movements use action, oftentimes direct action, in order to challenge those with whom they are in conflict. Opponents may include the authorities (e.g., government agencies), economic and social elites and other groups and movements whose values they find in conflict with their own (e.g., skinheads versus long-hairs during the 1970s in Britain).[23] In addition to sharing a common purpose based upon a grievance, movements coalesce when there is a sense of solidarity, when participants, or potential participants, come to the realization they share a common concern. "Movement entrepreneurs" are capable of promoting the sense of common concern and then mobilizing members to direct action on its behalf.

Further, if the conditions are right, if the structure of opportunity is appropriate (e.g., if the authorities do not know how to respond to the challenge), there is a tendency for social and political movements to develop a certain momentum. That is, the size of the movement will grow; it will spread to wider segments of the population and diffuse geographically to areas far from its original locale. Its "action repertoire" will also expand; new and different forms of direct action will be devised for use against appropriate targets.

Much of the attention researchers have focused on movements over the last few decades has been directed at "new social movements." The term has been applied to the array of movements that emerged from the turbulent politics of the 1960s in the Western democracies. In particular, the research and discussion has been devoted to such phenomena as the peace movement, anti-nuclear power movement, environmental movement, civil rights and gay rights movement, and the women's movement.[24] Almost without exception these new social movements were depicted as leftist or "new leftist" in orientation. But unlike leftist movements of an earlier era, the trade union movement in particular, the new ones seemed less concerned with material, bread and butter kinds of issues and more with a broad social agenda of goals, for example, environmental protection, nuclear disarmament, and the like, relevant to society as a whole.

Of particular interest to us is the fact that these new social and political movements seem to have had little difficulty in spreading from one continent to another, from North America to Western Europe or vice versa. For instance, from the mid-to-late 1960s on, the student movement committed to ending American participation in the Vietnam War was able to carry out common forms of direct action on both sides of the Atlantic. Thus, in the spring of 1968 as French students shut down their country's universities, University of California students expressed their solidarity by shutting down traffic along Telegraph Avenue in Berkeley. Opponents of racial segregation in the American South staged sit-ins at lunch counters and other segregated facilities. Shortly thereafter American students carried out similar sit-ins at administration buildings at universities in different parts of the United States as a way of expressing their opposition to the conflict in Southeast Asia. Later still, Italian students (some of whom painted their faces and called themselves "Metropolitan Indians") staged their own sit-ins at universities in Rome, Milan, and Turin.

In more recent years Americans and Europeans concerned about the degradation of the physical environment have coalesced around such international groups as Greenpeace and have undertaken actions designed to call air and water pollution problems to the public's attention. Likewise, something amounting to a Euro-American movement has developed over the protection of human rights, with Amnesty International taking the lead. And more recently still, the AIDS epidemic has engendered an international movement committed to pressuring governments on both sides of the Atlantic into elevating their support for AIDS research and reducing the sufferings of those already afflicted by the disease.

The Euro-American Condition

If we ask ourselves why these particular causes appear to have stimulated new social and political movements that mobilized a Euro-American base of support, the most obvious answer is that they represented responses to a common strain or a similar set of conditions, ones prevalent on both sides of the Atlantic. These factors were the necessary though not the sufficient conditions for the emergence of such movements. Other elements, notably a relatively permissive political environment (one with abundant opportunities for direct action and a high threshold for repression), access to modern forms of international mass communication along with the presence of energetic and skillful (at organizing and gaining attention) movement entrepreneurs seem to have been essential ingredients. In their absence it seems unlikely that these Euro-American movements would have emerged.

Are these same elements present with respect to a Euro-American radical right? We believe this question should be answered in the affirmative. We now propose to explain why.

First, the United States and the members of the European Union are relatively rich countries with aging populations surrounded by poor ones with largely youthful populations. These circumstances produce strong pressures for immigration, legal and illegal, as citizens of Mexico, Haiti, Algeria, Turkey, Romania and so on, seek to make better lives for themselves by finding jobs in the lands of the rich. Or, as other writers put it: "The growing income gap, as well as high rates of population growth in Third World countries, has encouraged migration towards the developed world. The communications revolution has resulted in a broad awareness of opportunities in Western Europe, and relatively easy, fast transportation has increased access. The force of these trends has been accentuated by war, the breakdown of order and the oppression and expulsion of ethnic minorities in the Third World."[25] This observation intended for Western European circumstances certainly applies to American ones as well.

On both sides of the Atlantic, the growing presence of third world immigrants has produced xenophobic reactions. On occasion, members of long-dominant ethnic groups, particularly youthful ones, have responded with violence to the appearance of "others" whose language and life-styles seem alien and threatening.[26] As we shall see, radical right groups and political parties in both the United States and Western Europe have sought to take advantage of these antiforeigner sentiments.

Next, the weakening of traditional family bonds is another common condition which plays a role in right-wing extremist activity. American observers are often so preoccupied with growing rates of divorce, illegitimacy, and female-headed households in the United States that they sometimes forget that similar trends have also been at work in most of the other advanced industrialized democracies as well.[27] The absence of fathers, or indeed the absence of stable family life in general, takes on political relevance when we consider the fact that this condition often yields large pools of directionless adolescents or postadolescents in search of personal identities, excitement, and, sometimes, political meaning for their discontents. Readers will surely not be astonished when we report that the members of various radical right aggregations—racist youth gangs, skinheads, Aryan warriors, neo-Nazis—active in both Europe and America, Berlin and Stockholm and Detroit, are drawn from precisely these pools of alienated young people.[28]

A third condition common to Western European and American societies concerns the changing nature of economic life. In both cases modern business firms confronted by competition from Japanese and other Asian-based corporations have sought to cut labor costs by having their products manufactured "offshore" in low-wage Third World countries. According to Robert Reich, the structural changes at work in the new global economy are producing very distinct categories of winners and losers within the Western democracies. As Reich sees it, the future belongs to highly educated and mentally nimble "symbolic analysts." Highly creative and organizationally adaptable, such individuals constitute the principal beneficiaries of the new global economy.[29] Not so fortunate are individuals holding "routine production jobs." Their work, typically in the manufacturing sector, is gradually being shifted to low-wage third world countries or being done by third world immigrants, legal and illegal, who have made their way to the U.S. or one of the prosperous E.U. countries. Of course, as Reich reports, there continue to be an abundance of jobs involving "routine in-person services." These include such low-wage service sector jobs as food server, cleaner, cashier, practical nurse, attendant, bank teller and so on. But there is also competition for these posts with third world immigrants and at least some of the jobs may be replaced by automated machines (i.e., the ATM machine). All these events are unfolding as governments are under increasing pressure to shrink public spending on "safety net" programs intended to soften the impact of the dislocations in the labor market they have caused.

In earlier times we might conclude that these economic conditions would grow increasingly ripe for some form of left-wing protest and mobilization. Present circumstances, however, work against this result. In most of the Western world, Marxist ideas have been discredited as a result of events in Eastern Europe and the former-Soviet Union. Market economics has triumphed. Trade union organizations have declined in membership and influence. Left-wing political parties ranging from the Spanish Socialists and German Social Democrats to the liberal wing of the Democratic party in the United States have fallen on hard times and in some instances, as with the Italian Socialists, have been overtaken by catastrophic financial scandals.[30] All this in a situation where large numbers of people of working-class or blue collar background would seem highly vulnerable to political appeals demanding radical change.

Under these circumstances parties of the extreme right may offer attractive alternatives for some. Given what we know about the susceptibility of the less educated and less economically secure to racist and xenophobic appeals, it is perhaps not surprising to discover that in France Jean-Marie LePen's highly xenophobic National Front has become the first party of the French working class.[31] A political space once dominated by leftist organizations of a socialist, social democratic, or even communist bent has become vulnerable to penetration by forces of the extreme right.

Along with these social and economic developments there is also some attitudinal evidence that pushes us further down the same road. Specifically, the public in most of the Western democracies has become progressively more disenchanted with the performance of their countries' democratic institutions in recent years.[32] Public confidence in the conventional spectrum of political parties has eroded along with, and correlatively, voter turnout at most national elections. Even at the elite level, the rush of self-confidence that followed the astonishingly rapid collapse of communist regimes in Eastern Europe and the subsequent disintegration of the Soviet Union has been replaced by a detectable malaise. The possibility that the dialectic of history has come to end with the triumph of democracy seems less convincing now than when it was first expressed. Furthermore, we are now far enough away from World War II and the experience of fascist and Nazi dictatorships for memories to have faded and for the relevant generation to have largely passed from the scene. Thus the remarkable nostalgia of disaffected youth—a disaffection often fed by movement elders—for such authoritarian figures as Stalin in Russia and Hitler in Germany, and indeed, throughout the Western world.[33] The antidotes may be wearing off with uncertain consequences.

We should also consider the fact that the contemporary radical right in Europe and America represents in part what the Italian political scientist Piero Ignazi has referred to as a "silent counter-revolution." Ignazi believes that the kinds of right-wing forces to have emerged in recent years are to a considerable extent reactions against the new social movements and their values.[34] In our terms, the appearance of women's, environmental, peace movements, and so on in the Western democracies itself became a condition promoting right-wing extremist activity in the countries where such "new" movements achieved widespread public visibility.

All this is to say that we have identified a number of social, economic, and political conditions common to American and Western European societies that make them vulnerable to a revival of right-wing extremism. We have not shown, as yet, how these commonalties are being transformed into a Euro-American radical right movement. It is to this task that we now turn our attention.

Locating the Movement

We devote the balance of this book to an account of the new Euro-American radical right movement. At this point what we wish to do is simply outline the major characteristics of this movement and then show by what means they are related to each other, how the parts fit together to make a whole.

First, if there is a Euro-American radical right, there is a Euro-American radical right culture or more appropriately a subculture. It consists of a shared set of myths, symbols, beliefs, and forms of artistic expression that set it apart on a transnational basis from other subcultures. There is some sense of mutual recognition. For instance, skinhead groups on both sides of the Atlantic share similar tastes in music and dress almost irrespective of the countries they inhabit. Another illustration: in Germany neo-Nazi groups make use of the fiery cross, a KKK symbol, because the public display of the swastika is banned.

Second, related to culture, is the matter of collective identity. Clearly vast numbers of people think of themselves as Americans, Austrians, Germans, Italians, and so on. But it is also possible to develop additional identities. Thus, AIDS sufferers having different national identities may also think of themselves as belonging to the former group, one with shared interests and shared fate. More commonly, this addition of international identities involves ethnicity. Thus America abounds with groups whose origins are European and many of whose members retain a strong sense of attachment to Finland, Ireland, Italy, Poland, and so on.

The Euro-American radical right movement is one whose followers are in the process of developing a common identity based upon a shared sense of racial solidarity, that is, as self-defined whites, "Aryans" or "Teutons," besieged by the threatening masses from the third world and of the prospect of multiracial societies. Or, if racialism is not the sole basis for the establishment of such an identity, cultural affinity and a sense of common historical experience and a shared ultimate destiny form yet other pillars of this shared identity.[35] The latter, in European terms is often expressed as a defense of Western civilization or Christian civilization threatened by a new Muslim invasion from the East. American radical rightists feel equally vulnerable to the perceived unchecked immigration from the countries of Latin and South America, Asia, ad infinitum. And just as American and European university students developed some sense of collective identity during the Vietnam era by holding common international days for peace rallies, so too in recent years Rudolf Hess Day has become an international event for right-wing extremists on both sides of the Atlantic.[36]

As has been true for the new social movements so too in the case of the Euro-American radical right, the capacity of the movement to grow and spread often depends upon the abilities of those individuals whom Tarrow refers to as movement entrepreneurs. The emerging Euro-American radical right does not lack such enterprising individuals. We will describe their highly important activities in some detail at a later point in this study. At this introductory stage of our inquiry it should be sufficient to mention a few figures and take some notice of the kinds of activities in which they seem to specialize.

The English historian of Nazi Germany David Irving is an interesting case of intellectual entrepreneurship. In his initial writings on the subject Irving did not deny the Holocaust had occurred. He wrote, however, that Hitler had not ordered the Jews to be killed. That decision, he maintained, was made and implemented by Himmler and other radical elements in the Nazi hierarchy. According to the American historian Deborah Lipstadt, though, Irving became converted to the cause during the 1980s and now conducts seminars and goes on lecture tours in Europe and throughout the United States to promote the Holocaust denial claim. In this connection Irving and the English Clarendon Club he organized have developed ties to the Los Angeles–based Institute for Historical Review, the most visible Holocaust denial organization in the United States.[37]

In a somewhat different métier, there is the case of the late Ian Stuart Donaldson who, until his death in 1993, led a far-right English skinhead band known as Skrewdriver. Donaldson was the pioneer of racist White Noise whose music and lyrics celebrated violence and white supremacy. The organization he founded, named for Skrewdriver's first album, *Blood and Honour*, continues but has had some difficulties in carrying on Skrewdriver's legacy.[38] Ian Stuart's political efforts were aimed at promoting a skinhead or neo-Nazi youth subculture that spanned the Atlantic.

Other examples come to mind. Among a long list of Americans there is the case of Gary Rex Lauck of Lincoln, Nebraska. Now under arrest in Germany, Lauck for many years was one of the principal suppliers of Nazi propaganda in the Federal Republic. Because the publication of such material is illegal in Germany, German neo-Nazis became dependent on Lauck whose racist and anti-Semitic writings enjoyed First Amendment protection in the United States.[39] Then there is Dennis Mahon, an American former Ku Klux Klansman now associated with the White Aryan Resistance (WAR). In addition to promoting the cause of white working-class revolution in the United States, Mahon has made sojourns to Western and Eastern Europe in order to promote the formation of the KKK and other racist aggregations.[40]

As these examples suggest, the activities of movement entrepreneurs often encompass two operations: first, the promotion and distribution of movement propaganda and, second, the development of organizational links between the various movement groups and constituencies both at home and abroad. (In some instances, as we shall see, the term "entrepreneur" can be taken quite literally because there are a number of visible movement figures who earn comfortable livings through the sale and distribution of radical right propaganda, including CD's, video cassettes, books, magazines, pamphlets, and paraphernalia). Further, as in the economic realm so too in the political, entrepreneurs often compete with one another for a share of the market, with one or another entrepreneur challenging the value or authenticity of the other's goods.

We believe the radical right movement should also be seen as consisting of a large number of extreme right groups (ERGs) and a variety of extreme right political parties (ERPs). In Europe and America there are literally hundreds of ERGs that conform to our definition of radical right.[41] It is also true that Western Europe abounds with ERPs. One recent compilation lists a total of 40 that were active during 1994.[42] Even in the two-party-dominated American system ERPs often contest elections. The Populist party and the Independent Americans are two recent examples.

One obvious way in which the ERGs and ERPs differ involves their size. Some ERGs consist of no more than a handful of members; such appears to be the case with the SS Action League in the United States or the Norwegian Boot Boys for example. On the other hand, there are ERGs on both sides of the Atlantic whose membership runs into the hundreds or higher; the Ethnically Loyal Extra-Parliamentary Opposition (VAPO) in Austria and at least in aggregate, the assortment of KKK organizations in the United States come to mind.

The same observation applies to the ERPs. In Austria the right-wing Freedom party of Jorg Haider was able to capture slightly less than 20 percent of the vote at the 1995 national elections.[43] The British National party, on the other hand, has not succeeded as yet in electing any of its candidates to the House of Commons, although it has had some limited success in electing members to local councils.

Other sources of variation among the ERGs and ERPs could be introduced, indeed they will inform our later discussion of the politics of right-wing extremism. But in this introductory part of our inquiry we want to pay particular attention to the scope of their operations. More specifically, some ERGs and ERPs are exclusively domestic in character, displaying no ties or linkages to groups outside their country's borders. The American Militia of Montana (MOM) offers an example, although MOM has a web page accessible to anyone in the world, and it would be surprising if their materials were not purchased in some other countries—if only for curiosity value.

There are other groups and parties, though, that should be identified as transnational because they operate in or bond with groups and parties in other European countries. ERP deputies in the European Parliament at Strasbourg belong to the same parliamentary group for example. Finally, there are transcontinental groups, ERGs almost exclusively, that have relationships that are truly Euro-American or even have global aspirations. They are the radical right equivalents of Greenpeace and Amnesty International. By way of illustration, there are the Storm Network and the recently reactivated Church of the Creator ERGs in Sweden. The latter was inspired by and has ties to the late Ben Klassen's neo-pagan, racist religious group in the United States, while the former neo-Nazi aggregation has developed links with the Afrikaner Resistance Movement in South Africa. The World Anti-Communist League of cold war vintage was able to cement links between ERGs on a worldwide basis with representatives from Asia, Latin America, Western Europe, and the United States interacting with one another on a regular basis.[44]

What are the types of relationships that link together the ERGs and ERPs belonging to the Euro-American radical right movement? In our view these link-ages vary in proximity.[45] In some cases the linkage is simply inspirational. There is no necessity for personal interaction between members of ERGs located in Western Europe and the United States. Neo-Nazi aggregations in the United States may be inspired by or seek to emulate comparable ERGs in Germany and Austria. Such American groups may use the paraphernalia and slogans of neo-Nazism, they may even celebrate Hitler's birthday or memorialize Rudolf Hess on the appropriate date, but their members lack personal contact with their European counterparts.[46] But in addition to this type of distant relationship, we intend to discuss an abundance of cases in which there is some form of personal interaction. The latter form may be limited to computerized encounters over the Internet. Presently Germany has its Thule Network and Canada and the United States have such World Wide Web sites as Stormfront and Ernst Zundel's Voice of Freedom site.[47] In this growing Euro-American "cyber community," radi-cal rightists are able to exchange ideas and even develop some sense of camara-derie without ever coming into face-to-face contact. But we also intend to explore instances in which there is such contact. Commonly, movement entre-preneurs like Gary Rex Lauck take it upon themselves to meet and discuss so-cial and political conditions with ERG leaders on the other side of the Atlantic. Their exchanges often take the form of transcontinental bridge building and or-ganization construction. Thus, in 1990 James Farrands, imperial wizard of the United Klans of North Carolina, aided in the formation of the British Ku Klux Klan.[48] Finally, there is a form of personal and organizational interaction that bears some resemblance to the franchising operations of a multinational corpo-ration. This is a situation where there is a degree of control and dominance at work. Not only is there personal interaction between individuals belonging to ERGs in different countries, transnational or transcontinental, but there is a sense that the ERGs are really part of the same multinational religious or political net-work. For example: the German-Austrian Institute for Contemporary History (DOIZ) is the Austrian branch of the Institute for Historical Review, the California-based group committed to Holocaust denial operations. Or, to cite another instance, during the 1980s the mercurial movement entrepreneur Lyndon LaRouche, an American and repeated candidate for president of the United States, created the European Labor party, an ERP with offices in Wiesbaden, Paris and other Western European cities, in order to promote his conspiratorial worldview.[49]

Conclusion

In this overview we have called the skeptical reader's attention to the fact there now exists a set of conditions common to America and Western Europe that draws right-wing radicals on both sides of the Atlantic closer together. These conditions, based upon demographic pressures, social dislocations, and economic change, have set the stage for the appearance of a new and troubling Euro-American radical right movement. This movement has been promoted by individual right-wing entrepreneurs who have taken advantage of the situation to forge ties between European and American radical right groups. We believe that to a significant extent these ties involve the formation of a common racial identity (unless Aryans, Nordics or Teutons recognize the danger and act accordingly, they face extinction). Given this existential discourse, the potential for violence seems considerable.

Despite the fact that the contemporary Euro-American radical right movement has emerged in response to circumstances and possibilities (e.g., the Internet) distinct to the end of the twentieth century, it is not unprecedented. Behind the movement there is a history, one rooted in the two decades between the end of World War I and the outbreak of World War II. And it is to this earlier experience that we now turn.

Chapter 2

The Euro-American Radical Right

A Brief History

Efforts by Americans and Europeans to create a Euro-American radical right did not begin in the 1980s. Rather, these undertakings date from the 1920s and 1930s. After World War II, which brought overwhelming defeat and discredit to the fascist and Nazi ideas on which they were largely based, there was a period of almost two decades before there was a major resumption of these activities. In this chapter we tell the story of the interwar period and then comment briefly on more recent developments, ones having mainly to do with the World Anti-Communist League and the World Union of National Socialists.

Until the First World War, and even during the 1920s, right-wing extremist movements in the United States were animated largely by nativist ideas. Such nineteenth-century movements as the Know Nothings, the American party, and the American Protective Association appealed to native-born Protestants fearful that new waves of European immigrants would bring ways of living along with religious and political views that would profoundly disrupt American society. Catholics and later Jews were suspected of being conspiratorially minded bearers of un-American ideas. For nativists, foreigners from Europe were identified with virtually every failing detected in American society. From excessive alcohol consumption to the diffusion of "white slavery" and the promotion of anarchist violence, radical rightists laid the blame on those recently arrived from across the Atlantic.[1] In their minds real Americans should have nothing to do with these alien imports.

Approximately the same thing may be said of the Ku Klux Klan. The original Klan, active in the Reconstruction-era South, was a secretive, vigilante organization devoted largely to racial repression. But the Klan, reborn at Stone Mountain, Georgia in 1915 and which became a mass movement throughout the country during the 1920s, had a strongly nativist Protestant agenda much like its nineteenth-century predecessors.[2] The anti-immigrant and anti-Catholic themes became so pronounced during the 1928 Democratic presidential election campaign of Al Smith that the journalist H. L. Mencken began referring to the Klan as the "secular wing of the Methodist church" in certain parts of the country. And the Klan's anti-Semitism became so pronounced that it even evoked some admiration in Weimar Germany. Thus, in 1923, the Reverend Otto Strohschein, a naturalized American and Klansman, returned to his native Berlin in order to form the German Order of the Fiery Cross, an organization with which he intended to use Klan-like techniques to rid the country of Jews.[3]

European Influences

Despite the Klan's nativist appeals over the decade, the 1920s also witnessed some signs that right-wing extremists might become amenable to ideas whose origins were European. After World War I, and especially in the aftermath of the Russian Revolution, the United States went through a "red scare." In 1919–1920 government officials, politicians, and journalists throughout the country became publicly fearful that communists, anarchists, anarcho-syndicalists, or various combinations thereof intended to copy Lenin's achievements and make a violent revolution. Federal, state, and local officials along with private employers used various forms of repression, legal and extralegal, to defeat this largely imaginary threat.[4] It was in the context of this antirevolutionary and anticommunist atmosphere that we may observe the appearance of radical right ideas of European origin. Communism represented a global threat, not simply a threat to America. And to defeat it both in the United States and elsewhere one needed to understand who was promoting it and for what reasons.

The answer for some was that communism was a Jewish invention and part of a global conspiracy, also involving control over the banking system, through which Jews would achieve world domination. Beginning in 1920, *The Protocols of the Elders of Zion*, the tsarist Russian secret police forgery which expresses these views in a luridly imaginative way (a tale replete with nocturnal gatherings of rabbis at a Jewish cemetery in Prague), began to circulate in the United States. Foremost among the *Protocols'* purveyors was Henry Ford, the automobile manufacturer.[5] His newspaper, the *Dearborn Independent*, not only published the *Protocols* but went on to wage an anti-Semitic campaign that extended until 1927. Ford himself promoted "The International Jew" series for his newspaper's campaign.[6] This essay, once again emphasizing the dangers of the Jewish world conspiracy, won praise from various figures at home and abroad. In the United States large numbers of Protestant ministers praised Ford's attacks from their pulpits. In Chicago leaders of both the Polish National Association and the Polish

Roman Catholic Union endorsed Ford's anti-Semitic attacks. While in Germany Adolf Hitler not only expressed admiration for *The International Jew* and its publisher, but was said to have incorporated some parts of it in his own volume *Mein Kampf*. Of Ford, the Führer wrote:

> It is the Jews who govern the Stock Exchange Forces of the American Union. Every year makes them more and more the controlling masters of the producers in the nation of one hundred and twenty millions; only a single great man, Ford, to their fury, still maintains full independence.[7]

The linkage between communist plans for proletarian revolution and the idea of a Jewish world conspiracy provides the leitmotiv for the appearance of right-wing Europeans who brought with them fascist and Nazi ideologies to the New World during the 1920s and 1930s. As we shall see, the organizations they promoted and the political doctrines they advocated were later emulated by "native fascists" who adapted them to fit American conditions during the Depression years. For now it is important to remember that the flow of radical right-wing views and those holding them was overwhelmingly from Europe to the United States and, further, that the initial appearance of fascists and Nazis was part of a political process involving émigrés and immigrants.

The three obvious cases involve the arrival of anticommunist Russians, pro-Fascist Italians, and spokesmen for the Nazi movement and the New Germany. In the cases of Italy and Germany we are dealing with dynamic mass movements that managed to win control of the state and establish formidable dictatorial regimes. In addition, in both instances there were millions of Americans of Italian and German origin who constituted potential pools of support for the Fascists and Nazis. The émigré Russian experience is, though, rather different. It was largely a one-man operation and one without active state sponsorship.

Anastase Vonsiyatsky was an anticommunist Russian exile who arrived in the United States during the 1920s after spending a few years in Paris. He married a wealthy American heiress, Marion Ream Stephens, who was willing to finance Vonsiyatsky's political activities. Operating from a small town in Connecticut, Vonsiyatsky established an All-Russian Fascist party in 1933 and proclaimed himself its *vozhd* or leader. Although he admired Mussolini and Hitler and sought to adapt their paramilitary organizational style to his own party, Vonsiyatsky's ideological affinity for the Italian and German movements was limited. It amounted to little more than shared feelings of detestation for Marxism-Leninism and the Soviet Union. The American vozhd sought to create a worldwide Russian Fascist Party apparatus and made trips to Berlin and Manchuria (the site of a large White Russian exile community) in pursuit of this objective. Rivalries developed between Vonsiyatsky and other Russian exiles, notably the Manchurian-based fascist Konstantin Rodzaevsky, so that he never achieved the kind of dominance for which he had hoped. Within the United States however, Vonsiyatsky used his wife's money to support an organization with several hundred members and which included, among other things, a small armory, a Russian fascist Bible school and a periodical, *The Fascist*.[8] Aside from occasional attacks on the All-Russian Fascist party contained in the American *Daily Worker* and other communist publications, Vonsiyatsky's activities had little to do with domestic political developments in the United States. The New England Duce's operations were focused on those Russian exiles who aspired to return to Russia once the Stalinist dictatorship had been destroyed. American politics during the Depression held little interest for them.

Italian Fascism

Italian Fascist activity in the United States was a far more substantial undertaking. In 1922, at the time of Mussolini's appointment as Italy's prime minister, there were more than four and a half million citizens or resident aliens of Italian descent living in the United States, many of whom continued to have significant ties to their original homeland. Furthermore, the new Fascist regime in Rome regarded these overseas Italians as a continuing part of the national community whose feelings of patriotism might be employed to promote the regime's interests. Illustratively, "when the March on Rome took place (28–30 October 1922), and Mussolini became prime minister, Di Silvestro [head of the Sons of Italy] hastened to hail these events as the beginning of a new era of glory and happiness in Italian history."[9] Other leaders of the Italian-American community also expressed support for Italy's new leadership. This new leadership in Rome could then count upon a certain amount of good feeling as it sought to build support for Fascism on American soil. Both initially and in the long term, Mussolini's dictatorship would benefit as well from its strongly anticommunist reputation.

With the advent of the Fascist regime, the state's Ministry of Popular Culture established a Bureau of Fascism Abroad, an organization intended to build support for the Mussolini dictatorship among the millions of Italians living in other countries.[10] Mussolini also formed a parallel body within the Fascist party to pursue a similar objective. The newly formed Fascio of New York was assigned the task of acting as the central clearinghouse for fascist operations in the United States. This body, in turn, was reorganized and eventually transformed into the Fascist League of North America. Between 1925 and 1929 the League was Fascist Italy's principal instrumentality in North America. Its directors and policies were determined by Rome. Among other things, it promoted visits by Italian-American youth groups to Italy in order to publicize fascism's successes.

Italian Fascist youth, members of the Ballila, reciprocated by visiting New York and other American cities.

The League's activities though were not confined to New York or the East Coast. Fasci were established in many cities. Working in conjunction with various Italian consulates, these units often intervened in domestic American affairs by waging campaigns, inter alia, against prominent anti-Fascists and by attempting to dominate and politicize local chapters of the Sons of Italy, an organization that previously had been given over to fraternal and cultural pursuits. Under the League's auspices, the American Fasci also sent delegates to attend congresses of the Italian Fascist party and, in turn, provided platforms for visiting Fascist speakers on missions from Rome. There was also the matter of "dual loyalty." Through League sponsorship, approximately 2,000 Italian Americans were registered as Fascist party members at oath-taking ceremonies at the Italian Consulate in New York City. By 1929, League membership itself was estimated to be 12,000.

However, the League's successes as an instrument of Fascist Italy in the United States heightened its visibility and made it a target of criticism. Complaints were raised in Congress about the intervention of a foreign power in American life. Expressions of protest by Senator William Borah, among others, led Secretary of State William Stimson to lodge a complaint with the Italian ambassador. On the basis of this representation, the League voluntarily dissolved itself in 1929. But this action did not put an end to Fascist operations in the United States.

Instead there was a proliferation of pro-Fascist bodies, for example, Italian Historical Societies, Afterwork (Dopolavoro), Disabled Italian Veterans, and others all clustered together at the local level as part of the Lictor Federation which coordinated Fascist activities in the United States. During the 1930s these organizations continued to promote Mussolini's interests in the United States. In particular, at the time of the Italian invasion of Ethiopia in 1935, the groups conducted a fund-raising drive in support of the military expedition and some 1,000 volunteers left the United States to serve in Italy's armed forces.[11] Also, at about this time an American representative of the Sons of Italy visited Rome to help celebrate the formation of a new, and as it turned out abortive, initiative to create a Fascist international.[12] Later, in 1937, after the formation of the Rome-Berlin Axis, pro-Fascist Italian Americans, dressed in black shirts, staged a joint parade with members of the pro-Nazi German American Bund at the latters' training site in Nordland, New Jersey. Leaders of both formations hailed the achievements of their respective dictatorships.

During the last years of the prewar decade the often pro-Mussolini Italian-American press joined with isolationists to promote American neutrality, asserting that events unfolding on the continent were better left for the Europeans to resolve. As in the 1920s, so too in the 1930s, anti-Fascist members of Congress took note of these intrusions in American politics, especially after the attack on Ethiopia soured U.S. relations with the Mussolini dictatorship. Among other investigations, the House Committee on Un-American Activities chaired by Martin Dies conducted an inquiry and held hearings concerning Fascism's involvement in American politics. But the Committee's interest in this relationship was clearly subordinate to its concerns about the dangers to American life posed by admirers of Nazi Germany. Furthermore, no matter the Dies Committee's level of interest, international events served to sever the relationship between Fascism and the Italian-American community. Italy's attack on France in 1940 and then American entry into the war against the Axis at the end of 1941 proved too much for all but a fanatical handful.

Nazi Germany

The Nazi presence in the United States was more serious and aroused far greater public concern than the Italian Fascists. Nazi and pro-Nazi activities in this country not only stimulated congressional investigation during the 1930s, but led to Justice Department sedition prosecutions in the middle of World War II.[13] In neither instance, however, did this organizational presence attract any more than a small handful of Italian or German Americans to their original countries' totalitarian causes.

Nazi activity in the United States began before the advent of the Hitlerite dictatorship in Germany. The Teutonia Association was organized in 1924, shortly after the failure of Hitler's Beer Hall Putsch in Munich. Teutonia, centered in Chicago, was led by Fritz Gissibl, a German national, who extended membership both to Germans living in the United States and Americans of German descent. In both instances there were few takers. Teutonia had no more than 100 members by the time it dissolved in 1932.[14] Its successor was a more serious undertaking.

As the Nazi party's electoral fortunes in Germany rose in 1932, the party's ambitious Foreign Section established an American branch. It sent a party member, Heinz Spanknoebel, to the United States to achieve this aim. Spanknoebel formed a group headquartered in Detroit, but with locals in New York, Cincinnati, Chicago, Los Angeles, and San Francisco. Its objective was to nazify the German Americans (racial Germans) throughout the country. Spanknoebel had some success in promoting National Socialist ideas and his recruitment effort surpassed that of the old Teutonia Association. By 1933, there were 1,500 members of this Nazi movement. However, its openly anti-Semitic activities, including physical attacks on Jews in a few cities and use of Nazi agents from Germany brought it to the attention of the U.S. State Department which proceeded to lodge a complaint with its German counterpart. Accordingly, in April 1933 the Nazi party in Germany issued an instruction calling for Spanknoebel's return to the Fatherland and the dissolution of the organization he had created.

In its place Rudolf Hess, Robert Ley, and other Nazi officials in Berlin created another American organization, the Friends of the New Germany. As short-lived as its predecessor, Friends of the New Germany embarked on an even more flamboyant campaign to promote National Socialist ideas in German-American communities throughout the United States, most particularly in the Yorkville section of New York City. Membership, estimated at approximately 10,000 in 1935 (60 percent of whom were German citizens), was of course substantially higher than the earlier Nazi groupings. Correlatively, the Friends' newspaper and other publications achieved a wider circulation, and its public demonstrations, often involving streetcorner brawling, gave them a considerably higher visibility than the earlier promotional efforts. Further, the Friends of the New Germany was able to establish some links to such emerging native fascist organizations as William Dudley Pelley's Silver Shirts.

But with Hitler firmly in power in Germany, the nature of National Socialism was becoming increasingly clear to American observers. Jewish groups, such as the American Jewish Committee, along with labor unions, acting under the auspices of the American Federation of Labor, staged their own protests, including a mock trial of Hitler in Madison Square Garden. Further, at the urging of Congressman Martin Dickstein, the speaker of the House of Representatives appointed a committee, under the chairmanship of Representative John McCormick, to investigate the Friends' substantial ties to Nazi Germany. This development along with practically unceasing internal rivalries among the Friends' leaders led Rudolf Hess to issue a directive in December 1935 requiring all Reich citizens living in the United States to withdraw their membership in the Friends organization, thereby bringing about its disintegration.[15]

Over the next few months, National Socialist activity in the United States went through a period of disorientation with various fragments of the Friends seeking to find a new format. Fritz Kuhn, a naturalized American citizen who had fought for Germany during World War I and had then joined the Nazi party afterward, succeeded in establishing a new American Nazi organization. At a meeting in Buffalo, New York, in March 1936, Kuhn and representatives of various splinter groups created the German American Bund. In contrast to its predecessors, the Bund would appeal to Americans and emphasize its American character. Kuhn indicated his goal was to promote German-American friendship and understanding. Symbolically, Bund rallies would include pictures of George Washington along with those of the Führer and American flags were conspicuously on display. For Kuhn and his followers the Bund was an attempt to Americanize National Socialism.

Kuhn's effort to divorce, or at least partially separate, the Bund from its roots in Nazi Germany produced ambiguous results, to say the least. Although its members were largely American citizens, many of whom were of German origin (according to the Justice Department, Bund membership achieved its highest level of 8,500 in 1937–38), the Bundists' organization mimicked that of the Nazis. Accordingly, the Bund divided the United States into three *gau* or districts (comparable to the Nazis' format in Germany), for the East, Midwest, and West. Each gau had its own *gauleiter* and staff to direct the Bund's operations in his region. In addition, Kuhn promoted the formation of a uniformed paramilitary unit, the Order Service, clearly modeled after the Nazi Brownshirt organization; and the Bund's Youth Division, from its public display of the swastika to the Hitler salute to the singing of the "Horst Wessel Song," represented a barely Americanized reproduction of the Hitler Youth. Even Kuhn's highly theatrical style of public speaking seemed patterned after that of the German dictator. And the fact that Kuhn and other uniformed Bund leaders were publicly photographed shaking hands with Hitler during a 1938 visit to Germany did little to promote the organization's reputation as an American entity.[16]

The highlight of the German American Bund's history was its 1939 Washington's Birthday rally (Washington's warning against America entangling itself in European affairs provided the theme) at Madison Square Garden in New York City.[17] Although Kuhn was able to fill the arena with 22,000 cheering supporters to hear him speak on the virtues of Christian Americanism, the gathering produced a massive backlash. Public officials and spokesmen for such groups as the American Legion denounced the Bund's alien ideas and ties to Nazi Germany.

Within several months of his Madison Square Garden triumph, Kuhn was indicted on charges of embezzlement for stealing funds from the Bund treasury and using them for various private purposes, including support for a female companion. With Kuhn's conviction and subsequent flight to Mexico to avoid incarceration, the Bund's fortunes declined rapidly; its activities were brought to an end with the American entry into World War II. Its effort to spread National Socialist ideas in the United States had been stymied by its transparent links to a foreign power. Nevertheless, it did achieve a few symbolic victories in this area, most conspicuously a joint rally with the Ku Klux Klan (at one of the Bund's New Jersey training camps) in 1940 and encounters with other American radical right groups, including such leaders as William Dudley Pelley and the Reverend Gerald Winrod.

Native Fascism

The Depression decade of the 1930s also witnessed the appearance of native fascist groups; that is, radical right groups with fascist ideas whose membership was mostly American. Before discussing their activities we will first consider their origins and sources of development.

First, as we have just described, fascist and Nazi ideas came to the United States principally in the context of émigré politics. Although the fear of communism and opposition to the Soviet Union clearly played roles, fascist and Nazi movements and regimes sought to promote their ideas among members of Italian and German immigrant communities residing in the United States. The organizations they promoted, the Fascist League, the German American Bund, and so on, tended to mimic their European models.[18] These groups operated on American soil, but were only marginally a part of American political life. Nevertheless, these immigrant-centered and mimetic fascist and Nazi groupings promoted the development of native American fascist groups by, among other things, offering personal contacts with their leaders (anti-Semitism, anticommunism, and isolationism, or keeping the U.S. out of another European war, provided points of convergence) and by providing paramilitary organizations that could be adapted to American circumstances.

Second, we should consider the era and international atmosphere in which the American fascist groups emerged. Consider the case of Art J. Smith, leader of the Khaki Shirts:

> Smith, an army veteran who had been a soldier of fortune in Africa,
> Russia and China, fancied the title "General" and wore a khaki shirt and
> riding breeches. He called his aides a "General Staff." He spouted anti-
> Semitic slogans and was reported to have threatened to "kill all the Jews
> in the United States." He proposed to lead a movement of veterans that
> would grasp power in America after a triumphal march on Washington
> in 1933, emulating the fascists' march on Rome.[19]

Where did "General" Smith and his miniscule faction of Khaki Shirts come from?

The period in which Smith proposed to stage his march was one in which there was widespread belief that the institutions of parliamentary democracy were ill equipped to cope with the profound economic crisis that gripped much of the Western world. Of course we can read history backwards and see that communist and fascist movements were doomed to failure. But for many observers looking at the world from the perspective of the mid-1930s, this did not appear to be the case. Quite the contrary. During the 1930s some Americans despaired of democratic capitalism and saw the wave of the future in Stalinist Russia. Others, including such writers as Lawrence Dennis and arguably James Burnham, thought the dynamic dictatorships of Fascist Italy and Nazi Germany represented a desirable model.[20] In short, the Depression era was one in which those alienated from the American economic and political system sought out possible alternatives. Among these citizens were those, like "General" Smith, who believed European Fascism offered a solution.

Third, there were the "political pilgrims," a term coined by the American writer Paul Hollander.[21] In developing this concept Hollander had in mind American intellectuals and other Westerners who visited Stalinist Russia in the 1930s (and later Maoist China and Castro's Cuba) and who came away enthralled by the societies they saw or the sections they were permitted to see. Hollander notes the disparity between the favorable impression and the catastrophic reality. At a time of the most brutal purges and when most Russians lived in grinding poverty, political pilgrims, sympathetic visitors from the United States, reported they had seen virtually the opposite. The communist system worked. There was full employment, political freedom and enough food and material goods to satisfy reasonable demand. And this was the story the pilgrims told when they returned home.

According to Hollander, the fantasy was the product of two processes. The responsible Soviet authorities stage managed the visits in such a way as to shield the pilgrims from reality. But, also, the visitors came predisposed to like what they were shown. Often alienated intellectuals or Communist party fellow travelers, the pilgrims were so critical of the American system they were prepared to believe that practically any alternative to it was an unqualified success.

Fascist Italy and Nazi Germany had their own set of political pilgrims from the United States and elsewhere who also came away expressing admiration for the achievements of these despotic regimes. A young Argentine army officer, Juan Peron, was profoundly impressed by Mussolini's Italy. Sir Oswald Mosely, the English Labour party politician, was so enthralled he later organized the British Union of Fascists, a movement replete with a paramilitary structure prepared for marches and streetcorner brawling.

Charles A. Lindbergh was the most illustrious American pilgrim to visit Nazi Germany, where in 1936 he and his wife were entertained by Herman Goering. He expressed admiration for that country's achievements under Hitler's leadership. But Lindbergh was hardly alone. Others on the list of pilgrims included such pro-Nazi Americans as Elizabeth Dilling, Gerald Winrod, and George Sylvester Viereck.[22] During these years, American scientists and other members of the eugenics movement visited Germany and expressed admiration for Nazi ideas and policies concerning the forced sterilization of the "biologically unfit."[23]

If we combine the effect of these political pilgrimages with the impact of personal interactions in America between fascist and Bund figures and native-born radical rightists with a political condition of growing skepticism about the viability of democratic capitalism, we can then understand the diffusion of fascism from European to American societies in these years. According to one estimate there were more than 100 such anti-Semitic fascist groups active in the United States during the decade leading up to Pearl Harbor.[24] It does not seem worthwhile to discuss all of these groups; most were small and without influence. But a few attained sufficient visibility to require some comment.

There is the case of the "Jayhawk Nazi" Gerald Winrod. In 1925, Winrod, a fundamentalist Protestant preacher from Wichita, Kansas, organized the Defenders of the Christian Faith. At first, Winrod through his sermons and speeches and the organization through its monthly publication the *Defender*, attacked theological liberals and religious modernism. He and his followers were millenarians who believed that a Second Coming was imminent. For the remainder of the 1920s, Winrod's political outlook was that of traditional nativism.

The Depression and Franklin Roosevelt's election to the presidency in 1932 heightened Winrod's political concerns. He condemned the New Deal as not only ineffective, but a conspiracy designed to rob Americans of their freedom.[25] It did not take Winrod long to identify the source of this conspiracy. He concluded, based on his reading of *The Protocols of the Elders of Zion*, that Jews were conspiring to control the United States by infecting it with liberalism. He placed this perceived Jewish threat squarely within the context of the standard conspiratorial scenarios of the far right, identifying the Illuminati and the Jews among a host of others as direct instruments of Satan on earth.[26] From the crucifixion of Christ to the torture of Russian Christians and the plowing under of Kansas wheat in a hungry nation, Winrod said that a "Jewish elite had played satanic roles [sic] in a divinely directed drama now drawing to a close."[27] The presence of such Jewish figures as Bernard Baruch in the circle of Roosevelt's advisers led Winrod to this judgment.

Although he was initially critical of Hitler, Winrod came away from his visit to Nazi Germany in 1934 with a favorable impression of the dictator and his new regime.[28] Winrod was able to overlook the Nazi movement's manifest paganism because of its violent opposition to the Anti-Christ, Communist Russia, and the satanic Jews behind it. From 1934 on, Winrod and his Defenders of the Christian Faith offered their followers a distinctive kind of American fascism, a mixture of pro-Nazi ideas and religiously derived traditional American nativism. Early on, Winrod came to champion Christian Identity—a faith he may have passed on to the most influential Identity pastor of the twentieth century, Wesley Swift. Winrod's Identity legacy passed down to his sons who, after a brief and highly unsuccessful attempt to transplant their Identity community to rural Alaska, have endeavored to carry on the remnants of the Winrod ministry from the comfort of their native Kansas soil.[29]

Winrod, a handsome man and a persuasive preacher, was able to achieve a certain degree of national attention. The Defenders of the Christian Faith had several thousand members, and its publications, the *Defender* and the more clearly political *Revealer*, reached more than 100,000 readers at the height of their popularity. Winrod himself ran for a U.S. Senate seat in the Republican party primary in Kansas in 1938. He finished second after winning approximately 20 percent of the vote.[30]

William Dudley Pelley was another figure who sought to synthesize European fascist views and American religious ones. Pelley, unlike Winrod, was neither handsome nor an effective orator. He was the son of a Protestant minister (although the senior Pelley turned from the pulpit to the manufacture of bathroom tissue later in his career) whose spiritual concerns preceded his political involvements. Pelley's religious perspective was far more exotic than Winrod's comparatively mainstream conservative Protestantism. Between 1930 and 1933 Pelley, a journalist and writer, published *Liberation* and later *New Liberator*, magazines largely devoted to spiritual reflections. The latter included a belief that a "Great Time of Troubles" was at hand, a period during which humanity's current state of softness and greed would be corrected.

Pelley was a political pilgrim of another sort. As a young man, Pelley set out in 1918 armed with an expense account and the rank of "consular courier" for the United States to Russia. Appalled by the violence he witnessed there, Pelley became a life-long anticommunist. Convinced that communism was a Jewish plot, Pelley became a passionate anti-Semite. This anti-Semitism would become increasingly virulent with Pelley's sojourn in Hollywood, California. A would-be screenwriter, Pelley had spent a number of years in Hollywood during the 1920s. He came away from this experience with an abiding hatred of Jews, a people he came to believe not only dominated the motion picture business, but the world in general and who had used their power to thwart his career. Pelley best describes this unfortunate experience in his 1935 autobiography:

> The fleshpots of Hollywood. Oriental custodians of adolescent entertainment. One short word for all of it—JEWS! Do you think me unduly incensed about them? I've seen too many Gentile maidens ravished and been unable to do anything about it. They have a concupiscent slogan in screendom, "Don't hire until you have seen the whites of their thighs!" For six years I toiled in their galleys and got nothing but money.[31]

As the Depression era progressed into the 1930s, Pelley's anti-Semitic and religious views tended to fuse with explicitly political ones. He became convinced that an international Jewish conspiracy was the key to everything. And when Hitler became chancellor of Germany in 1933, Pelley formed the Silver Legion. He wished its paramilitary unit the Silver Shirts to replicate the performance of the Nazis' Brownshirt formations.[32]

This was not to be. Until American entry into World War II, the Silver Shirts engaged in various violent adventures. In 1939, for example, five Chicago-area Silver Shirts threw rocks at the windows of Goldblatt Brothers department store. More often than not however, the Silver Shirts' efforts to take politics into the streets met physical opposition from counterdemonstrators. And on several occasions Pelley's followers had to ask for police protection to shield them from attack by violent antifascist demonstrators.

While movement figures claim 100,000 members for Pelley's organization, the true figure for membership in the Silver Legion was probably fewer than 15,000 at the height of its popularity.[33] Still, Pelley never lost hope that his dream of replacing Roosevelt and the New Deal with a Christian Commonwealth with himself at its head could be realized. He believed that the spread of anti-Semitism around the Western world made victory in the United States all the more likely. He did not ignore the fact that anti-Semitic attitudes also reached exceptionally high levels throughout the United States over the course of the 1930s.[34] Public opinion surveys conducted in these years revealed that large numbers of Americans held highly negative stereotypes of Jews and often regarded them as both powerful and dangerous. Pelley was certainly not deluded as to the presence among Americans of widespread hostility to Jews in this era. Further, when Pelley looked to Europe, he not only saw what Hitler was able to achieve in Germany, but he was able to applaud the appearance of the British Union of Fascists, the French Croix de Feu, the Romanian Iron Guard and other likeminded groups. In other words, Pelley saw his Silver Legion as part of a thriving Euro-American radical right, a movement bound together by anticommunism, anti-Semitism and a belief that constitutional democracy had probably reached the end of the road.

Defenders of the Christian Faith, the Silver Shirts, and a handful of other native fascist organizations to appear during the Depression era; George Deathrage's Knights of the White Camellia and the Black Legion, and, arguably, the Rev. Gerald L. K. Smith's Committee of One Million, represented an amalgamation of European fascist ideas and strands of American Protestantism. But the profascist American public figure to reach the widest audience during the 1930s was in fact a Catholic, Father Charles Coughlin.

Coughlin began his career during the 1920s as a parish priest at the Church of the Little Flower located in Royal Oak, Michigan, a working-class suburb of Detroit. Royal Oak was in the 1920s a hotbed of Ku Klux Klan activity, and in reaction to the anti-Catholic bigotry of the 1920s-era Klan, Fr. Coughlin in 1926 took to the airwaves on Detroit station WRJ with a message of tolerance and religious brotherhood. He proved to be an exceptionally effective speaker and the number of stations carrying his presentations grew quickly. As a social and political thinker Coughlin had been influenced by papal encyclicals, *Rerum Novarum* ("Of New Things" 1891) and *Quadragesimo Anno* ("After forty years" 1931), that expressed concern for the sufferings of the poor in industrial society.[35]

Rerum Novarum was an encyclical issued by Pope Leo XIII which was of considerable importance to the American Catholic faithful. Breaking with the Church's withdrawal from the world of secularism and modernism with which the United States in particular was seen to be deeply infected, *Rerum Novarum* upheld the right to private property and strongly condemned socialism, but at the same time upheld the rights of workers to unionize and to live at a decent standard, with fair wages and reasonable working conditions. *Quadragesimo Anno*, the Depression era follow-up to *Rerum Novarum*, upheld the principles of the 1891 encyclical, but strongly condemned both communist tyranny and capitalist greed. Significantly, no mention was made of European fascism in this document.[36] Fr. Coughlin's early broadcasts were not marked by significant or controversial political commentary. Following the pattern of a number of American populist voices however, the Depression changed this.

At first Coughlin, like many an American populist, expressed strong support for Roosevelt and the New Deal. Indeed, he was at first welcomed by the Roosevelt White House, and Coughlin in return did not hesitate from signing his letters to the new president with the declaration "I love you" and publicly blessed the New Deal as "Christ's Deal." However, like his close associates Gerald L. K. Smith and the apostle of the universal pension system Dr. Francis P. Townsend, Fr. Coughlin felt the need to explain the suffering of the Depression to his ever growing audience. This explanation was not long in coming. By 1934, Coughlin had declared America a Christian nation, and he endorsed *The Protocols of the Elders of Zion*.[37] This transformation from a moderate left-wing populism to the singling out of the Jews as the primary cause of the nation's suffering was heralded by the public assertion that the continuing Depression was the product of flaws in the monetary system and the machinations of "international bankers."

On the radio waves however, Fr. Coughlin was still circumspect with regard to overt public expressions of anti-Semitism at this stage of his career. By the mid-1930s however, Fr. Coughlin began to take a far more critical attitude toward Roosevelt, especially after the president rebuffed his attempts to gain a direct influence on public policymaking. Growing increasingly frustrated by developments in Washington, he was adamant, for example, in his opposition to the administration's attempt to have the U.S. join the World Court, Coughlin created the National Union for Social Justice. At the time, 1935, Coughlin claimed no less than 8.5 million active supporters, although he later offered the more realistic figure of 1.6 million active members and 6 million "passive supporters."[38] He hoped to mobilize this vast audience on behalf of issues and candidates he favored. Coughlin went on public speaking tours in order to raise support for his social justice agenda. In 1936 he also promoted the third-party presidential candidacy of Congressman William "Liberty Bell" Lemke. When the latter, in the context of the Roosevelt landslide, failed to win a significant percentage of the vote, Coughlin informed his followers that he was retiring from public life.

But less than two months later he resumed his career by delivering Sunday sermons on the CBS radio network. By 1938 and after, the tone of Coughlin's remarks became increasingly anti-Semitic, linking Jews to the spread of communism and to the nefarious activities of international bankers. He began to see virtues in the Nazi and Fascist dictatorships that he had overlooked in the past. *Social Justice*, the Coughlinite periodical, serialized *The Protocols of the Elders of Zion* and Coughlin himself attacked the role of Jews in the Roosevelt administration.[39] It is also at this stage of his career that Coughlin urged his followers to create paramilitary units under the name Christian Front in order to combat a largely imaginary communist menace. Obviously modeled after European fascist groups, Christian Front organizations were established in New York, Boston, Hartford and a few other East Coast cities. The Christian Front groups, composed largely of young toughs, carried out streetcorner attacks on Jews and other passersby in these communities. One of these local groups, the Christian Mobilizers led by Joe McWilliams, achieved some prominence in New York City in the summer of 1939 when it held a rally and paramilitary display jointly with Kuhn's German American Bund.

World War II and After

With the outbreak of World War II in Europe, Coughlin urged American neutrality and blamed Jews for seeking to drag the country into the conflict. He also praised the kind of "New Order" Hitler was seeking to impose on the Continent. A few months after Pearl Harbor, Coughlin's public career was brought to an end when, with the threat of prosecution hanging over his head, the Detroit Archdiocese officially demanded his silence.

As a result of his compliance, Father Coughlin was more fortunate than some of the other pro-Nazi and pro-Fascist figures whose outlook he came to approximate. During the war the Justice Department brought charges of sedition against Pelley, Winrod, McWilliams, and a long list of others (United States v. Winrod [1942] United States v. McWilliams [1944]) it believed were involved in promoting the Axis cause.[40]

In the immediate postwar years there appears to have been a cessation in efforts to link together radical right groups active on different sides of the Atlantic. But neither in America nor Western Europe did such right-wing groups disappear from the political landscape, and attempts at continued linkage by a cadre of dedicated individuals did continue. Illustratively, in post-Fascist Italy the neo-Fascist Italian Social Movement was formed in 1946. And in West Germany a neo-Nazi Socialist Reich party was organized in 1949.[41]

In the United States, an Anti-Defamation League study reported a total of fifty-seven racist and anti-Semitic groups active in the country in the period 1945–1950. In none of these cases though, does the report refer to European or international connections.[42]

Despite the general absence of direct cross-Atlantic linkages, there were certain developments underway in these years that would promote the appearance of a Euro-American radical right in more recent times. These developments concern the matter of the Christian Identity movement.

In southern California and western Canada during the 1940s and early 1950s a new religious movement was emerging that would become an important part of the contemporary radical right's view of the world. British-Israelism, a nineteenth-century religious formulation of English origin, was transformed into Christian Identity, the movement with which so many contemporary right-wing extremist groups have come to be associated.

As originally articulated in England, British Israelism was a set of beliefs that, among other things, stressed the idea that Anglo-Saxons or the Britons were literally the descendants of the Israelites depicted in the Bible. During the early decades of the twentieth century this relatively exotic doctrine crossed the Atlantic and gained adherents in both Canada and the United States. According to Michael Barkun, its handful of adherents in these countries began to emphasize and elaborate upon the latent anti-Semitic elements in the teaching and to attach them, in turn, to the politics of right-wing extremism. But it was in the Los Angeles area during the 1940s and early 1950s that British-Israelism was finally transformed into Christian Identity.[43]

If we think in broad sociological terms, the Los Angeles area in these years was the locale of a profusion of small fundamentalist, evangelical, and Pentecostal religious groups. It was also a region where a number of professional anti-Semites had established themselves during the war years; the most prominent of the latter was the Reverend Gerald L. K. Smith. Smith, a former aid to governor Huey Long of Louisiana and an ex-member of Pelley's Silver Shirts during the 1930s, used his publication *The Cross and the Flag* and his public speaking appearances in postwar Los Angeles to stress the destructive role of Jews in American life.[44]

Operating in this milieu were other preachers and advocates of British-Israelism including Joe Jeffers, Clem Davies, Conrad Gaard, Jonathan Perkins, Bertrand Comparet, William Potter Gale, and, most important, Wesley Swift. Swift, a former born-again Methodist, was attracted to Gerald L. K. Smith's anti-Semitic sermons and, for a while, became the latter's assistant. In time Swift and Smith became estranged from one another as the former developed his own religious perspectives and band of followers. In 1948, Swift founded his own church in Lancaster, California, a community northeast of Los Angeles on the edge of the Mojave Desert. Over the next decade, Swift, preaching from his pulpit in Lancaster, came to imbue Identity theology with a syncretic mixture of Christian religious, cultic, and racist ideas.

Modern Christian Identity advocates the view that Aryans, defined in racial terms, are the true descendants of the biblical Israelites and that God gave America to these Aryans for their exclusive control and use. The people known as Jews are literally the biological offspring of Satan and Eve. For some Identity theorists, Asians, African-Americans, and Hispanics are "mud people," racial inferiors and the genetic consequence of a pre-Adamic creation, while for others these races are the result of a separate creation identified in Genesis as the "beasts of the field" over whom white Adamic man has been given the responsibility of benevolent stewardship. Armed with this Identity doctrine, Swift and his principal disciples William Potter Gale, a retired Army officer and head of the Christian Defense League, Richard Gint Butler, a Lockheed Aircraft Company engineer, and James K. Warner, a veteran of George Lincoln Rockwell's American Nazi party and then the spiritual leader of the New Christian Crusade Church in Los Angeles, catalyzed a movement far more racist and anti-Semitic than the rather benignly philo-Semitic British-Israelism cult upon which it was based. By the end of the 1950s, Identity theology had spread throughout California to western Canada and beyond. As we will see, the Identity teaching would later cross the Atlantic from West to East and provide one of the bases for a common Euro-American racial identity.

The Internationals

At about the same time as Identity views began to be taught to small numbers of adherents in the United States, another problem of identity was emerging on the extreme political right in Western Europe. One of the central characteristics of most pre-World War II fascist movements was their ultranationalism. But many of the neo-fascist groups and political parties that formed in postwar Western Europe were influenced by writers and led by figures who emphasized the value of a common European identity based upon a common European civilization, one challenged by both the Soviet Union and the United States.[45] Inspired in part by the Italian philosopher Julio Cesare Evola and by the example of the Waffen SS during the war in its "heroic" defense of European values against the advancing Red Army, leaders of the extreme right sought to create a European-wide neofascist network to advance this outlook.

The Italian neofascists took the initiative. In 1950 the Youth Front of the Italian Social Movement sponsored an exploratory meeting in Rome attended by neo-Nazis and neofascists from all over Europe. The outcome of their deliberations was a common "European" platform. A second gathering of like-minded figures in Malmö, center of Swedish neo-fascist activity, was convened in 1951 and led to the formation of the European Social Movement (MSE) or "Malmö International." Leaders, like Per Engdahl (Sweden), Maurice Bardèche (France), and Augusto De Marsanich (Italy), committed the Movement to a European wide struggle against communism, a struggle they believed weak democratic governments were incapable of waging with any hope of success.[46] For some neo-fascists and neo-Nazis, the European Social Movement appeared too conservative in as much as it was insufficiently committed to the cause of racism and anti-Semitism. Thus, only four months after the Malmö meeting, opponents of the MSE's moderation convened in Zurich, Switzerland, and established the European New Order (NOE). The latter's program included the "third force" aspects of the MSE, but went on to express racist themes, calling, inter alia, for a prohibition on marriages between Europeans and non-Europeans and advocating genetic research aimed at improving the hereditary qualities of the European population. Anti-Semitic themes were not long in coming.

The MSE and NOE represented the first, but not the last, efforts by right-wing extremists to erect a common European identity through the use of "internationals." During the late 1950s and early 1960s the cause of Algerie Française, the fight to maintain French control over Algeria, as well as opposition to Belgian withdrawal from the Congo, provided the basis for another initiative. The Belgian neo-Fascist Jean Thiriat launched Jeune Europe in order to rally popular support for a continued European presence in Africa.[47] He warned that a French defeat in Algeria would lead inevitably to a new Muslim challenge to European civilization. In addition, leaders of the more prominent radical right parties in Western Europe met in Venice in 1962 under the auspices of the Italian Social Movement to form the National European party. The Pan-European Protocol issued at the conclusion of the meeting called for the creation of a supranational European government and an end to American and Soviet domination of European life.

The evolution of the Identity belief system in the United States and the various attempts undertaken by radical rightists to forge a Pan-European identity during the postwar period were largely independent initiatives. Developments in America and Europe had no immediate impact upon one another. As the 1960s progressed, though, the situation changed considerably. There were two transcontinental organizations established that require our attention.

The first of these is the World Anti-Communist League (WACL). The WACL was created in 1966 under the sponsorship of the South Korean and Taiwanese governments along with an organization known as the Anti-Bolshevik Bloc of Nations (ABN).[48] The goals identified by the WACL's founders stressed the defense of freedom and opposition to communism through both psychological and physical means. As an organization the WACL's founders aspired to make it not merely Euro-American but global in character, bringing together anticommunists from Asia, North and South America, and Europe.

Commitments to the defense of freedom and the defeat of communist movements did not make the WACL a radical right organization by any stretch of the imagination. Nor did the fact that over the years it attracted to its membership rolls American congressmen and senators, members of the British Parliament and distinguished religious leaders from various countries. But there are other aspects to the WACL, aside from its public presentation of itself, that, though they confirm the authenticity of its anticommunist credentials, suggest its defense of freedom has been something less than total. In Latin America, for instance, such Death Squad leaders as El Salvador's late Roberto D'Aubuisson was a prominent WACL figure.

With respect to our focus on the appearance of a Euro-American radical right, the WACL provides an exceptionally compelling subject for inquiry. During the 1970s, it became an umbrella organization under which could be found several radical right groups and personalities with transatlantic ties. There is the case of Roger Pearson, an Englishman, who founded the Northern League (N.L.) in 1957. The N.L. was a group committed to the promotion of unity among all "Teutonic" nations in the North Atlantic area as well as Australia, New Zealand, and white South Africa. Besides Pearson, its other leaders, including Franz Altheim a former assistant to Heinrich Himmler, were explicitly concerned about promoting the interests of the "Nordic" race. Pearson later moved to the United States, where, during the 1970s, he became president of the Council on American Affairs, an American branch of the WACL.[49] Pearson's background and involvement were not unique. The American Security Council, another WACL group, included among its members various Eastern European immigrants to the United States who had become the heads of "captive nations" committees, organizations, such as the Bulgarian National Front, committed to freeing their homelands from communist control. In many cases these committees were headed by figures who had been Nazi and Fascist collaborators during World War II or by individuals accused of war crimes because of their participation in atrocities during that conflict.[50] In short, the WACL provided a Euro-American network for anti-Semites, racists, and other right-wing extremists.

While the WACL also was able to win the support of many widely known and democratically minded politicians and others concerned about communism, the World Union of National Socialists (WUNS) could make no such claims to respectability. Its founder was also the founder and leader of the American Nazi party, George Lincoln Rockwell.[51] Rockwell's initiative was unusual in its point of origin. The other efforts to establish a Euro-American radical right movement with which we have been concerned were almost exclusively of European origin. WUNS, on the other hand, began as an American export.

According to a recent biography, Rockwell, a former U.S. Navy flier and commercial artist, defined the ultimate goal of National Socialism as the establishment of an Aryan world order.[52] Thus, almost simultaneously with the beginning of the American Nazi party in the 1958–59 period, Rockwell thought about the desirability of a worldwide Nazi movement that would be built around an Anglo-American-German axis. As Rockwell imagined the shape of things to come, Germany would be liberated from its decadent democracy after his Nazi movement came to power in the United States. However, before the latter event was scheduled to occur, Rockwell made contact with a number of European neo-Nazis, the most important of whom were the Englishman Colin Jordan, leader of the British movement, and Bruno Ludtke, a German neo-Nazi writer. Jordan was able to put Rockwell in touch with other European neo-Nazi figures who were just surfacing after the postwar hiatus. Ludtke had grown up in Nazi Germany and was able to convey to Rockwell in their correspondence the excitement and joy associated with that experience. Ludtke was able to persuade both Rockwell and himself that the former was destined to become the new Führer.

The immediate outcome of these discussions was a July 1962 meeting in the Cotswolds in Gloucestershire (England) between Rockwell and neo-Nazi leaders from Britain, Germany, France, Austria, Ireland, and Belgium.[53] Their deliberations produced a document, the Cotswolds Agreements, that called for National Socialist world revolution that would feature prominently a final reckoning with the Jews, and an organization, the World Union of National Socialists (WUNS), intended to achieve these goals. Rockwell was its leader and the Englishman Jordan its second in command, with particular responsibility for European operations.

WUNS had to confront serious problems almost from its beginning. Rockwell had to conduct almost all its business by correspondence since no nation would grant him an entry visa. The British authorities prosecuted and imprisoned Jordan for his Nazi activities and the German authorities did not regard Ludtke's activities with favor. Despite these problems, WUNS was able to establish or develop affiliations with neo-Nazi groups in some nineteen countries by the end of 1965. According to Rockwell's biographer, WUNS chapters were particularly strong in Iceland, Denmark, Belgium, France, and, under Jordan's leadership, Great Britain. Eventually, WUNS was able to develop ties with groups on all the continents including South Africa, Australia, and such Latin American countries as Chile and Argentina, where ex-Nazis seemed to rise to the bait.[54]

At the same time, the importance of WUNS should not be overestimated. While Rockwell himself enjoyed considerable favor in European National Socialist circles, the United States was thought of in terms heavily clouded by its World War II role in the defeat of Nazi Germany and in the nearly universal perception among European N.S. sympathizers that America was too much under the influence of the Jews to be trusted. This feeling is best expressed by Göran Assar Oredsson, who in 1956 founded the Nordiska Rikspartiet (Nordic Reich party) in Malmö, Sweden:

> The Nordic Reich Party was never part of WUNS. I was opposed to this because I have personally never been a friend of the USA. I can never forgive the USA's war against Europe, even if the guilt is not to be put on the US National Socialists . . . and I could never accept the idea that the headquarters for a World Union of National Socialism should be in the USA.
>
> But I want to stress that my friendship with Lincoln Rockwell was total, and so was our co-operation with him as a person and American NS-leader. Instead of WUNS I was one of the founders of the Northern League together with Colin Jordan, and he in return has had an intensive co-operation with WUNS [and] Lincoln Rockwell.[55]

Rockwell's own American Nazi party had little money to support itself, much less provide funds for an organization which aspired to worldwide status. However, the American Nazis were able to use the mail to distribute neo-Nazi propaganda material to WUNS chapters whose own countries barred its publication domestically. Despite the predictable struggles for dominance within various national chapters—the French, Belgian, and Canadian organizations had particularly acute problems—WUNS was able to survive for a considerable period the Rockwell's assassination by a member of his own party in 1967.

Conclusion

In this brief review of earlier attempts to promote a Euro-American radical right, a few tendencies stand out. First, until the formation of WUNS or more problematically the WACL, the flow of right-wing ideas and political influence was from Europe to America. Initially, the ideas, typically involving anticommunism and anti-Semitism, and those immigrants or state representatives expressing them arrived in the United States from European Fascist and Nazi points of origin. Second, once in the United States, a process of diffusion and adaptation took place. As these radical right ideas and practices were taken up by Americans they were modified to fit American circumstances and culture. Specifically, the role of religion and religious practitioners became far more important in the United States than had been the case with Fascist and Nazi movements in Europe. And, finally we should notice the tendency towards "privatization" that seems to have been at work. During the 1920s and 1930s, Fascist Italy and Nazi Germany were interested in promoting sympathy for their programs through the formation of organizations of well-wishers in the United States. With the defeat and disappearance of these dictatorships after World War II, efforts to forge links between radical rightists on the two sides of the Atlantic became an essentially private endeavor, lacking obvious forms of state sponsorship. With these generalizations in mind we may now turn our attention to the emergence of the contemporary Euro-American radical right.

The Politics of Right-Wing Extremism

To UNDERSTAND the nature of the Euro-American radical right movement today we need to develop some sense of the elements from which it is composed.
Not all right-wing extremist activity in Western Europe and the United States
contains a transcontinental or even a transnational component. But unless we
are able to comprehend the general structure or organization of the radical right
in the Western world we will not be able to discuss the Euro-American movement with much clarity. So the first task in this chapter is to describe in some
detail what the Western European and American radical rights look like: what
groups are involved, what they want, what they believe, what they do, who sup-
ports them, who leads them. It is only after answering these questions that we
can hope to be clear about the emerging Euro-American movement. It may be
true, as the German political scientists Erwin Scheuch and Hans-Dieter
Klingemann have suggested, that right-wing extremism represents a "normal"
pathology to which all advanced industrialized societies are susceptible, but the
particular manifestations will show variations from one country or one continent to another.[1]

Chapter 3

Radical Right Political Parties in Western Europe

One of the most striking differences between radical right-wing activity displayed
in Western Europe and the United States is an organizational one. In some of
the European countries with which we are concerned—Austria, France, and Italy
come to mind immediately—there are radical right political parties whose leaders, Jörg Haider, Jean Marie Le Pen, and Gianfranco Fini, have managed to transform their organizations into significant forces at the polls. For reasons to be

explained later, this has not been the case in the United States, where such radical right undertakings as Willis Carto's Populist party have failed to achieve much visibility, much less to win more than a handful of votes. Another way of distinguishing the role of parties on the two sides of the Atlantic is to point out the differences in the legal environments. In view of their historical experiences with fascist dictatorship or Nazi occupation during World War II, several of the Western European democracies impose constitutional bans on explicitly antidemocratic right-wing parties. Such provisions may be found in the constitutions of Austria, Germany, Italy, and France among others.[2] In these countries radical right parties are able to persist or even thrive (witness the above examples), but they must take some care in their actions and pronouncements in order to avoid the possibility of legal proscription. In the United States, on the other hand, the First Amendment makes it virtually impossible to outlaw parties of the far right no matter how extreme their outlook.

The first place to begin an examination of Western European radical right parties is by identifying who they are (see Table 1). This profusion of parties (there are thirty-eight listed in Table 1) is a bit deceptive if we take their sheer number to be of much significance. Some count for very little at the polls while others are serious contenders for power. For example, neither the British National nor National Democratic parties have much hope of achieving representation in the House of Commons while the Italian National Alliance on the other hand not only has a substantial parliamentary delegation, but actually participated in the governing coalition during the mid-1990s. The reader should be aware that there are other important variations. Some parties reflect and are structured around the personal outlook of vigorous or wealthy individuals, for example, "Pino" Rauti and the Italian Social Movement–Flamed Tricolor or Gerhard Frey and his German People's Union, while others have a well-developed organizational base.[3] Especially notable for our purposes is that some parties are relatively parochial undertakings while others, like the Swedish Sverigedemokraterna (Sweden Democrats), have extensive international connections, often with neo-Nazi groupings in Europe and America.

Academics, journalists, and other observers of extreme right-wing parties in Western Europe have noticed that their level of electoral support has displayed considerable volatility. Over almost the entire course of the post–World War II era in Western Europe, the voter appeal of radical right parties has tended to come and go in waves to an extent much greater than other formations of the left, center, or moderate right. The initial observation was made with respect to the German situation, where radical rightist parties surged and then rapidly declined in the early 1950s, mid-1960s, and late 1980s.[4] But the French case, among others, is similar; in France Pierre Poujade's violent Shopkeepers and Artisans Defense skyrocketed in voter support during the mid-1950s only

Table 1
Radical Right Parties of Western Europe

Country	Party
Austria	Action Committee for Democratic Politics
	Austrian Freedom Party
Belgium	Vlaams Blok
	Front National
	Walloon Party (AGIR)
Denmark	Progress Party
	Well-Being Party
Finland	Agrarian Party of Finland (SMP)
France	National Front
	National Republican Party
Germany	National Liberal Party
	German League for the People and the Homeland
	German People's Union
	National Democratic Party
	Republikaner
Greece	Greek Political Party
Ireland	n.a.
Italy	National Alliance
	Northern League
	Italian Social Movement - Tricolor Flame
The Netherlands	Democrats of the Center
	National Popular Party/Party of the Center '86
	Dutch Bloc
	Dutch Citizens Party
Norway	Progressive Party
	Fatherland Party
	Stop Immigration
Portugal	n.a.
Spain	Alliance for National Unity
	Spanish Democracy
	Falange Espanola de las Jons
	Spanish Right
Sweden	Ny Demokrati
	Sverigedemokraterna
	The 'Heimat' Party
Switzerland	Swiss Democrats
	Tessino League
United Kingdom	British National Party
	National Democratic Party

SOURCE: Jean-Yves Camus ed., *Extremism from the Atlantic to the Urals* (Paris: European Center for Research and Action on Racism and Antisemitism, 1996).

to virtually disappear a few years later. Currently Jean Marie LePen's National Front may follow the same trajectory.[5] In this instance however, it may be too soon to tell. (The American pattern at the level of presidential elections at least bears some resemblance to the European experience. The Dixiecrat ticket in 1948, headed by Strom Thurmond, and George Wallace's Independent American party run on the White House in 1968 did well. But both these right-wing initiatives collapsed within a short time.)

Table 2
Average of Fascist and Extreme Right Vote: Interwar Period and 1980s–1990s

Country	Interwar	1980's–1990's
Austria	5.46%	10.77%
Belgium	7.49	3.00
Denmark	0.64	4.72
France	–.—	8.01
Germany	16.67	0.95
Italy	19.24	7.90
The Netherlands	4.06	0.74
Norway	2.02	6.88
Spain	0.70	–.—
Switzerland	1.47	4.40
United Kingdom	0.16	0.00
Average	5.22	4.92

SOURCE: Leonard Weinberg, William Lee Eubank, Allen Wilcox, "A Brief Analysis of the Extreme Right in Western Europe," *Italian Politics & Society*, (Spring 1995), 42. [In those countries where the fascists competed in only one election, the percentage of the vote garnered by the fascist parties is used in lieu of the mean.]

Another way of understanding the contemporary level of support for radical right parties among Western European voters is to compare it with the electoral performance of fascist parties during the 1920s and 1930s; a period thought to be the golden age of right-wing extremism in the Western world. Here we should also keep in mind the fact that the 1980s and early 1990s are often depicted as a period when the right-wing phenomenon has taken hold once again.[6] When we examine this phenomena in graphic form as in Table 2, however, we see some interesting data.

When we calculate the average level of voter support for fascist and extreme right parties for those Western European countries that experienced both types of organization we discover two quite interesting things. First, overall the average (mean) level of support for the contemporary radical right at the polls is approximately the same as that received by fascist parties during the interwar period. Second, in both cases the average support is not astonishingly high. It congregates around 5 percent in recent years as it did in the 1920s and 1930s.[7] These findings lend themselves to a number of interpretations. The most apparent are these: Despite vast differences between the two historical eras, the radical right is about as popular (at least in electoral terms) now as then. And, second, again put in the aggregate, the radical rights in the two periods only have had a limited appeal to Western European voters. There are obviously deviations from the mean. Most conspicuously, the radical right, the Nazis, were a formidable electoral force in Germany at least in the early 1930s while the National Front displays similar prowess in our own time. Nevertheless, all things considered it seems remarkable that the average level of voter support would be so similar over a span of forty to fifty years.

Despite the overall similarity in electoral performance we should stress however that the contemporary radical right parties are not simply the offspring of the old fascist parties of the interwar period. Such political scientists as Hans-George Betz, Herbert Kitschelt, and Piero Ignazi have emphasized the differences.[8] Among other things, given the new times and the new legal setting, few if any of the current parties have developed the kind of paramilitary organizations—Blackshirts, Brownshirts, and so on—with which the old fascist parties presented themselves to the public. The new radical right parties are by contrast organized by a comparative handful of professional managers, a small number of party activists, and a few highly media conscious leaders. Correlatively, the kind of young people susceptible to the appeals of right-wing extremism in recent years do not respond to the values of discipline, order, and hierarchy characteristic of right-wing youth of the post-World War I generation.[9] Characteristically, contemporary right-wing youth show more enthusiasm for White Noise music than the elephantine operas of Richard Wagner.

Betz, Kitschelt, Ignazi, and others make a distinction among the Western European radical right parties listed in Table 1. They assert that some of them, the German National Democratic party or the Italian Social Movement–Flamed Tricolor for example, do seek public support on the basis of ideas, slogans and grievances left over from the earlier era. In other words as with the fascist originals so too here these parties are rooted in the industrial-era conflicts of interwar Europe. In that sense they are similar to the handful of unreconstructed communist parties still visible, though barely, on the European scene. Their voter appeal is based on nostalgia and therefore quite limited. This is not true however with the more electorally successful radical right parties. The latter operate in the present and are concerned with the social and economic problems of Western Europe's advanced industrial societies.

These problems include the serious dislocations caused by the globalization of the world economy, associated with competition from low-wage third world countries and the East Asian "tigers"; pressures to downsize enterprises or close unprofitable plants and factories completely; the shrinkage in the size of the traditional blue collar working class—along with growing rates of youth unemployment, early school-leavers especially; the decline in the agricultural sector; pressures to cut spending for welfare state programs; strains on family life linked to growing divorce rates and increases in the number of children reared without a father on the scene; and the highly visible presence of millions of Commonwealth immigrants, asylum-seekers, and guest-workers from countries outside the European Union.

Based upon the above considerations, the new and electorally viable radical right parties seek to win voter support based upon a combination of appeals.

According to Kitschelt and others, the latter involve antistatism and support for capitalist enterprise. In vivid contrast to the corporatist and strongly statist orientations of the interwar fascist parties, the new radical right parties advocate tax reduction; Jean-Marie Le Pen has referred to the National Front's "Contract with France," the privatization of public enterprise and the reduction of the welfare state, or at least limiting its benefits to native-born citizens—welfare state chauvinism. In addition, the new radical right parties characteristically play upon racist/xenophobic sentiments in the population, feelings aroused by the presence of so many newcomers from Third World countries. These individuals are blamed for stealing jobs from the locals and virtually every social problem besetting the countries involved. (The racist/xenophobic outlook has virtually replaced the kind of extreme nationalism with which many of the old fascist movements were associated.)

As with the old fascist movements, the new radical right parties exhibit a strong authoritarian bent. But unlike the interwar fascists with their veneration of the strong state and craving for the leadership principle, the new parties' authoritarianism often expresses itself in the form of a cultural critique. In particular, the new or newly remodeled parties of the extreme right encompass an outlook that represents a backlash against the "silent revolution" of the 1960s and 1970s.[10] The latter decades witnessed the formation of new social movements committed to women's equality, environmental protection, and the celebration of ethnic diversity (that is, multiculturalism). Furthermore, not uncommonly the new social movements, the West German Greens for example, used unconventional forms of political participation (e.g., nonviolent civil disobedience) to convey their message. If these values and that style represented a silent revolution then the new radical right may reflect a silent counterrevolution. Because the new parties of the extreme right typically endorse the preservation of traditional gender differences, oppose multiculturalism in the name of cultural uniformity or racial supremacy, stress the importance of industrial production and saving jobs at the expense of environmental concerns (the Swiss Automobilists' party would be an example), and support the authorities in general and the police in particular in punishing the new social movements' unconventional political displays. To the extent that the new radical right parties are authoritarian in an immediately political sense, they are supporters of their countries' respective police and military establishments.

Under What Circumstances Do the New Parties of the Extreme Right Thrive?

The electoral success or failure of these parties depends in part upon what observers of political movements refer to as the "opportunity structure" prevailing in the countries where they vie for power.[11] The best opportunities arise in the advanced industrial democracies, Kitschelt and others discover, when major parties of the moderate right and moderate left move towards one another or in other words converge towards the center of the political spectrum. In this condition, an electoral space is created which may be filled by the new radical right. Thus, if the moderate parties' attitudes towards immigration coincide and reflect a relatively temperate approach to the issue, the new radical right party can win support by adopting a policy of bellicose opposition, accompanied by demands for the return of "foreigners" to the countries from which they have come.[12] France for the French. Germany for the Germans, and so on. In addition to this consideration, the evidence suggests that the new radical right parties do well at the polls in those countries where new left or libertarian left parties also do well. Usually this means the prosperous, postindustrial democracies of Northwest Europe where the Greens or other parties committed to environmental protection began to perform well at the polls by the 1970s. The latter parties elicit a backlash from which the new radical parties later derive some electoral benefit.

Despite the existence of these opportunities, not all parties respond to them equally well. Opportunities may be lost as well as taken. In newly reunified Germany the new radical right Republicaners have so far failed at the polls (at the national level at least) because of serious leadership problems involving their erstwhile chairman Franz Schonhuber. On the other hand, next door in Austria, the Freedom party has thrived under the astute and telegenic leadership of Jörg Haider.[13] In France, a country where the skills of political rhetoric are widely admired, Jean-Marie Le Pen has developed a reputation for speaking a language ordinary Frenchmen can understand, in contrast to the arcane expressions of the country's technocratic elite.[14] Likewise in Italy the National Alliance's Gian Franco Fini and the Northern League's Umberto Bossi have emerged as flamboyant public personages on a political stage crowded with gray figures displaying professorial styles.[15] In these cases new radical right leaders have come forward with some sense of what it takes to build a mass following in a political setting where television has replaced industrial-era organizational structures as the most important device for winning voter support.

Who Votes for the New Radical Right Parties? And Why Do They Do It?

First, such Western European democracies as Greece, Spain, Portugal, and Ireland are not the countries where new radical right parties seem to do well. Instead electoral support for the latter appears strongest in the wealthier and most industrialized or postindustrialized nations. Within this context, countries with traditions of state centralization, for example, France and Italy, are most vulnerable. The new radical right parties are able to tap popular resentment against the remote and unresponsive state apparatus. This seems to be the case especially in countries where the conventional political parties, as in Austria and Italy, have come to share power with each other and monopolize the major centers of power in the country, that is, "partocracy."[16] For those alienated from these arrangements, the new radical right parties offer an opportunity to express their resentments. Next, analysts seeking to explain variations in the level of radical right voting in the Western democracies report, unsurprisingly, that countries experiencing economic downturns along with large inflows of refugees and asylum seekers are likely to evoke strong support for right-wing extremism.

Third, beyond these structural features we are concerned with who votes for the new radical right parties. The evidence is far from clear cut and there is significant country-to-country variation. But a few things seem clear. Unlike the fascist parties of the interwar period, the new radical right ones have little appeal for white collar workers or public employees, state functionaries of one kind or another. Spokesmen for the latter miss few opportunities to attack the public bureaucracy. Further, the historic fascist parties did well in the countryside, among farmers especially. This appeal apparently persists in our own time, but the farming sector itself has declined dramatically over the intervening decades. In his detailed analysis of the available data, Kitschelt identifies the two occupational groups most susceptible to the appeals of the far right parties: small businesspeople (along with farmers) and blue collar workers. In other words, for Kitschelt the new radical right electorate in Western Europe represents a social coalition.[17] The components of the coalition reflect somewhat different orientations. The small business element is attracted by the new radical right parties' procapitalism, promarket outlook while the workers find the racist, xenophobic themes and authoritarian tone most alluring. Among other things, these voters are bound together by their limited exposure to formal education. But the radical right's electoral base is susceptible to fracture as well as coalition. The working-class component typically does not share the small businesspeople's enthusiasm for market solutions—particularly when this translates into cutbacks and layoffs.

Radical Right Groups in Western Europe

The new radical right parties are normally compelled by law and the discipline imposed by electoral competition to articulate their support for the democratic order, to disavow too visible traces of a fascist or Nazi past, and to express their commitments to the peaceful resolution of political problems. These inhibitions have far less meaning for the large number of extreme right-wing groups that are active in Western Europe.

Table 3
Estimated Number of Extreme Right-Wing Groups Active in Western Europe, 1994 and 1996

Country	Number of groups 1994	Number of groups 1996
Austria	24	28
Belgium	12	31
Denmark	6	4
Finland	5	4
France	22	15
Germany	41	23
Greece	3	3
Ireland	1	1
Italy	8	7
Netherlands	12	7
Norway	12	11
Portugal	5	5
Spain	9	4
Sweden	12	15
Switzerland	6	8
United Kingdom	13	5
Totals	191	171

SOURCES: *Political Extremism and the Threat to Democracy in Europe: A Survey and Assessment of Parties, Movements, and Groups* (London and Paris: Institute of Jewish Affairs and the European Centre for Research and Action on Racism and Antisemitism, 1994); *Extremism from the Atlantic to The Urals*.

We have no wish to convey a false sense of statistical precision, but it does make some sense to begin our examination of these groups by calling the reader's attention to a few numbers at least.

The summary figures recorded in Table 3 represent the estimates provided by groups of researchers working for the Paris-based European Center for Research and Action on Racism and Anti-Semitism. The results of their research, supported by the European Parliament and the European Commission, consists of two reports on the status of right-wing extremism in Europe; the first published in 1994 and the second in 1996.

These endeavors strike us as providing a reasonably accurate assessment of the more visible extraparliamentary right-wing organizations active in Western Europe during the early-to-mid-1990s. The more obscure or short-lived organizations (e.g., skinhead youth gangs) are less likely to have been included. The sharp decline in the number of German groups reported between 1994 and 1996 probably reflects the German authorities' crackdown on these organizations in the wake of a wave of antiforeigner violence the country experienced in these years.[18]

If we simply compare the number of groups with the population size of the countries concerned it looks as if Austria, Belgium, Norway, and Sweden are substantially overrepresented while Italy and the United Kingdom have fewer groups than their relatively large populations would predict. But the sheer number of visible groups need not reflect the overall strength of the radical right movements in the countries concerned. For instance, there is no relationship between the number of active right-wing groups in a country in 1994 or 1996 and the size of that country's radical right electorate, that is, the percentage of the popular vote won by political parties of the extreme right.[19]

There are also problems when it comes to estimating membership figures for the groups involved. There is typically a gap between the numbers the groups claim for themselves and the estimates produced by the relevant police authorities. The groups routinely inflate their membership size in order to appear more important than they are in reality. Further, multiple memberships are not uncommon; a single individual may belong to more than one group simultaneously. Also, joining a far right group is not the equivalent of receiving tenure at a university, there is a significant amount of membership turnover often associated with young people dropping out as they assume adult responsibilities. In some cases membership may simply mean feeling some sense of attachment to an ephemeral group or considering oneself to be part of a "scene."[20] Having said this, the Federal Office for the Protection of the Constitution estimated there were slightly over 12,000 right-wing extremists (not affiliated with one of the radical right political parties) in Germany during 1994. Our effort to estimate a total for Western Europe as a whole based upon the *Political Extremism and the Threat to Democracy in Europe* study yields a figure of approximately 19,000 for the previous year. Assuming these numbers are in the ballpark, we are likely dealing with somewhat under 25,000 individuals in Western Europe during the mid-1990s.

The next questions it seems logical to pose are: Who joins these extreme right wing groups? What do they believe? And how do they go about achieving their objectives?

There is by now a conventional stereotype concerning the kinds of people who become attached to radical right groups in the countries of Western Europe. The image that is normally called to mind is that of the ethnocentric young male from a broken home who has grown up in a decaying high-rise on the periphery of Berlin, Brussels, Rome, Milan, Marseilles, and so on. He is an early school leaver, unemployed with very limited life prospects. His anger at foreigners is fueled by alcohol and some version of "white power" music. In short, he is a marginalized youth. To what extent does the stereotype conform to reality?

The political scientist Helmut Willems conducted an inquiry into the social backgrounds of some hundreds of Germans arrested in connection with attacks on foreigners during the early 1990s.[21] He reports, in effect, that the stereotype fits the kinds of individuals he characterizes as "criminal youth" and "ethnocentric youth," but this is by no means the end of the story. Those Willems identifies as right-wing activists, individuals with a coherent set of political ideas, and their fellow travelers came from substantially different social backgrounds. Their largely middle-class or lower middle-class families tended to remain intact. Further, they were relatively successful at school and in job training programs; and they were not unemployed.

At the level of the groups' visible leadership there is even more grounds for skepticism concerning the stereotype. Illustratively, Gottfried Kussel and Gunther Reinthaler, two leading Austrian neo-Nazis, come from wealthy circumstances, live (when they are not in prison) in expensive apartments in Vienna and Salzburg respectively and drive to meetings in BMWs.[22] Likewise, the influential German neo-Nazi leader Christian Worch is a multimillionaire who uses his inherited wealth to subsidize the cause of racial supremacy. In Italy such "Aryan aristocrats" as Franco Freda and Giovanni Ventura come from highly privileged family backgrounds.[23]

There is even some reason to question the essentially male composition of the radical right groups. It is certainly true that men constitute the overwhelming majority of individuals arrested in connection with violent attacks on foreigners and others. But there is evidence from Germany and Norway, for instance, that increasing numbers of young women are now being drawn into the cause of racial supremacy. For example, the extraparliamentary right in Germany now includes such groups as Women for Aryan Unity and the German Women's Front.[24]

No doubt part of the reason for the emergence of the social stereotype of right-wing activists in the first place is the inclination to see radical right groups in general as more or less politicized street gangs. The generalization applies to many skinhead and paramilitary groups, certainly those that receive the most publicity but not others. In fact we would have to include among the radical right groups active in Belgium, France, and other Western European democracies various study groups and literary circles, for example, the Friends of Drieu la Rochelle in Belgium, Groupement d'Etudes et de Recherches pour la Civilisation Européenne (GRECE) and Synergies Européenes in France, and Third Position in Great Britain. Or, for example, the English historian and Holocaust denier David Irving regularly conducts seminars in order to publicize his ardently anti-Semitic views. The adherents to these groups, though far from the European mainstream, are often highly educated types more committed to the publication of books and journals than brawling in the streets.

We know that West Europe's radical right political parties, at least the ones able to achieve some measure of success at the polls express some blend of xenophobic and promarket views. But what about these extraparliamentary organizations, what do their leaders believe, what do they advocate?

Without the need or interest in expressing electorally palatable views, these groups reflect a more heterogeneous constellation of outlooks than the parties. Further, once upon a time the cause of anticommunism was central to the worldviews of radical right groups in Europe as well as those active in the United States. But with the disintegration of the Eastern bloc and the collapse of the Soviet Union, the cause of fighting the "reds" has lost much of its salience. With what kinds of views then are we dealing?

The virtual disappearance of communism has hardly brought an end to the view that the countries of West Europe singly and collectively face a serious threat. Opinions among the various right groups vary concerning its nature, but the discourse of threat is common to all the groups with which we are concerned.

For some the threat is religious in nature. In France, Switzerland, and elsewhere, there are groups committed to the view that traditional Catholicism is menaced by the penetration of Muslim civilization into Europe. Freemasons and Jews, according to this outlook, continue to play their habitually destructive role in undermining traditional worship.[25] But for a long list of groups, ones active especially in Germany and the Nordic countries, the religions involved are hardly Christian. If anything they are anti-Christian. These are neopagan groups who reject the "Judaized" message of Christianity and seek to replace it with the tribal or racially based religions of pre-Christian Europe. These sects have in mind Wotan and the old Norse gods. "Odin rather than Jesus" is the slogan of one of the *volkish* German groups.[26] Anti-Semitic and racist religions formed in the New World have also attracted some adherents in Scandinavia. The Church of the Creator, "Our race is our religion," currently has a Swedish web site and Identity theology has attracted believers in most of the Nordic countries.[27]

Conspiracy theories often provide a bridge between the religious and secular aspects of the radical right belief system. There is a certain irony involved. Among some of the Western European groups, French and Italian ones for example, it is common to believe that a Wall Street or New York-based Jewish conspiracy exists to undermine European civilization and cripple the economies of those countries that manifest it.[28] Across the Atlantic in the United States various "Patriot" and militia groups have won adherents to a New World Order conspiracy theory by emphasizing European-centered schemes often involving Belgian and Russian troops lurking in the background waiting to seize control.[29] In other words, if you are American the conspiracy originates in Europe, while if you are European, the conspiracy has been made in America.

The one conception that seems to bind the two conspiracies together is ZOG, the Zionist Occupation Government. Various Norwegian and Swedish groups have come to believe, like their counterparts in the United States, that governments in Oslo and Stockholm are under the control of ZOG in the same way that Aryan Nations, and other groups do, concerning the American gov-

ernment. Israel is usually identified as the international headquarters of this conspiracy.[30] The ZOG discourse is not universal however. ZOG has not arrived in
Germany for example. There, followers of such neo-Nazi aggregations as National Alternative assert that the Bonn Republic is simply and unambiguously
under the control of Jews or an international Jewish conspiracy without benefit
of the ZOG doctrine.[31]

ZOG or no ZOG, explicit anti-Semitism seems to be a characteristic shared
by virtually all of Western Europe's right-wing extremist groups. There is a certain amount of what psychologists identify as cognitive dissonance involved here
because hostility to Arabs and others from the North Africa and the Middle
East whose views of Israel and Jews in general may match those of the right-
wing Europeans is widespread as well.

Associated with, but not as ubiquitous as, anti-Semitism is the Holocaust
denial phenomenon. There are any number of far right study groups, the German-
Austrian Institute for Contemporary History for example, that specialize in promoting the notion that Nazis' attempt to exterminate the European Jewish
community is a lie foisted on well-meaning Europeans in order to win unwar-
ranted sympathy and financial support for Israel and the Jews.[32] But of course
in Austria and Germany there are various right-wing publicists who have developed computer games about Auschwitz, the purpose of which is to lead Jews
into cyberspace versions of the gas chamber.

Racism seems to be virtually the sine qua non of the radical groups with
which we are concerned. Before World War II, on the other hand, extreme nationalism was a perspective common to the extreme right. In fact, fascist movements, Italian Fascism prototypically, were less racist than ultranationalist in
outlook.[33] For years Mussolini and other Italian Fascist leaders were openly contemptuous of what they perceived to be the Nazis' crude racial theories. The
contemporary situation is very different. Both radical right parties and extraparliamentary groups in Eastern Europe, the Balkans especially, and Russia continue to exhibit ultranationalism replete with chauvinist displays and irredentist
demands.[34] But in Western Europe as in the United States the focus is overwhelmingly on racial difference.

There is however a distinction to be made among contemporary radical right
racial theories. The groups, neo-Nazi and otherwise, that derive their inspiration from German National Socialism emphasize the biological nature of race
and racial hierarchies. Members of more sophisticated new right study groups
and literary circles in France and Germany, on the other hand, discuss race in
terms of culture and the limits of cultural assimilation rather than biology.[35]

Finally, by contrast to the political parties, the extreme right groups seem
far less enthusiastic about the marketplace and capitalism in general. The critique takes on two forms. First, there are the followers of the late pro-Nazi Italian

philosopher Giulio Cesare Evola who find the consumerism and materialism of the Western European economies morally repugnant and Judaized. Man, they believe, is made for higher and more "spiritual" endeavors than simply making money.[36] Second, there are the openly neo-Nazi bands active in various countries that contain Strasserite elements, leaders and factions that stress the socialist part of National Socialism as reflected, they believe, in the views of the Strasser brothers during the Nazi movement's Weimar phase.

Now that we know what the groups say and, approximately, who belongs to them, we must specify what they do. Violence is obviously the most conspicuous activity but hardly the only manifestation of extraparliamentary right-wing activity in Western Europe.

First, the groups with which we are concerned place strong emphasis on ritual and ceremony. Neo-Nazi, pagan religious, skinhead, and even the more cerebral aggregations both recognize and practice various ceremonies and rituals intended to commemorate the movement's past achievements, among other things.[37] Thus, for the neo-Nazis the date of Adolf Hitler's birth and Rudolf Hess's death have become nostalgic occasions with groups from various European countries assembling together to venerate the departed. These ceremonies and rituals appear to have a therapeutic function. Not only are they occasions for the expression of racial or ethnic solidarity, they also call attention to a sense of collective superiority, usually rooted in past greatness. The events we have been describing often involve the symbolic degradation of "out-groups." Jews in particular are singled out for highly stylized forms of symbolic degradation, sometimes involving the location of Stars of David inside toilets. (This form of degradation equating Jews and excrement is consistent with Elizabeth Young-Bruehl's personality theories concerning the obsessive nature of anti-Semitism.[38])

Displays of physical prowess are often celebrated by the right-wing groups, either as part of their ceremonial repertoire or as part of confrontations with their enemies. To quote the former Berlin-based neo-Nazi leader Ingo Hasselbach: "There's a unique thrill to being in the middle of a violent dangerous crowd and slugging, slamming and kicking your way to victory."[39] The latter observation also contains a message about radical right attitudes towards violence. Rather than regarding the use of violence as solely instrumental, behavior that may be useful in advancing a movement's political objectives, members of right-wing extremist groups often appear to treat it as an expressive activity. Violence may be used to express who one is as much as it is directed at achieving a political end. Right-wing violence is often violence with a smile because the perpetrators are enjoying themselves so much.

Second, as is apparent many of the extraparliamentary radical right groups in Western Europe do get caught up in political violence. According to the Israeli political scientist Ehud Sprinzak, contemporary right-wing violence is a case of "split delegitimization."[40] Briefly, Sprinzak believes that there is, in effect, a choreography to attacks staged by radical right groups. They begin with campaigns of private violence by staging attacks against despised minorities, perhaps gypsies or other unpopular groups (for example, homosexuals) in the population. When the national government involved does not respond by taking action against the despised minorities, the radical rightists come to regard the authorities themselves as illegitimate. When this happens the radical right groups often launch campaigns of violence directed against the government itself or particularly hated members of it.

Whatever the merits of Sprinzak's argument—it may come closer to fitting the American case than the European—it seems clear that contemporary radical right violence in Western Europe differs significantly from the fascist violence of the interwar period. In the 1920s and 1930s much of the violence was the work of disciplined paramilitary organizations often composed of World War I veterans. These organizations staged street battles against the private militias of left-wing political parties, communist or socialist. The current situation however is one that more closely resembles the kind of mob violence associated with the pogroms of an earlier era. The groups involved are far less disciplined than their interwar predecessors, and their targets are commonly unorganized members of racial or religious minorities who happen to be in the wrong place at the wrong time.[41] Public officials, for example, those in Austria who become identified with the rights of asylum seekers, may become the targets of more calculating aggressions, as the recipients of letter bombs.

Third, in addition to the ceremonial and violent activities, right-wing extremist groups and individual publicists in Western Europe specialize in the cultivation and dissemination of ideas emerging from a cultic milieu.[42] That is, the more literary and philosophically focused groups promote, publish, and distribute small-circulation periodicals and monographs, videocassettes, as well as websites on the Internet.[43] These productions are given over to the promotion of ideas and understandings that have usually been rejected by the mainstream mass media as outside the realm of acceptable or scientifically verifiable knowledge. Holocaust denial is an important theme, but there are many others. The overall impact of these endeavors is to maintain and reinforce a distinct radical right subculture throughout Western Europe whose members view the world around them in ways unlike the bulk of the population.

The American Scene

In at least four ways the contemporary radical right's situation in the United States differs significantly from its Western European counterpart. First, the legal milieu poses fewer barriers to the operations of the right-wing extremist movement. Secondly, the organizational bases of the two movements differ in meaningful ways. Party politics plays a lesser role in the American context; small, extraparliamentary, organizations are correspondingly more important. Third, religious beliefs are more central to radical right operations in the U.S. than they are in the more secularized societies of Western Europe. Fourth, at least some of the radical right groupings have declared war on the United States and are presently engaged in a form of armed insurrection against it based on the principle of leaderless resistance.[44] The only situation in Western Europe that approximates the latter is drawn from the recent past. In Italy, from the late 1960s to the early 1980s, various neofascist bands waged a terrorist campaign aimed at toppling Italian democracy and replacing it with a military-police dictatorship.[45] The foregoing items do not exhaust the list of differences, but they are the most striking.

With respect to the first consideration, the U.S. Constitution or at least prevailing interpretations of its First and Second Amendments make possible right-wing extremist activities and expressions that are hard to match among the other Western industrialized democracies. In most of the European countries with which we are dealing there are legal restraints on hate speech. Individuals and groups may be prosecuted for seeking to incite racial or religious hatred. Holocaust denial is now a prosecutable offense in Germany, France, and Italy. In the German case, obviously the most sensitive, the courts have found Holocaust denial to be a violation of the federal criminal code's provisions pertaining to defaming the memory of the deceased. Also in Germany, Italy, and other European democracies the authorities possess the ability to dissolve organizations, the extraparliamentary ones along with political parties, that are opposed to the constitutional system. Thus, since 1989 the German interior ministry has formally dissolved such neo-Nazi organizations as the Viking Youth, Nationalist Front, German Alternative, German Comrades League, National Front, and National Bloc.[46] Earlier, Italian authorities via the courts had dissolved such neofascist bands as the New Order, National Vanguard, and Mussolini Action Squads. In the United States, by contrast, the First Amendment makes it exceptionally difficult for the government to pursue similar actions against comparable expressions and groups.

As we mentioned earlier, unlike those in Western Europe right-wing extremist parties rarely amount to much at election time. This failure is not from want of trying, however. Over the last few decades a number of parties have contested national elections. The now defunct Populist party, a creation of the sly anti-Semitic publicist Willis Carto, sought to tap farm discontent during the 1980s by running the former Olympic pole vault champion Bob Richards, erstwhile neo-Nazi pamphleteer and Ku Klux Klan entrepreneur David Duke, and Vietnam veteran and anti-Semitic land developer Charles "Bo" Gritz for president at different times over this period. In no instance did they receive close to 1 percent of the vote.[47] The American Independent party, an outgrowth of the George Wallace for President movement of the 1960s and the John Birch Society, continues to field candidates for office in a number of western states in the 1990s, but has had virtually no success other than remaining on the ballot.

The most successful third-party initiative undertaken by the extreme right over the last three decades was Wallace's run for the presidency in 1968. Not only did Wallace win close to 13 percent of the vote nationally, but his thinly veiled race-based appeals for law and order and his populist attacks on Washington bureaucrats established themes that other right-wing candidates would later follow. In fact, in *The Politics of Rage*, Dan Carter argues that since Wallace, American politics in general has undergone a "southernization."[48] We should also remember that the Wallace movement attracted a number of groups and individuals who belong to the American radical right. In many states members of the John Birch Society offered their assistance. The late Ben Klassen, founder and leader of the anti-Semitic and racist Church of the Creator, was a Wallace activist as well.[49]

Given the openness of both major American parties to penetration by groups from the outside, it is not surprising to discover that the Democrats and Republicans have proven vulnerable to radical right maneuvering. The Democrats in Illinois were embarrassed in 1986 when followers of Lyndon LaRouche were able to win statewide primaries for lieutenant governor and secretary of state. But in general the GOP has provided a more hospitable environment for right-wing extremists. During the cold war era the Republicans provided an umbrella for ardently anticommunist émigré groups from Eastern Europe, the National Republicans Heritage Groups Council, whose central figures had begun their political careers in their homelands as members of interwar fascist movements.[50] During the Reagan years British-born Roger Pearson, a former leader of the Northern League (a London-based organization devoted to proclaiming the racial supremacy of the Nordic peoples) played a prominent role in the GOP administration. During the Bush years, 1988–1992, David Duke, a former Klansman and neo-Nazi leader, won Republican primaries and then campaigned under the party label for senator and governor in Louisiana.[51] More recently, it was discovered that Larry Pratt, head of the Gun Owners of America and a key organizer of paramilitary militia groups throughout the country, was active in a number of GOP campaigns, most visibly the 1996 presidential primary campaign of Pat Buchanan.[52]

Other individuals might be mentioned. But the important thing to bear in mind is the more general phenomenon. Whether it is the New Christian Crusade of the Reverend Pat Robertson or the Buchanan for President movement in 1996, the GOP right wing, particularly that faction of it defined by its social conservatism, provides a milieu within which right-wing extremists feel at home.[53] And so while there are no parties in the United States comparable to the French National Front et al., the American two-party system's permeability has made one of the major parties vulnerable to the participation of radical rightists.

The American experience also differs from the Western European over the matter of religion. As any number of observers have pointed out, Americans tend to be more religious both in terms of belief and practice than their counterparts on the other side of the Atlantic.[54] Because of this persistent difference, the United States has been the site of a marriage between certain forms of religion and right-wing extremism. Not all aspects of the marriage can be discussed here. It should suffice to say that there is a long history of interchange between evangelical Protestantism and such radical rightist organizations as the Ku Klux Klan and between the former and such radical right leaders as the Reverends Gerald Winrod and Gerald L. K. Smith. The current controversy over abortion has served to sustain the relationship. But the particular marriage that flourishes in the United States as nowhere else is that between Nazism and Christianity. After years of publicity seeking during the late 1950s and early 1960s George Lincoln Rockwell, the founder and leader of the American Nazi party, reached the conclusion that National Socialism's appeal in the United States was quite limited so long as it continued to be perceived as an alien doctrine. But if it could be married to more authentically American beliefs Nazism's prospects would be enhanced.

One observer has gone so far as to posit that Identity Christianity in its present form is the result of this line of reasoning.[55] Whatever the merit of this thesis, we need not go into much detail at this stage of our analysis. It should be sufficient to point out that this religious doctrine represents a synthesis of Nazi-based biological racism with an especially exotic biblical interpretation according to which Aryans are God's Chosen and Jews are the biological offspring of Satan. The Identity movement has spread to Europe, as we shall see, but it has achieved its fullest expression and widest influence in the United States.

The fourth way in which the American radical right differs from the Western European movement concerns the use of violence. Unlike the current situation in Europe, there is an armed insurrection presently underway in the United States. Since the Ruby Ridge and Waco incidents of 1992 and 1993 respectively or, arguably from the terrorist campaign of the Order or Silent Brotherhood during the 1983–84 period, a variety of small, loosely connected rightist groups, some fueled by apocalyptic end-of-the-world visions, have carried out numerous attacks on government facilities, civilian and military, federal, state, and local; banks, railroads, health clinics, and other public institutions; and members of racial and religious minority groups.[56] Whether these operations represent simple copy-cat behavior enhanced by readings of *The Turner Diaries* or the Book of Revelation or some kind of leaderless resistance remains unclear, one attempt by the federal government to prove seditious conspiracy failed in 1988, but what is clear is that no other Western democracy confronts the same kind of violent threat currently posed by America's right-wing extremists.[57] In Europe, Italy in the 1970s aside, the targets of attack are essentially private, racial and religious minorities and their institutions, not the state itself as in the United States.

Now that we have noted the most important ways in which the American and Western European radical rights differ, we need to identify the central features of the American movement in approximately the same way as we did for the Europeans. Let us begin, therefore, with an assessment of the American radical right's overall size and strength.

Estimates concerning the latter show considerable variation. One longtime observer, Laird Wilcox, publishes a *Guide to the American Right* on an annual basis. The 1995 edition produces an estimate of approximately 2,200 right-wing groups active in the country during that year.[58] This figure no doubt exaggerates the size in two respects. First, as Wilcox himself points out, many of the "groups" consist of no more than one or two individuals with a post office box and a commercial interest in selling books, pamphlets, audio and video cassettes, and more exotic forms of right-wing paraphernalia. Second, along with the conventional categories of hate groups (e.g., Klans, Neo-Nazis),Wilcox also lists libertarian and pro-free market groups and campus conservative organizations that don't appear to share the conspiratorial, racist, and anti-Semitic worldview we have come to associate with the radical right. By contrast to such watchdog organizations as Klanwatch and the Anti-Defamation League, Wilcox himself believes that the number of adherents these groups attract is quite limited, their size often exaggerated.[59]

If we confine our analysis of the American radical right to hate groups and use data compiled by Klanwatch or the ADL the following picture emerges.[60] Klanwatch estimated there were 157 hate groups active throughout the United States during 1995. This total is divisible into fifty-eight Klans, twenty-eight neo-Nazi, twenty-five skinhead, and thirty-five religious and racial supremacist organizations. If anything these numbers represent an underestimate because they do not reflect the branches or local chapters of major organizations. Illustratively, in our rendering, Aryan Nations is only listed once, yet it is an organization with more than twenty-five congregations scattered around the country. Further, if we are willing to assume that the Western European and the American figures cited above are reasonably accurate, it appears that the United States by itself has approximately the same number of radical right hate groups as all the countries of Western Europe combined.

The American organizations are by no means evenly distributed around the country. They are more prevalent in some states than others. Pennsylvania,

Florida, Tennessee, Michigan, Wisconsin, Illinois, Ohio, Texas, and California stand out. The Klan, unsurprisingly, is most common in the states of the Confederacy while neo-Nazi and other aggregations are most frequently found in the Middle West. There is also an urban-rural difference. Neo-Nazi and skinhead groups are a predominantly urban phenomenon while the Klans and the religiously grounded groups are often located in rural or small town settings. An interesting feature of at least some of the religiously inspired radical right groups is their pursuit of physical isolation. These "compound dwellers" can be found at such locations as Adair County, Oklahoma (Elohim City), and Hayden Lake, Idaho (Aryan Nations).[61]

In addition to the hate groups no description of the American radical right would be remotely complete without at least a brief account of the "Patriot" or militia movement.[62] This is, of course, the milieu from which Timothy McVeigh and Terry Nichols, the Oklahoma City bombers, emerged.

There are predecessors to be sure. The Minutemen of Robert DePugh of the 1960s and the Posse Comitatus of William Potter Gale and Gordon Kahl during the 1970s and 1980s provide precedents.[63] But the immediate causes for the formation of the Patriot movement were events of the 1990s. The latter were the Ruby Ridge and the Waco (Branch Davidian) incidents, cases where federal authorities were widely perceived as using excessive force against peaceful (though gun-bearing) citizens; and the enactment into law of the Brady Bill and another modest gun control measure.

In terms of the rhetoric many of its spokesmen articulate in public, the Patriot movement is free of racial and religious bigotry, its followers are simply concerned Americans afraid of a federal government that has exceeded all constitutional restraints and has become tyrannical in character. Sometimes the appearance of federal tyranny is linked to the emergence of a New World Order conspiracy under the auspices of the United Nations, international bankers, or other nonsectarian evildoers. The reality is somewhat different however.

According to Morris Dees and a long list of other observers, the public expressions of the Patriots obscure a more sinister reality. Individuals with long histories of involvement in the racial supremacy movement have seized on the opportunity offered by Ruby Ridge, Waco, and popular fears about the consequences of gun control legislation to reach a far wider constituency than would be possible based solely on their longstanding appeals to anti-Semitism and racial supremacy doctrines. Thus, John Trochmann, co-founder and leader of the Militia of Montana, was a featured speaker at the 1990 Aryan Nations World Congress and has a long history of involvement in and support for the Christian Identity movement.[64] In short, the Patriot movement constitutes a "popular front" that is manipulated, penetrated and often controlled by figures from the less publicly palatable world of racial supremacy and Jew hatred.

Table 4
Number of Patriot Groups Active in the United States, 1994–1996

State	Number of groups	State	Number of groups
Alabama	26	Missouri	25
Alaska	5	Montana	16
Arizona	27	Nebraska	5
Arkansas	9	Nevada	10
California	61	New Hampshire	8
Colorado	38	New Jersey	3
Connecticut	4	New Mexico	12
Delaware	2	North Carolina	14
D. C.	2	North Dakota	2
Florida	70	Ohio	25
Georgia	17	Oklahoma	17
Hawaii	6	Oregon	15
Idaho	20	Pennsylvania	32
Illinois	15	Rhode Island	3
Indiana	29	South Carolina	8
Iowa	5	South Dakota	4
Kansas	13	Tennessee	14
Kentucky	6	Texas	37
Louisiana	7	Utah	9
Maine	3	Vermont	2
Maryland	3	Virginia	10
Massachusetts	6	Washington	17
Michigan	88	West Virginia	2
Minnesota	9	Wisconsin	21
Mississippi	6	Wyoming	3
New York	15		

SOURCE: *False Patriots* (Montgomery, AL: Southern Poverty Law Center, 1996), 58–68.

The Militia Task Force of Klanwatch, the watchdog arm of the Southern Poverty Law Center, conducted a survey of Patriot activity in the United States during the 1994–1996 period. The somewhat questionable result of its work is a list of 809 groups located in the states as listed in Table 4.

Under the heading of Patriot groups, the Task Force included not only militia organizations, but also "common law courts" and "freemen" groups that defined themselves not as defending Americans or the United States against conspiratorial threats or the federal government's excesses, but as sovereign individuals or state citizens who have no ties whatsoever to the United States. For example, the widely publicized Republic of Texas, an organization built around the belief that Texas never really joined the United States, would be identified as a Patriot group by the Task Force's criteria.[65] More questionable, in our judgment, is the Klanwatch decision to include Christian Identity churches in their compilation. The latter belong, unambiguously in our view, to the racial supremacy movement. So its constituent parts get counted twice, once under the hate group heading and then as part of the Patriot movement.

Even with this defect and even considering the likelihood that a good number of militia members are not active anti-Semites and racial supremacists, we are still dealing with a right-wing phenomenon of considerable size. In 1995 the ADL estimated there were about 15,000 members nationwide.[66] There is some variation, but the states (see Table 4) where the Patriots are most common also tend to be the frequent locales for Klanwatch's hate groups, for example, Florida, Michigan, Pennsylvania, Texas, and California. Some of the countries in Western Europe have radical right organizations that engage in paramilitary training surreptitiously from time to time, but nothing on the size or scale of the American militia organizations.

The Hate Group Elite

Who leads the right-wing extremist groups in the United States? Where do they come from and what are they like? One way we may respond to these questions is by providing the reader with colorful or hair-raising biographical accounts of a handful of individuals who have achieved some degree of public attention. Such accounts may be highly illuminating, but at this stage of our analysis we think it best to provide a more general picture of the radical right elite in the United States. To do this we rely on two sources. First, the ADL's 1996 *Danger Extremism* volume which contains capsule biographies of fifty-nine hate group leaders or luminaries. Second, Klanwatch's *False Patriots*, also published in 1996, reports biographical information 117 prominent Patriots active in the 1994–1996 period.[67] Both accounts are hardly neutral in tone. The ADL and Klanwatch are watchdog organizations who regard the members of the radical right elite as opponents or enemies (the feelings are reciprocated). The reader should bear this in mind in considering the following accounts.

When we examine the ADL's collection of hate group leaders, the first thing that comes to our notice is that minorities are underrepresented. Of course the surprising thing is that they are represented at all. But they are. Harold Von Braunhut, a longtime Klan and Aryan activist and financial contributor, is a Maryland businessman of Jewish background. And Don Brock is an African-American white supremacist, Holocaust denier, and writer for Liberty Lobby's *Spotlight*.[68] Two women make the list. One, Rose Mokry, is a lone wolf who writes anti-Semitic tracts and then distributes them on Manhattan's Upper West Side. The other, Ingrid Rimland, writes a column for Holocaust denier Ernst Zundel's web site, The Zundelsite.

The other members of the hate group elite are white males, overwhelmingly middle-aged but with a handful of individuals in their seventies and eighties and a small number in their twenties. In terms of their occupations, there are a number of ordained or practicing ministers on the list: Peter "Pete" Peters, Thom Robb, E. Stanley Rittenhouse, Ralph Forbes, and Richard Butler, for example. Most of the individuals on the list, to the extent that they do not engage in radical right activity on a full-time basis, appear to be employed in middle-class or lower middle-class level occupations. Tom Metzger, the leader of the White Aryan Resistance, owns an appliance repair store. Klan leader and editor of *The Truth at Last* Dr. Edward Fields is a chiropractor. But there are a handful of wealthy investors and land developers along with a few individuals serving time after violent felony convictions at the other end of the spectrum. One relatively surprising biographical characteristic of this elite is the high percentage of its members who were born in or who have continuous ties to other countries. We reserve much of this commentary for our account of the Euro-American right in the next chapter. For now we should point out for example that neo-Nazis Gary Rex Lauck and Harold Covington have longstanding involvement with neo-Nazi groups in Germany and South Africa. Also of note, we believe, is the fact that approximately 17 percent of these hate group leaders (ten of fifty-nine) were born and in some cases raised in Europe. If we deduct from the list those individuals identified as Ku Klux Klan leaders (we assume the KKK is a nativist movement centered in the South whose members are not amenable to foreign-born leadership), then the percentage increases. In this case approximately 21 percent (ten of forty-eight) of the leadership group is composed of immigrants from Europe.

In terms of their ethnic background, we are struck by the relatively high percentage of individuals in the elite of German origin, both those born in Germany itself like Hans Schmidt, head of the German-American National Public Affairs Committee, as well as American-born figures such as Mark Weber, a Holocaust denial propagandist. If we rely simply on their surnames then we can report that 25 percent (15 of 59), one quarter, of the hate groups leadership is of German origin.

There is some overlap between the ADL's list and Klanwatch's collection of 117 "prominent patriots." Aryan Nations and Identity figures Louis Beam, Richard Butler, Pete Peters, and Kirk Lyons, for instance, appear on both lists. The overlap is surely not coincidental since the racial supremacists have sought to promote and manipulate the "patriots" for their own purposes. In general the Patriots are a more heterogeneous cast of characters, but one thing they have in common with the hate group elite is gender. Linda Thompson, an Indianapolis attorney who produced two widely distributed videos attempting to show that the Waco siege was part of a broader government conspiracy, is one of only two women on the list. The latter includes a number of prominent political figures such as Congressman Steve Stockman (Texas), former Arizona governor Evan

Meecham, state legislators Charles Duke (Colorado), Don Rogers (California), Larry Pratt (Virginia) and county commissioners, such as Dick Carver (Nye County, Nevada). The Patriots also seem distinguishable from the hate group elite by virtue of their military-police backgrounds. To a much greater extent than the former, the Patriots are people who have served in the military, often at officer rank, or have pursued careers in law enforcement such as Jack McLamb, a retired Phoenix police officer who wrote *Operation Vampire Killer 2000*, a widely circulated New World Order conspiracy tract. Both lists have in common a significant number of Christian ministers, either Identity or fundamentalist. And in both cases racial and religious minorities are few and far between. Beyond this, the Patriots are more likely to be involved in ranching and farming and to reside in the western states compared to those on the hate group list.

The best way to understand the beliefs of the contemporary American radical right is by dividing our discussion into two parts. First we offer an account of the hate groups' views and then, second, a description of the Patriots' outlook. In neither case do we aim to be comprehensive. Our goal is to provide some sense of how the leaders of these organizations view the world.

Rather than attempting to simply report what the hate groups have to say we think it beneficial for the reader to get some sense not only of what they believe, but also how they express themselves. So we have recorded below excerpts from the basic statements of the Knights of the Ku Klux Klan, Aryan Nations, National Alliance (the organization of William Pierce, author of *The Turner Diaries*), and the World Church of the Creator from their respective websites.

Knights of the Ku Klux Klan:

[T]he Klan today does not exist just as a memorial to past accomplishments, but as a living instrument for the ideals of Western Christian Civilization and the one element that makes them possible: the White race. . . . From out of its international headquarters in North Salem, IN . . . the Knights of the Ku Klux Klan sends out a message of hope and deliverance to White people throughout the world. In each country Klansmen are encouraged to have nationalist pride in their own country and at the same time work for world wide White racial unity! In America, members of other countries have a similar platform, but naturally are devoted to their own nationalistic heritage: 1. The White Race; the irreplaceable hub of our nation our faith, and the high levels of western culture and technology. 2. America First: First before any foreign or alien influence or interests. 3. The Constitution as originally written and intended. The finest system of government ever conceived by man. 4. Free Enterprise: Private property and ownership of business, but an end to high finance exploitation. 5. Positive Christianity: The right of the American people to practice their faith, including prayers in the school. 6. The Family: We believe the strength of any nation must be based upon strong family units, commonly called the traditional family. (http:/www.capecod.net/~ndemonti/kkk.htm>)

Aryan Nations:

We believe in the preservation of our race, individually and collectively, as a people as demanded and directed by Yaweh. We believe our Racial Nation has a right and is under obligation to preserve itself and its members. We believe that Adam, man of genesis, is the placing of the White Race upon this earth. Not all races descend from Adam. Adam is the father of the White Race only. . . . We believe that the true, literal children of the Bible are the twelve tribes of Israel, now scattered throughout the world and now known as the Anglo-Saxon, Germanic, Teutonic, Scandinavian, Celtic peoples of the earth. . . . We believe that there are literal children of Satan in the world today. . . . We believe that the Cananite Jew is the natural enemy of our Aryan (white) Race. We believe that there is a battle being fought this day between the children of darkness (today known as Jews) and the children of light . . . the Aryan race, the true Israel of the Bible. . . . We believe that there is a day of reckoning. The usurper will be thrown out by the terrible might of Yaweh's people, as they return to their roots and special destiny. (http://www.stormfront.org/aryan_nations/)

National Alliance:

There is no greater power in the world today than that wielded by the manipulators of public opinion in America. No king or pope of old, no conquering general or high priest ever disposed of a power even remotely approaching that of the few dozen men who control America's mass news and entertainment media. . . . And who are these all-powerful masters of the media? . . . In each case that man has been a Jew. . . . Only one in 36 U.S. citizens (2.8 per cent) is a Jew. But nearly all of the men who shape young Americans' concept of reality, of good and evil, of permissible and impermissible behavior are Jews. . . . The suppression of competition and the establishment of local monopolies on the dissemination of news and opinion have characterized the rise of Jewish control over America's newspapers. . . . Once we have absorbed and understood the fact of Jewish media control, it is our inescapable responsibility to do whatever is necessary to break that control. We must shrink from nothing in combating this evil power which has fastened its deadly grip on our people and is injecting its lethal poison into their minds and souls. If we fail to destroy it, it certainly will destroy our race. (http://www.natvan.com/whorules/whorules.html)

World Church of the Creator:

After six thousand years of recorded history, our people finally have a religion of, for and by them. Creativity is that religion. It is established

for the Survival, Expansion and Advancement of our White Race
exclusively. Indeed, we believe that what is good for the White Race is
the highest virtue, and what is bad for the White Race is the ultimate
sin. We have come to hold these views by observing the Eternal Laws of
Nature, by studying History, and by using the Logic and Common Sense
everyone is born with: the highest Law of Nature is the survival of one's
own kind; history has shown us that the White Race is responsible for
all that which we call progress on this earth. . . . Our people have faced
threats throughout history, but never before has our people faced as
grave a threat as it is facing today. Today, our people's very continued
biological existence on this planet is in doubt. (http://www.creator.org/
about.html)

The common theme that runs throughout these views is that of a white
race, the sole source of all human achievement, in imminent danger of extinction. The authors write on behalf of and appeal to members of the race. The
racism is based upon different foundations, ranging from traditional Christianity in the case of the KKK to Identity for Aryan Nations (really a mix of biological racism and Biblical interpretation) to History and Nature for the Creators.
The source of the threat is Jewish, a powerful Jewish conspiracy (for the National Alliance centered in the mass media) to poison and control the minds of
whites. The Jews intend to destroy the white race by promoting its mongreliza-
tion. African Americans represent an affliction, but they are not the real source
of the threat. What is to be done? The Creator position especially emphasizes
the development of race consciousness as a way of inoculating whites. William
Pierce's far more literate presentation (he has a Ph.D. in physics) offers a thinly
veiled appeal for genocide. As the psychologist Rafael Ezekiel has observed, there
is a division of thought at work among the members of hate groups. The rank-
and-file members direct their hatred and hostility toward blacks and Hispanics,
while the leaders are obsessed (in perhaps a clinical sense) with Jews to whom
they ascribe almost supernatural powers.[69]

The Patriot movement sees things somewhat differently. Its spokesmen have
no doubt about the existence of a global conspiracy but the emphasis, by and
large, is nonsectarian. Here, for example, is an excerpt from *The Shadow
Government*:

A key question about the Shadow Government is how does it make
decisions and carry them out. Where is the center? Some think it lies in
a few major financial institutions. . . . Still others that it has no permanent center, but operates by consensus, with shifting factions that confer
through various mechanisms. Some think that those mechanisms are
reflected in public associations such as the Council on Foreign Relations, the Tri-lateral Commission, the Bilderbergers, the Federal

Reserve, the World bank, or the International Monetary Fund. . . . Most available evidence indicates that the center is in the intelligence apparatus.[70]

Here is a brief quotation from a widely distributed movement tract, *Operation Vampire Killer 2000*:

> As patriotic Americans of all races, religions and political beliefs, we claim our right to defend our Republic from all enemies foreign and domestic. . . . Many of our nation's INTERNAL PROTECTORS know of the well-laid plan which will culminate in the year 2000, to usher the United States, along with the rest of the nations of the world, into a "utopian" global community allegedly under the control of a "philanthropic" United Nations.[71]

And the following is an excerpt from the *Mission Statement of the United States Militia Association*:

> The United States Militia Association is organized for the purpose of returning America to the organizational structure and purpose of the organic "Original Constitution" with the Bill of Rights secure and intact for all citizens regardless of race, religion or political persuasion. . . . We believe in the sanctity of life, liberty and property; further, that a citizen has the right of self defense of the same, as the sovereign of this nation.[72]

The rhetoric of the Patriot movement, the way it presents itself to the public, is far more compatible with the American tradition than that of the hate groups. There is no reference to race, an identity that transcends national borders. The appeal is to Americans and their Lockean-based natural rights. Rights that are threatened by the federal government and those conspirators plotting to give over its powers to a New World Order, represented by the United Nations or some other alien entity. The rhetoric appears to be a combination of the American credo linked to made-for-television science fiction ideas (e.g., *Red Dawn*) about foreign troops located in out of the way bases prepared to seize control of the country after it is softened up by "black helicopter" operations, currency debasement, and gun control legislation.[73]

If this is the rhetoric, what is the reality? In practice Patriots often make a distinction between original, "state" citizens and Fourteenth Amendment citizens. The former possess rights based upon the original Constitution, while the latter have had them granted by the federal government in the wake of the Civil War.[74] In other words, there are first- and second-class citizens.

Fourteenth Amendment citizens are obliged to obey laws of the federal government, the entity from which they derived their status. But this is not the case for sovereign state citizens. State citizens have been misled to thinking they are obliged to obey the federal government's rules, that they pay income taxes for example. But this is not true. Citizens may revert to their original state or sovereign status by breaking their tacit contracts with the government, by destroying their drivers' licenses, social security cards, marriage certificates, and so on. These ideas provide the bases for the refusal to pay taxes and for claims to be "freemen" totally exempt from all government rules and regulations.

Now that we have some understanding of what radical right groups in the United States believe it is time to consider what they do. Although there is in practice an overlap between the hate groups and the Patriot movement, with the latter often constituting a front for the former, we believe it makes the discussion clearer if we retain the distinction.

So far as the Patriots are concerned, we are dealing with a movement which is to a considerable extent built around gun worship. Mao's famous observation that "power comes out of the barrel of a gun" is rivaled or outdone by the Patriots' more particularistic bumper sticker slogan, "God, Guts and Guns Made America Great."[75] In practice, militia organizations are highly visible at gun shows around the country, locations their leaders believe will provide new recruits and well-wishers. At these highly popular and largely male gatherings militia organizations sell video cassettes and print publications. The cassettes and the pamphlets are often of a how-to variety. For example, *How to Open a Bank Account without a Social Security Number* lists "The six steps to financial freedom!!" and *How to Start and Train a Militia Unit* informs the reader about "Breaking out of Encirclements." ("When surrounded, stage your breakout as soon as possible. The longer you wait the stronger the enemy will become.")[76]

The linkage between the patriot movement and firearms is hardly confined to the hotel convention sites where many of the gun shows are held. The militia groups engage in paramilitary training exercises around the country and, on occasion, attempt to put their training into practice. For instance in 1996 authorities arrested members of the Mountaineer Militia in West Virginia and the Arizona-based Viper Team after they had planned attacks on federal facilities in these states.[77]

But the patriot movement is not limited to the militia organizations and to paramilitary activities. There is also the matter of "paper terrorism." Klanwatch has identified 131 common law courts that were active in a total of thirty-four states during 1996.[78] The most spectacular of these "courts" was the Freemen/ Justus Township in Jordan, Montana, a ranch where some two dozen freemen claimed immunity to American law and held federal authorities at bay for over a month before surrendering.[79] In 1997 a similar case arose in Davis County Texas where followers of Republic of Texas "ambassador" Rick McLaren proclaimed their autonomy from normal state and local law enforcement authorities for some time. But they (with two exceptions), like their Montana counterparts, eventually gave themselves up, in this instance to the Texas Rangers after being "indicted" by their own putative organizations for treason.

Common law courts are pseudo-judicial bodies that issue bogus liens, arrest warrants, and various fake judicial rulings. They are intended to harass real judges, county recorders, other public officials, and private citizens who stand in the freemen's way in one fashion or another. Not uncommonly the members of these common law courts are ranchers and farmers unable or unwilling to pay the taxes on their property and looking for a way out of their dilemma, or the victims of scam artists who have persuaded these innocents that their unsecured personal checks are the equivalent of real money.

Goals and Methods

Hate group operations in the United States encompass a wide range of activities not least of which is the penetration and control of many organizations inside the Patriot movement. If there is an overall goal to these activities it is RaHoWa, short for racial holy war.[80] The term is a slogan for groups ranging from the World Church of the Creator to skinhead white power rock bands. The hope is that RaHoWa can be unleashed throughout the United States the outcome of which will be the establishment of a white supremacist regime, the expulsion or subordination of the "mud people" or "beasts of the field" and an end to Jewish domination, preferably with the physical destruction of the Jews themselves.

The model for this cataclysmic showdown is of course William Pierce's *The Turner Diaries*, a novel that has served as a source of inspiration for both the late Robert Mathews and his Silent Brotherhood and Timothy McVeigh, the Oklahoma City bomber.

If RaHoWa is the goal, leaderless resistance is the method. The term was popularized by the former Klan leader and Aryan Nations militant Louis Beam.[81] Some years ago Beam came to the conclusion, accurately enough, that conventional right-wing extremist groups were too easily penetrated by the authorities. What was called for were small autonomous groups operating independently of one another but taking cues from the same events: "The bulk of our resistance forces should be comprised of individuals, or small nuclear units of teams no larger than five or six members. These individuals or nuclear units will conduct their resistance efforts in whatever capacity they feel capable of instituting."[82]

Some analysts of right-wing extremist politics see Beam's conception of leaderless resistance as highly original. Nothing could be further from the truth. Anarchist groups and individuals in America and Europe functioned in this fashion in the last decades of the nineteenth century.[83] More recently, during the 1970s and early 1980s, left-wing terrorists in Germany and Italy (e.g., Worker

Autonomy) practiced "diffuse terrorism" in an effort to avoid detection by the police.

In any event, short of the achievement of RaHoWa, any number of racist groups in this country hope to establish a separate white bastion in the northwest corner of the United States. It is not totally accidental that Aryan Nations, the National Socialist Vanguard, the Volksfront and other like-minded organizations have established bases of operation in Oregon, Washington, and Idaho. If Nordics are unable to overcome their racial enemies then at least they may be able to establish an existence and raise their families, separate from them and in an environment that bears some resemblance to their race's ancestral homeland in Northern Europe.

We have hardly exhausted the possibilities. Hate group operations in the United States include such activities as the promotion of Holocaust denial through the mass media and efforts to recruit new adherents via the Internet— by now most of the significant groups have their own web sites—or by direct contact in the armed forces. But our rendering should at least give the reader some sense of their range and significance.

Conclusions

The Western European and American radical rights appear different in ways we have sought to describe. Further, within the United States the concerns and rhetoric of the Patriot movement appear to differ from those of the racial supremacist organizations. But there is at least one thing that seems to bind them together: identity. European and American radical rightists, though they may stress their respective national identities on occasion define themselves as belonging to a common race, one that is victimized by a variety of social forces and, indeed, may be in danger of extinction. The Patriots may not be as openly racist at least in terms of their rhetoric. We cannot help but notice though that the Patriots include many freemen, Republic of Texas believers, and so on, who repeatedly deny they are American citizens in any conventional sense. For them as well as the racists then the issue of personal as well as social identity is at play. And it is on the basis of this observation that we now turn our attention to the emerging Euro-American radical right.

Chapter 4

The Ties that Bind

The Euro-American Radical Right's "Special Relationship"

By DESCRIBING in the previous chapter the major characteristics of the contemporary radical right in Western Europe and the United States we have set the stage for our account of the emerging Euro-American radical right, a movement that spans the Atlantic and transcends national boundaries. But before we can provide such an account there are still a few obstacles to be overcome, a few a priori reservations to be addressed.

Problems and Possibilities

First, one of the common themes in the discourse of radical right leaders in Western Europe is hatred of the United States. The source of this hatred is threefold. For neo-Nazis in Germany and elsewhere as well as Italian neofascists the United States is loathed because of its role in the defeat of the Axis in World War II. But the disdain extends beyond the historical. America is hated because of the multicultural or multiracial nature of its society. It is precisely this sort of growing social pluralism that European radical rightists from LePen and Haider to such minor figures as the Norwegian Arne Myrdal find so alarming. For them America represents an antimodel, something to be avoided at all costs. Furthermore, many European radical rightists despise America because its various cultural artifacts—films, music, fast food restaurants—have a corrupting effect on their own societies. Given this view of the United States, how is it possible for the Europeans to make common cause with American radical right groups?[1]

Second, there is the matter of organizational disunity. Radical right groups on both sides of the Atlantic and within the particular countries involved show a strong tendency to split into progressively smaller, self-absorbed fragments, ones usually centered around a single leader. In this context there have been, over the years, various attempts to forge a transnational rightist movement in Europe. During the 1930s, for example, there was an Italian-led effort to create a Fascist International for European youth based upon the presumed universally valid principles of Mussolini's movement.[2] But internal divisions led to a collapse of this initiative within a few years. After World War II, there were several attempts to forge a neo-Nazi or neofascist international—the European Social Movement (Malmö Movement),the New European Order, Young Europe, Euro-Ring, and the World Union of National Socialists—including a Belgium-centered Nazi aggregation during the 1960s. But as with their predecessors these efforts collapsed as the result of personal or national egoisms.[3] There may be the irreducible problem of competing nationalisms. One story, for example, has it that at a recent celebration of Rudolf Hess Day in Belgium young British and German neo-Nazis initially got along well with one another, expressing a common racial solidarity. But after a long night of drinking the sense of racial solidarity dissolved, British-German hostility surfaced and the proceedings concluded in a drunken brawl. So much for Rudolf Hess.[4] In view of this tendency toward fission how is a Euro-American radical right possible?

Neither of the objections noted above pose an insuperable barrier to the emergence of the kind of transatlantic movement with which we are concerned. Many of the American radical rightists and many of the relevant American radical right organizations that belong to the movement hate the United States with as much or more intensity as their European counterparts. It would be hard for a European right-wing extremist to outdo the rhetoric Robert Mathews composed for the Silent Brotherhood's Declaration of War against the United States in 1984:

> It is now a dark and dismal time in the history of our race. All about us
> lie the green graves of our sires, yet, in a land once ours we have become
> a people dispossessed. . . . By the million, those not of our blood violate
> our borders and mock our claim to sovereignty. . . . All about us the land
> is dying. Our cities swarm with dusky hordes. The water is rancid and
> the air is rank. Our farms are being seized by usurious leeches and our
> people are being forced off the land. The capitalists and communists
> pick gleefully at our bones while the vile hook-nosed masters of usury
> orchestrate our destruction. What is to become of our children in a land
> such as this? Yet still our people sleep.[5]

In earlier times it was common for analysts to refer to such 1950s or 1960s American radical right organizations as the John Birch Society or the Minutemen as "patriotic" or "super-patriotic." This characterization probably still applies to some of the contemporary militia groups. But for the racial supremacist groups, the basic allegiance is to race not nation and their feelings towards the United States are hostile in the extreme. They believe it is a profoundly corrupt country largely populated by, and under the control of, their racial enemies. They are hardly patriots, super or otherwise. In short, these radical right groups are every bit as anti-American as their European counterparts.

The second barrier, really a conceptual problem more than anything else, to the appearance of a Euro-American radical right is the tendency towards division and fragmentation. We believe that the Euro-American radical right is a movement, and "movements are sustained interactions between aggrieved social actors and allies, and opponents and public authorities."[6] That is, we do not believe that a movement is or needs be a single cohesive organization with a clear hierarchy. We are dealing with "aggrieved social actors and allies" operating on two continents, a collection of groups, organizations, and individuals sharing a relatively common outlook and similar grievances, not a singleminded conspiratorial organization. Given this view there is nothing incompatible between the tendency toward fission and the presence of a Euro-American radical right. Movements may be fragmented. The latter may influence their effectiveness but will not determine their existence.

What we need to stress here is that the emergence of the Euro-American radical right movement should be best seen in a more general political context. For various reasons there has been a growing tendency in recent decades for political forces on both sides of the Atlantic to have more exchanges with one another. Thus, the highly successful 1997 Labour party campaign of Prime Minister Tony Blair not only involved the emulation of U.S. President Bill Clinton's speeches and campaign techniques, but also included personal encounters between Labour and Democratic Party strategists. In the late 1980s and early 1990s there were extensive contacts between Republican campaign advisors in the United States and their Conservative party counterparts in Britain. Earlier still, there were the widely publicized exchanges between Ronald Reagan and Margaret Thatcher. After the Newt Gingrich–led Republican success in the 1994 congressional elections in the United States, LePen, the French rightist, began talking about the National Front's "Contract with France."[7] Viewed in this light and in an era of globalization, it is not surprising to discover that adherents of extreme right-wing views are also having more to do with one another. And while in the interwar period right-wing extremist influences tended to flow from east to west, from fascist forces in Europe to their North American admirers, the contemporary situation is much more one of balance where right-wing ideas developed in the United States are as likely to cross the Atlantic from west to east as the other way around.

Émigré Politics

This is not to say however that the kind of émigré politics that perhaps typified right-wing extremist activity in the United States during 1920s and 1930s has completely passed from the scene. There is, for example, the case of post-Soviet Ukrainian nationalism.

During World War II the paramilitary wing of the pro-fascist Organization of Ukrainian Nationalists in conjunction with special Ukrainian battalions of the Nazi SS carried out ethnic cleansing operations against Poles living in the eastern regions of the Ukraine. The objective was to make this area part of the Ukraine. After the war many of the Ukrainians involved, including war criminals, fled to safety in West Germany, Canada, and the United States. They and their descendants pursued their ultranationalist objectives from exile. When the Ukraine became an independent country in 1991, the enthusiasm of the émigré organizations for a new wave of Ukrainian irredentism was revived. Literature promoting the incorporation of Eastern Poland into the Ukraine was sent from Canada and the United States to Kiev and elsewhere. In 1997 the Ukrainian Congressional Committee of America met at its New York headquarters, under the auspices of some veterans of the World War II ethnic cleansing atrocities—including former SS men—to commemorate their activities and to consider new measures to advance their cause.[8]

On a somewhat broader canvas, approximately the same picture may be painted of German immigrant activities in North America. In the United States there are the obvious cases of Hans Schmidt and George Dietz. Older men, both were ardent members of the Hitler Youth before leaving Germany after World War II. Despite the changed circumstances, both Schmidt and Dietz retained their virtually unrestrained enthusiasm for National Socialism. Schmidt, a veteran of the Waffen SS and an American citizen, organized the German-American Public Affairs Committee (GANPAC). The latter, run successively from Santa Monica, California; Burke, Virginia; and Pensacola, Florida, is committed to promoting the cause of Holocaust denial and anti-Semitism. Among other things, Schmidt waged a vigorous campaign against the construction of the national Holocaust Museum in Washington. In 1995 Schmidt was arrested in Germany for incitement to racial hatred and Holocaust denial activities. He has come to regard the government in Bonn as treasonous and under the control of "top Jews" (*Oberjuden*).[9]

The Dietz case is similar though his ambitions seem higher. Dietz is a successful West Virginia businessman who uses his Liberty Bell Publications to publish anti-Semitic, racist, and pro-Nazi tracts in English, German, French, and Spanish. This output is then distributed, often surreptitiously, in those countries where the laws prohibit the dissemination of this kind of material; German authorities have found Dietz's publications in the homes of neo-Nazis. Dietz has also been involved with a Josef Schaller, a German citizen, in a plan to use the Union of German Interests, based in Germany (Generalsekretar of the Dachverband Deutscher Interessen), to promote the unification of various radical right groups around the world.[10]

Canada has not been immune to the radical right politics of pro-Nazi German immigrants.[11] During the nineteenth century the area of Ontario, including the communities of Waterloo, Kitchener (whose name before World War I had been Berlin), and Guelph was the site of a significant wave of German immigration.[12] Prior to World War II elements within this economically successful immigrant community were supportive of the Third Reich. After the war ethnic Germans from Eastern Europe migrated to these communities. It is apparently from the latter that pro-Nazi sentiment has surfaced in recent years. The situation is rather odd in that all the secondary schools in the Waterloo County school district teach a compulsory section about the Holocaust in contemporary history courses.[13] Despite (or perhaps because of) this instruction, the area has become a center for Holocaust denial in Canada. Robert-Jan Van Pelt, a historian at the University of Waterloo and the co-author of a widely known volume on the history of Auschwitz, has been the target of repeated insults, threats, and warnings from local residents since the latter's publication. Van Pelt also reports that there are now public celebrations of Hitler's birthday and other milestones on the Nazi calendar.[14]

But the most widely known pro-Nazi German immigrant to Canada is Ernst Zundel. Co-author of *The Hitler We Loved and Why*, for more than two decades the Toronto-based Zundel has promoted the cause of Holocaust revisionism and exalted the National Socialist movement through his Samisdat publishing firm and more recently over the Internet where his homepage, Zundelsite, provides pro-Nazi material in English, French, and German. Zundel is nothing if not indefatigable. He has been tried twice in Canada for his activities and the German authorities arrested him for the dissemination of Nazi propaganda while on a visit to the Federal Republic. In spite of these seeming setbacks, Zundel's business continues to thrive. Officials at the Federal Office for the Protection of the Constitution in Germany regard Zundel as one of the most energetic foreign Holocaust deniers whose efforts they monitor.[15] In fact it is partly because of Zundel's Internet propaganda operations that the German government has sought to restrict its citizens access to America On Line (AOL).

Dietz, Schmidt, Zundel, and a handful of others like them, active in North America, are German immigrants who have defined themselves as defenders of German culture and civilization against all those they perceive as maligning them. Schmidt writes, for example, "GANPAC is the only organization politically defending and representing the interests of the 60 million Americans who declare themselves German Americans, this nation's largest ethnic group. It is

GANPAC's aim to fight the constant defamation of all things German by the American media, to inform the American public of the great contributions by the German-Americans and Germans to the growth and well-being of this nation, and to help build a better society for all."[16] But it is a curious kind of ethnic defense in which these immigrants are engaged in that they are defending a Germany that no longer exists in a struggle with largely imaginary or symbolic enemies (e.g., the film *Schindler's List*). The Federal Republic of Germany is a prosperous, peaceful parliamentary democracy, a country with substantial cultural and scientific achievements to its credit. But Dietz, Schmidt, Zundel, et al., regard this country with the utmost contempt, regarding it as under the control of the despised Oberjuden. Instead they exalt the Germany of the Third Reich, a regime that brought ruin, defeat, and death to virtually all it touched and won for Germany the condemnation of civilized peoples. This sort of émigré politics bears some resemblance to that of white Russian exiles after the Bolshevik revolution (including the Russian fascist movement discussed in chapter 2), with the Nazi dictatorship taking the place of tsarist autocracy. But the comparison requires a fantastic equation of the Federal Republic and the Soviet regime.

Nazi Worship

Dietz, Schmidt, and Zundel and the émigré politics they represent are helpful though in that they point us toward one of the dominant features of the contemporary Euro-American radical right: an admiration for and in some cases worship of the Nazi regime and its Führer. The admiration concerns race and power. Here, for example, is an excerpt from Jost of the NS Kindred, a now-defunct neo-Nazi-oriented Odinist group based in Northern California which will be considered at greater length in the context of communalism:

> National Socialist Germany was a highly successful Aryan Folk-
> community. It provided a natural environment to bring forth a higher
> species of mankind, while demonstrating the amazing social and
> economic viability inherent in Folk-communities. . . . National Social-
> ism is simply a change of consciousness, a change from the usual narrow,
> individual interests to Folk-consciousness: a willingness to place the
> welfare of the Folk above all personal desires and interests.[17]

And, a recent issue of *Calling Our Nation*, the periodical of Richard Butler's Aryan Nations-Teutonic Unity of Hayden Lake, Idaho, shows photographs of Wehrmacht troops on parade in Berlin under the caption "An Awesome Display of Military Might."[18] The message conveyed to those who belong or believe they belong to the appropriate Aryan category is one involving a common bond to a superior and physically powerful community. If you are weak, alone, and defense-less, membership in the "Folk-community" can make you feel strong and full of might. Along with the veneration of Hitler as a wise racial leader, messages such as these are communicated by radical right groups on both sides of the Atlan-tic, from California to the Oder River and beyond and therefore represent an appropriate place from which to describe the Euro-American radical right.

The Euro-American Radical Right

The first thing we should mention in this regard is the radical rightists' social backgrounds. There may be some country-to-country variation to be sure, but what seems clear is that by and large we are dealing with the same kinds of people irrespective of the countries they inhabit. This generalization is not all that as-tonishing in light of the common economic and social conditions we mentioned in chapter 1, but it is worth emphasizing nevertheless. Here we should distin-guish between the members and supporters of militant right-wing extremist or-ganizations and the far larger electorates of radical right parties and factions. The latter seem substantially more heterogeneous than the former. Our primary focus in this analysis is on the extremist organizations, but a few words about the electorates are in order.

In appealing for votes, candidates and parties of the radical right typically have to play down the most extreme aspects of their policy proposals and per-sonal backgrounds. This practice applies as much to David Duke and Pat Buchanan in the United States as it does to Jörg Haider and Gianfranco Fini in Austria and Italy. Thus, in attempting to expand their electoral bases they usu-ally have to make their constituencies more diverse. Despite this logic there is some evidence that voters attracted to such populist candidates and parties on both sides of the Atlantic are drawn disproportionately from males, blue collar and the self-employed or white collar (employed in the private sector) segments of the population. These tend to be individuals whose policy preferences include opposition to free-trade arrangements (NAFTA in the United States, Maastricht in Western Europe), a desire to shrink the state, the welfare state especially (at least the benefits they perceive as directed at undeserving minorities), a xeno-phobic reaction to minorities and various out-groups (e.g., homosexuals), and an authoritarian reaction to cultural diversity and law enforcement problems. These sentiments are not always compatible and there is, as a result, a certain amount of tension built into the relationship between the candidates, the par-ties, and the voters to whom they appeal.[19]

But it is among the members and followers of the right-wing extremist or-ganizations that the similarity of social background is most apparent.[20] The Nor-wegian analyst, Tore Bjørgo, calls attention to the fact that on both sides of the

Atlantic these organizations have developed out-reach programs in the prisons. These programs are intended not only to maintain contact with "political prisoners," that is, members who have been convicted of hate crimes, but more importantly, to recruit new supporters from among the regular prison population. As an example, one of the first acts of the Volksfront, a racial supremacist group formed in Portland Oregon, in 1994, was to establish *Thule*, a journal of "Philosophical, Spiritual, Historical, Political and Tribal Discourse for . . . Political Prisoners and Incarcerated European-Americans."[21] As in Oregon so too in the Federal Republic. In his memoirs, the former German neo-Nazi leader Ingo Hasselbach recalls becoming attracted to the cause while serving time in a Berlin jail.[22]

More generally, in analyzing the social backgrounds of the Euro-American radical rightists it is necessary to pay some attention to what the organizational spokesmen have to say about themselves and their recruits. Here is an account, once again, from the Volksfront:

> The Volksfront was founded by twelve young men who felt the current social and political situation in this nation was quickly becoming irreversible, and genocidal to our European people. In the last two years the Volksfront has grown into the largest Aryan cultural organization in the Northwest United States. Volksfront is part of an international network of like-minded Aryan organizations, our ideology transcends national barriers and thrives where ever (sic) Aryan blood flows.[23]

The following is an excerpt from the Dennis Mahon's White Aryan Resistance newsletter, the *Oklahoma Separatist*:

> A lot of people have contacted us about who we are and who is our "target" group within the White Working people in our Nation. Many folks tell us they really identify with the viewpoints found in the Separatist and wonder if their lifestyles are similar to those of the various authors in our publication. You bet they are WORKING MAN! . . . We draw no distinction between any of the social strata within the working class. We've got Cowboys, Bikers, Skinheads, average workers, college students, ex-street gang members, preachers— you name it, and they get along just fine. So don't get caught up in worrying about Social distinction. . . . Heil.[24]

And here is a brief self-portrait from the London-based European Liberation Front about whom more will be said in chapter 5:

> Who We Are and What We Represent—We are an association of White Peoples, resident in many parts of the world, all our work is voluntary and gratis, we all subscribe, work and expenses are contributed

by a small reliable and dedicated group; Regretfully anonymity is the key to our survival and ultimate success. Our anonymous H.Q. is in London, England, known only to 'Our inner circle.'[25]

The first two appeals for support are aimed almost exclusively at white "Aryan" males. The first appeal is made on the basis of race not class, while the opposite is the case with the second, although racist and anti-Semitic attitudes pervade the whole document. The impression conveyed is that those making the appeals are of about the same social extraction as those whose support they seek. Further, there is an obvious preference for German locutions "Volksfront" in Portland, "Heil" in Oklahoma—as if the German language or Germany was the center of the racial struggle in which these groups have embarked. The third appeal is more circumspect. The European Liberation Front appeals to whites all over the world, without social distinction, but retains social anonymity because "Our inner circle" would be endangered by "the outer forces" lurking in the background. The stress on gender, race, and class combined with the preference for things German (derived from the Nazi past) and the sense of suspicion that "outer forces" (i.e., Jews) are threatening the movement and its goals unless precautions are taken provides us with a reasonably accurate self-portrait of the Euro-American movement's sociology and temperament.

Personal Contacts

But for the movement to coalesce, to be more than simply groups of like-minded people from similar backgrounds located in the various countries of North America and Western Europe there is a need, inter alia, for personal contacts and communications. In this regard there are a number of leaders, not necessarily from the same social milieu as their followers, who have taken on the responsibility of crossing the Atlantic and developing a rapport with their transcontinental colleagues. These entrepreneurial figures include both Americans who visit Europe and Europeans who travel to the United States (or Canada). We think these individual cases should suffice to illustrate the general phenomenon.

Manfred Roeder, the German neo-Nazi leader visited the Reverend Richard Butler in the early 1980s at his Aryan Nations headquarters in Hayden Lake, Idaho. "Roeder traded names of sympathizers with Butler, providing him with contacts in Spain, Switzerland, Scandinavia . . . Australia and New Zealand."[26] In 1995 the American William Pierce, head of the National Alliance and author of the widely discussed *Turner Diaries*, delivered the keynote address to a general meeting of the British National party in London. The same organization hosted Louis Beam, the former American Klan leader and proponent of the idea of "leaderless resistance," a few years earlier.[27] David Irving, the English historian, currently spends half the year in Florida working with Don Black, leader of the Stormfront organization. Some years ago Andy Strassmeir, a right-wing German army veteran, spent some time as a resident of Elohim City, a Christian Identity settlement in Oklahoma, where he became "head of security." Dennis Mahon, the American ex-Klan and neo-Nazi leader, has visited the Netherlands and Germany in order to help locals establish Klan organizations in their respective countries. The American neo-Nazi figure Harold Covington spent some time in Rhodesia and the United Kingdom, where in 1991 he developed ties to Combat 18, the violent racist and radical right British organization (the 18 stands for the first and eighth letters of the alphabet, a and h, in other words Adolf Hitler). In a letter obtained by *Searchlight*, the English antiracist journal, and published in 1992, Covington wrote that he was in the U.K. to drum up British and European support for "a worldwide racial resistance—nothing less than the return of National Socialism to the sacred soil of the German Fatherland."[28]

Roy Godenau (aka Armstrong), a former American G.I. stationed in Germany, became a neo-Nazi sympathizer and married a German woman active in the radical right politics of the Republikaner party. Using his American passport, he now travels to various parts of the world distributing anti-Semitic and pro-Nazi propaganda. Although deceased, we think the late David McCalden is worth mentioning here. Born in Northern Ireland but a long-time resident of Great Britain, McCalden founded the racial supremacist British National party. After some years he moved to California where, using a pseudonym, he became the director of the Institute of Historical Review, the most vigorous of the various Holocaust denial organizations in the United States.[29] McCalden died of an AIDS-related illness in 1990, after a decades-long campaign to stimulate hatred of Jews on both sides of the Atlantic. Last on our short list of Euro-American radical right figures is Gary (aka Gerhard) Rex Lauck of Lincoln, Nebraska. Lauck is presently (1998) in a German prison after having been convicted of violating the Federal Republic's criminal code's prohibitions on the publication and distribution of Nazi propaganda. In addition to his role as an American supplier to Germans of illegal Nazi material, Lauck—a Nebraskan whose mock-German accent is the subject of much mirth in the American movement—is the head of the National Socialist Workers party/Overseas Division (more commonly, NSWP/AO), a modest organization but one with ties to likeminded individuals in the Federal Republic and other European nations.[30] Jörg Haider, the forty-seven-year-old leader of Western Europe's most electorally successful radical right party, the Austrian Freedom party, has been a student at a Harvard University seminar on International Development.[31]

Communications

Not only do members of the Euro-American radical right movement communicate with one another in person, they are able to exchange ideas and information through the print media and over the Internet as well. There is developing, then, a thickening web of associations, attachments, and interactions. The volume of information available on this subject is growing and is already so voluminous that we can only provide the reader with a brief accounting.

Illustratively, the January 1996 issue of the radical right-wing British newsletter *Candour* (whose motto is: "To defend national sovereignty against the menace of International Finance"), contains an article by Pastor Earl F. Jones of Denning, New Mexico, in which the author identifies the Aspen Institute as part of the New World Order conspiracy and goes on to point out some of the latter's Zionist, plutocratic, Bolshevik, and capitalist (!) participants.[32]

Pastor Jones's account is then followed by an article by another and more widely known American, Phyllis Schlafley, who attacks the opinions of Justice Ruth Bader Ginsburg.[33] An article in another issue of the same periodical quotes Pat Robertson on the dangers of a New World Order and refers to the threat to Poland's independence posed by the World Bank and Harvard economist Jeffrey Sachs.[34] *Candour's* advertisement section contains ads for video cassettes on ostensibly American themes: "Waco: The Big Lie" and the life of "Father Charles Coughlin." The advertisements for these cassettes appear side by side with ones calling for support of the right-wing government in Croatia.

In the United States, radical right publications often provide coverage of developments abroad. For example, the July/September 1994 issue of Rick Cooper's *NSV Report* ("A Quarterly Overview of the National Socialist Vanguard") of The Dalles, Oregon, reports on the trial and sentencing of the violent Austrian neo-Nazi leader Gottfried Kuessel. Readers are asked to write him and express their solidarity. The same issue also laments the conviction in London of Lady Jane Birdwell, one of Britain's most widely known Jew haters, for the dissemination of anti-Semitic material.[35] The *ANP Newsletter* ("the official internal organ of the American Nazi Party") does not ignore European developments either. In one issue its survey of "World News Briefs," for example, reports a story on the alleged murder of Rudolf Hess along with an account of a German ceremony marking the fiftieth anniversary of the Allied bombing of Dresden.[36] And on both sides of the Atlantic radical right publications often devote space to the state of Israel and its various iniquities or alleged iniquities. The plight of the white minority in South Africa attracted considerable attention in these publications particularly as that country's leaders were contemplating a turn away from the apartheid system.

But these days it is on the Internet where radical right organizations have become most visible. The availability of World Wide web sites, e-mail, news groups and chat rooms have provided racist, anti-Semitic, and right-wing extremist individuals and groups with previously undreamed of opportunities for communication and interaction on a global basis. Internet technology is being used to perform a number of functions. First, there is the dissemination of publicity. Various organizations on both sides of the Atlantic, the World Church of the Creator, Institute for Historical Review, or the Zundelhaus, for example, have developed home pages in several languages on which the group's doctrines are attractively packaged and explained in varying degrees of detail. For example, there is now a "White Calendar" available for downloading: "This calendar came about through a desire to give white people around the world a look at what our history is and what we have given the world." The intent is to use the calendar to build a sense of racial solidarity by noting the births and deaths of such illustrious whites as Richard Wagner, Paul Revere, and Gabriel Fahrenheit.[37]

Second, the Internet has offered an enormous opportunity for radical rightists to interact with one another across national boundaries: "Norwegian neo-Nazis have published an international contact list giving the country, Bulletin Board names, System Operators, contact numbers, etc. for over forty neo-Nazi groups in Sweden, Germany and the USA."[38] The Norwegian case is not unique, such American groups as Stormfront do likewise. Further, these cyberspace interactions, via the use of mailboxes, create an opportunity for radical rightists to plan personal encounters in ways the authorities find hard to detect. The Thule network in Germany, for example, has been used to plan a transnational get together commemorating Rudolf Hess's death so that the authorities were unaware of its location and precise time.[39]

And third, the radical right presence on the Internet can be used to stimulate violence. Computerized bombmaking manuals coming from the Lauck's NSDAP/AO in the United States have been transmitted to Austria, Germany, France, and the Netherlands for instance.[40] Similar information concerning guerrilla warfare techniques is available from the "Aryan Guerrilla Resistance Warfare" site and elsewhere.

In view of the above it is hardly surprising that various Western governments, Germany's especially, and private watchdog organizations have become interested in limiting the ability of hate groups to gain access to the Internet.[41] Because of the First Amendment, American efforts to censor such speech, along with pornographic displays, have met little success. But in European countries where hate speech is criminalized, the prospects, for better or worse, seem brighter. In Germany, for example, investigations have been undertaken of America On Line and CompuServe because of their willingness to permit the relevant groups to use their Internet facilities.

The Radical Right Subculture

The increased personal interactions and the improved means by which radical rightists can communicate with one another has helped promote the consolidation of a distinct Euro-American radical right subculture, or what we labeled in the previous chapter a cultic milieu. We mean by this term a variety of cultural expressions, both of form and substance, that separate those who share the radical right outlook from the general population on both sides of the Atlantic. It makes some sense to distinguish between the religious and secular aspects of this subculture or milieu. Before we do however we note that there is at least one feature of the subculture that appears common to both religious and secular components: admiration for the Nazi dictatorship and related phenomena.

For the secular skinhead part of the subculture with its "skinzines," white power music, Doc Marten Boots, tattoos and related tough-guy paraphernalia, there is a common Euro-American stress on the slogans and symbols of the Nazi dictatorship. In Italy and Norway just as in the United States there are Reich Skins and Boot Boys whose skinzine publications use German or German-looking words (one Italian skinzine is named *Blitz-Krieg*) to express their preference for Aryans and violent hostility to racial minorities and foreigners, particularly ones from Third World nations.[42] "Sieg Heil" (Hail Victory!) either translated into the local language or in the German original is a common exclamation for neo-Nazi groups on both sides of the Atlantic. The psychologist Raphael Ezekiel reports that members of Detroit area Death's-Head Strike Group were attracted initially to the neo-Nazi movement by watching old World War II films on TV and being impressed by the brutality and strength of the German Wehrmacht.[43] It is also not uncommon for members of such groups to use as salutations "88" (for the eighth letter of the alphabet, H, or Heil Hitler) or "for 18" (for Adolph Hitler).

But the slogans and symbols of German National Socialism seem equally pervasive within the religious part of the subculture. Thus the editorial staff of *Calling Our Nation*, the periodical of Aryan Nations, the Identity Christian organization, include "Col. Gruppenfuhrer" Tim Bishop and "Maj. Sturmbann-fuhrer" C. W. Nelson.[44] Within this subculture there is a strong tendency to treat Hitler not merely as an inspirational political leader, but as a quasi-religious figure worthy of veneration or in some cases as a savior to whom votive candles are offered.[45]

More commonly in Western Europe than the United States, the Waffen SS has taken on a particular subcultural meaning. Because this combat branch of the Nazi SS recruited volunteers from various countries, Belgium, the Netherlands, Denmark, and so on, during World War II, contemporary European radical rightists often have used it as a symbol of the common bond that links all enlightened Europeans together in the defense of Western civilization variously threatened by Bolshevism, Zionism, and Islamicism.

The religious component of the Euro-American radical right subculture includes both pagan and Christian or pseudo-Christian elements. So far as the latter is concerned, Christian Identity, as we have seen, represents a set of beliefs that combine an exotic biblical interpretation with biological racism.[46] In the United States, Identity ideas have come to influence much of the radical right. Adherents seem to be drawn from fundamentalist Christian denominations particularly ones that have grown sympathetic to Israel and the Zionist cause. In the far more secularized countries of Northern Europe, the impact has been far more limited. ZOG or the Zionist Occupation Government, a term used by American Identity followers to describe the government in Washington, has crossed the Atlantic and is now widely used by right-wing extremists in Europe. Also, Identity ideas about the establishment of a separate white Aryan "bastion" or territory have achieved some visibility in Great Britain, but especially in the new South Africa.[47]

While Identity is a religious conception that attempts to synthesize biological racism with a number of Christian beliefs, the other religions that form part of the Euro-American subculture make no such concessions to the Western world's dominant religion. They are explicitly pagan in outlook and tend to derive their inspiration from pre-Christian Norse or German tribal ideas or post-Christian New Age formulations. All equate religion and race.

The pagan religions to which we refer are Odinism, Creativity, and Cosmotheism.[48] So far as the latter is concerned, Cosmotheism is largely the work of William Pierce, author of *The Turner Diaries* and head of the National Alliance. Centered in Pierce's compound in Pocahantas County, West Virginia, it is a religious outlook that looks forward to and indeed seeks to promote the worldwide domination of the white race by a combination of consciousness-raising (for the Aryans) and racial warfare.

Pierce's focus is primarily on the United States and the appeal of his religious ideas outside the country, his Euro-American reputation as a racial theoretician aside, is quite limited. Odinism, on the other hand, travels well. Based upon worship of the old gods of the Norse or Teutonic pantheon, there are followers and sects not only in the United States but also in Germany, Scandinavia, Britain, and South Africa. Accounts suggest the groups involved place strong emphasis on the revival of the festivals, rituals, and customs of the pre-Christian era.[49]

Creativity or the World Church of the Creator ("Our Race is Our Religion") was the invention of the late Ben Klassen, a Ukrainian émigré to the United States.[50] Klassen and his successors repudiate Identity and all other forms of Christian belief on the grounds they are irretrievably corrupted by Jews and Judaism. The leader or "Pontifex Maximus" (the term is derived from Roman religious tradition), currently Mat Hale in the United States, propounds a god-free doctrine that seeks to promote a global Racial Holy War (RaHoWa) against the Jews and the establishment of a new world dominated by the source of all human creativity, the Aryans. While Odinism obviously was a European import to the United States now in the process of being exported back to Europe, Creativity is a purely American invention, but one that has now attracted followers in the Scandinavian countries—there was a Ben Klassen Academy in Sweden under the leadership of Tommy Rydén, and the Creativity Website provides access to a Swedish language home page—as well as South Africa.

In thinking about the secular part of the Euro-American radical right subculture we think it best to make a distinction between its lowbrow and highbrow elements. The first is a manifestation of popular youth culture while the second is the product of intellectuals on both sides of the Atlantic.

For more than a decade white power music and the skinhead subculture have attracted young people all over Europe and North America. Of British working-class origin, the skinhead gangs represented a reaction against long-haired anti-Vietnam youth of the 1960s. The "scene" quickly caught on in the United States and on the Continent: "The intimidating look favored by male Skinheads is instantly recognizable: a shaved head or closely cropped hair; jeans; thin suspenders or braces; combat boots; a bomber jacket, and tattoos of Nazi symbols and slogans."[51] We should add that the uniform and the intimidating look described by the writer are instantly recognizable to citizens of virtually all the countries of Europe and North America from Norway, Sweden, and Canada to Italy, Spain, and Portugal; the "look" of skinhead gangs is certainly Euro-American. The same may be said with respect to the music.

The goal of the youthful Canadian entrepreneur George Burdi, the late English musician Ian Stuart Donaldson, and other young leaders of a racist vanguard is to build a "global community of young neo-Nazi skinheads."[52] To accomplish this task, Burdi and the others have promoted a long list of white power bands, such as Blood and Honor and No Remorse, whose rock music, as performed on CDs, videos, and at in-person concerts all over the Western world, is intended to attract young people to the cause of racial supremacy and racist violence. And to some extent these music promoters and the virtual movement entrepreneurs of the Internet seem to have made some progress. Writing in the *New York Times*, Stephan Talty quotes a twenty-seven-year-old white power music devotee and computer engineer from Dallas as saying, "I have received more contacts, good ones, over the Internet in four months than I have in all four years. I get E-mail from other white-power skins from Sweden, Norway, Finland, Germany, Holland, Luxembourg."[53]

There is a highbrow or at least upper-middlebrow version of the Euro-American radical right subculture as well; one replete with little magazines, scientific or at least pseudo-scientific inquiries, institutes and international conferences. These various endeavors are largely given over to two subjects: scientific racism and Holocaust denial.

In France the Group for the Research and Study of European Civilization (GRECE) has been active since the 1970s. Its inquiries seem to stress a new, nonbiological form of racism—one that emphasizes culture and cultural essences over genetic determinism. To some extent GRECE has been influenced by the late Italian fascist philosopher Julio Cesare Evola. The intellectuals involved in the work of GRECE tend to be ardently anti-American for all the usual reasons. However, one of its publications is the *Nouvelle école*, a periodical promoted by Roger Pearson, an Anglo-American race theorist long active in the United States and former head of the World Anti-Communist League.[54]

In the United States Pearson's work has received the support of the Pioneer Fund. The Fund, created in 1937 by the late textile millionaire Wicliffe Draper, promotes research designed to show that race differences promote inherent differences in intelligence and other traits. Accordingly, over the decades the Pioneer Fund has given millions of dollars to researchers on both sides of the Atlantic who seemed able or likely to demonstrate the accuracy of this view.[55]

Holocaust denial, the belief that the Nazis did not exterminate the European Jews after all or that the killings have been vastly exaggerated for purposes of winning undeserved money and sympathy for Jews, constitutes a second part of the Euro-American radical right's highbrow subculture. That is to say, there are individual "researchers" in Europe and America whose professional careers are given over to promoting the cause of Holocaust denial. The most prominent of these individuals include the French historians Robert Faurrison and Henri Roques, and the Americans, "chemist" Fred Leuchter and Arthur Butz, a professor of electrical engineering at Northwestern University. There are publishing houses (Grabert-Verlag in Germany and Noontide Press in the United States), professional journals (e.g., *Mankind Quarterly* in Britain, *Journal of the Institute of Historical Review* in the United States), and periodically international conferences all given over to the promotion of Holocaust denial. As the Holocaust itself recedes in history, it seems likely that the deniers' activities will intensify, since there are new generations to be won over.[56]

Organizations

The Euro-American radical right is a movement within a movement or, more precisely, a movement within movements. It takes on a variety of organizational expressions. There are, first of all, a number of small groups whose aspirations are Euro-American but whose realities fall far short of the goal. In the United States for example there is the CAUSE Foundation (the acronym stands for

Canada, Australia, United States, South Africa, Europe) established by Kirk Lyons, a Texas lawyer. Lyons adopted the acronym to call attention to the common racial bonds linking beleaguered whites on a worldwide basis. For the most part though CAUSE has confined its operations to providing legal assistance to racists and right-wing extremists who have been accused of crimes in Canada and the United States. The Euro-American Alliance of Milwaukee, Wisconsin, is another small operation whose aspirations well exceed its capacities. Under the leadership of "Major" and "Commander" Donald Clerkin, the Alliance purports to operate a paramilitary unit, the Euro-American Brigade, and does in fact publish two small periodicals on an intermittent basis.[57] Both publications express the need to achieve Aryan unity around the world and the hope of a white separatist homeland far removed from Jewish control and nonwhite contamination.[58] Here is an example of Clerkin's thoughts on American life:

> Whites are beginning to feel the pressure of dispossession. Amerika (sic) is beginning to look like images in National Geographic, its cities resembling Mexico City and Calcutta. The U.S. Armed Services are turning Black, Brown and Yellow. . . . Hi-Tech (sic) jobs are going overseas. The universities fill up with Asians. . . . Media preach a steady stream of "minority rights" propaganda, telling young Whites that they must share their country with the refuse of the entire world. The same message is spread into each and every White country in the world . . .[59]

It should not be hard for the reader to identify the particular conspiratorial force behind these developments.

Not all organizations belonging to the Euro-American radical right movement are the kind of limited virtual one-man bands as CAUSE and the Euro-American Alliance. There are more serious undertakings.

The organizations involved in the Euro-American radical right movement hardly constitute a secret conspiratorial endeavor. Rather, they might best be regarded as separate channels or networks with transatlantic links of varying intensity and with intermittent contacts across the different networks. These Euro-American networks consist of organizations devoted to Holocaust denial, the revival of Nazism, or neo-Nazism in both secular and religious forms, racist skinhead activities and, sui generis the World Anti-Communist League. We should add to this mix the concept of emulation,[60] for in addition to the organizational networks that we have described, there are radical right groups on both sides of the Atlantic who adopt the rhetoric, style, and modus operandi of others without the need of direct contact between them.

Here we have in mind the fact there are now Ku Klux Klan organizations replete with Confederate flags in the Netherlands, France, Germany, and a few other European countries as well. In these cases there may have been some original involvement of American servicemen stationed in Europe. But after their initial organizational support the locals have been left to their own devices. In the United States there are an abundance of neo-Nazi groups. Klanwatch reports a total of twenty-nine active during 1996.[61] In some instances there are transatlantic contacts, as we shall see, but in most cases the American neo-Nazi groups simply emulate the National Socialist originals in Germany without any direct contact with their contemporaries in the Federal Republic. Approximately the same may be said with respect to the skinheads: in some cases there are Euro-American exchanges, but in most it is a matter of emulation or simple copycat behavior. Thanks to television and the other mass media, it is possible for fashions and styles to cross the ocean without the need for direct and personal forms of communication.

The cause of Holocaust denial has stimulated a robust Euro-American radical right network. This has come about for at least three reasons. First, persuading the public on both continents that the Holocaust did not occur is a high priority concern for radical rightists and Nazi apologists interested in reviving popular support for the National Socialist cause. Second, in a number of countries it is illegal to print and distribute Holocaust denial material. As a consequence, if this material is to be produced and distributed, it requires the participation of individuals from more than one country. And because of First Amendment protections in the United States and the high level of freedom printers enjoy in the United Kingdom, Holocaust denial writings in various languages may be printed in these countries and then distributed secretly in the targeted nations.[62] Third, there is a substantial amount of money involved. For example, the Institute for Historical Review in the United States has been the beneficiary of a multimillion dollar bequest left to it by a wealthy patron.[63] Reputedly some wealthy German rightists like Gerhard Frey have been willing to spend money to have this material printed elsewhere and smuggled back into Germany.

We are able to provide a few illustrations. The German-Austrian Institute for Contemporary History is the Austrian arm of the Institute for Historical Review in California.[64] According to the Anne Frank Institute in Amsterdam, the latter organization has a British outlet as well, the Historical Review Press, which has links to other far right groups in the U.K.[65] In Belgium there is the Foundation for Free Historical Research, which specializes in attacking Anne Frank's memory by claiming her diary to be fraudulent. Also active in the Netherlands, the Foundation likewise has ties to the California-based group. The editorial board of the *Journal of Historical Review*, the Institute's principal publication, is composed of an international who's who of Holocaust deniers. According to Gill Seidel, "The international networks advertise each other's publications, contribute and translate articles for fascist journals, attend fascist gatherings, attempt to penetrate other organizations and forums to gain a platform for their ideas."[66]

In an earlier chapter we sought to trace the history of Euro-American neo-Nazi organizational cooperation. At this point we think it a good idea to bring the story forward in time.[67] In the late 1970s and early 1980s the Belgian neo-Nazi organization Flemish Militant Order took the lead in promoting European-wide cooperation among the various groups. In 1979 the Aid Association for National Political Prisoners and Their Relatives was formed for the purpose of coordinating neo-Nazi operations. In 1987 a European neo-Nazi congress was held in Antwerp, Belgium. More than 250 neo-Nazi delegates from the different West European democracies attended the gathering which, among other things, passed a resolution in support of a fight for a "free and white Europe." When German police authorities became fully aware of the network's activities, in the course of arresting one of its leaders, they reported that American neo-Nazis played an extensive role in promoting the work of their European counterparts and of the success they enjoyed in fund raising in the United States. Although the police were successful in dismantling the Belgium-centered initiative, particularly after the arrest of one of the key Germans involved, Manfred Roeder, this has hardly been the end of things.

In the mid-1980s the late German neo-Nazi Michael Kuhnen and several of his collaborators in the Federal Republic had some success in creating a New Front, another loosely tied collection of European neo-Nazi groups. From our perspective, the most interesting feature of this operation was the role played by the American Gary Rex Lauck, the Nebraska-based leader of NSDAP/AO. Although the Front continued on after Kuhnen's death and the German authorities' dissolution of various neo-Nazi groups after the country's upsurge in racist violence in the early 1990s, it is Lauck's role that attracts our attention.

The level of support for Lauck's organization within the United States was quite limited. It was known for years that his stock-in-trade was the publication and surreptitious distribution of neo-Nazi propaganda material in Germany (typically smuggled in via Denmark).[68] But it is only in recent years that the full extent of Lauck's activities have become widely known.

According to the former German neo-Nazi leader Ingo Hasselbach, in fact Lauck was the key figure in the Euro-American, and even international, neo-Nazi network. Lauck's NSDAP/AO became an umbrella organization for many neo-Nazi groups in North and South America, South Africa as well as Europe. Lauck became particularly adept at bridging generational differences between old and new Nazis. In visits to South America and South Africa he succeeded in raising money from old Nazis who had become wealthy farmers and businessmen and then funneling it to the various neo-Nazi groups. Hasselbach reports that the entrepreneurial Lauck also provided him with connections to American radical rightists: Hasselbach met Tom Metzger of the White Aryan Resistance and the KKK figure Dennis Mahon through Lauck.[69]

Fortunately for those opposed to a Nazi revival, Lauck was arrested by Danish authorities in 1995. And despite resistance from his attorneys, he was subsequently extradited to Germany where he was tried and convicted of distributing illegal propaganda, incitement, encouraging racial hatred, and belonging to a criminal group. From his German prison, Lauck continues to write to his colleagues and his work evidently has been taken up by others.

Both Norway and Sweden have become sites for Euro-American radical right organizational activity. This activity has involved both secular and religious aspects. For example, the violent White Aryan Resistance (VAM) in Sweden took its name from Tom Metzger's California-based organization. Likewise its leaders came to see that ZOG had come to control the Swedish government in Stockholm as well as Washington.[70] A Norwegian branch of White Aryan Resistance also stressed the role of ZOG in Oslo.

As we discuss in a subsequent chapter the Scandinavian countries have also been the beneficiaries of some American religious ideas. The Church of the Creator operates in Sweden where, inter alia, a Ben Klassen Academy has been established. Not surprisingly Odinism has managed to attract some followers as well. There are skinhead gangs in virtually all the countries of Western Europe and North America. The Anti-Defamation League (ADL) finds these youth gangs to be in action all over the world including such unlikely locales as Japan and New Zealand.[71] In some cases the gangs are apolitical and in groups such as SHARP (Skinheads Against Racial Prejudice) they actively oppose racial and religious bigotry. But the most visible groups display racist, anti-Semitic, or pro-Nazi sentiments. They are also exceptionally violent. The ADL reports they have been responsible for thirty-seven murders in the United States alone. Racial or ethnic minorities and homosexuals are favorite targets. In Europe the gangs often attack nonwhite foreigners, gypsies, guest workers, political asylum seekers, the homeless, and others who appear to be weak and defenseless.[72] Our concern though is the extent to which these youth gangs have developed Euro-American organizational ties.

The first thing we should mention in this connection is that there is often an overlap between the gangs and neo-Nazi organizations operating in the countries with which we are concerned. In Austria, for example, most skinheads belong to VAPO, an illegal neo-Nazi formation. In Italy, before it was outlawed the Political Movement (MP) led by Maurizio Boccacci served as an umbrella organization for the country's three major skinhead groups: Skinhead Action, Autonomous Base, and Veneto Skinhead Front. In the United States, the Aryan Nations has held skinhead music festivals as a way of attracting youthful recruits to the movement. In any case, to the extent that the neo-Nazi organizations possess Euro-American links and associations they are also relevant to the skinheads' operations. Thus, when Gary Lauck was able to smuggle neo-Nazi propaganda into Germany, he was also able to promote the distribution of a favorite skinhead video game KZ or Concentration Camp at the same time.

Second, beyond the type of linkage mediated through neo-Nazi organizations, skinhead groups in the different countries also have direct contacts with each other. For instance in 1993 and again in 1995 the Portuguese police confirmed that groups in their country were in contact with their counterparts in Spain, Germany, Italy, France, and Switzerland.[73] These contacts are sustained through rock concert performances and white power rock bands that perform in one country after another and cross the Atlantic in both directions. George Burdie and other racial supremacist musical entrepreneurs promote these initiatives in the hopes of strengthening cross-national racial identity among the youth of the different countries. An ADL report on the *Skinhead International* summarizes the situation: "The skinhead movements in these . . . countries are extensively linked to one another. This 'Skinhead International' is maintained through the travels abroad of popular Skinhead rock bands and their fans; the world-wide marketing of Skinhead paraphernalia and recordings; the sale and trading of publications known as 'skinzines'; the wide exchange of propaganda materials and other correspondence; and, increasingly, the utilization of electronic communications."[74]

If the skinheads constitute an international or Euro-American radical right youth movement, then the World Anti-Communist League (WACL) represents an older, more mature constituency, but one attracted to approximately the same kinds of ideas. The WACL was formed in the late 1960s with the financial backing of the South Korean and Taiwanese governments for the purpose of fighting communism on a worldwide basis. Unlike the free-floating, diffuse skinhead movement, the WACL has been a formally organized umbrella organization for various ardently anticommunist conservative groups along with unsavory racist and radical right ones existing in the different countries. So far as the latter are concerned, the *Washington Post* reported that the WACL's 1978 gathering in Washington was attended by delegates from the neo-Fascist Italian Social Movement, such American groups as the National Alliance, Liberty Lobby, and the Anti-Bolshevik Bloc of Nations, the British Crown Commonwealth League of Rights, and so on.[75] Both before and after that occasion, the WACL has provided an institutional setting where leaders of Central American "death squads," East and West European fascists, American and European racial supremacists, and neo-Nazis can encounter one another on a regular basis in a desire to form a radical right common front in the name of anticommunism.[76] The end of the cold war and the disintegration of the Soviet Union has eliminated the WACL's original raison d'être. It is presently a shell of its former self.

Goals

What is the purpose of the Euro-American radical right? What do members of this movement within movements hope to accomplish? There is a strong element of fantasy in many of their writings so it is often hard to distinguish their utopian visions of a racial holy war or the establishment of a separate country from more realistic objectives. Some of their writings and actions appear to be more expressive than instrumental. Despite all this one purpose seems clear.

Most of those involved in the Euro-American radical right seek to achieve a common identity based upon racial affinity. As observers presently engaged in the study of nationalism have pointed out, the tendency of people to identify themselves with particular ethnic groups and nations requires the development of a subjective attachment. It is learned rather than genetically determined.[77] In this context we should point out that in Western Europe and North America national and even ethnic identities are in a state of flux.

The Freemen, Identity Christians, compound dwellers, and so on, in the United States reflect a desire felt by some to disengage personal identities from the American one, from what Gary Rex Lauck refers to as the "Jew'nited States." There is evidence of identity problems in Western Europe as well. There is talk about the formation of a European identity directed toward the European Union.[78] There is some evidence that national loyalties are weakening as ethnic or regional attachments become more salient as in the case of the Northern League in Italy. The percentage of French, German, Italian people who report strong feelings of patriotism has declined over the last few decades.[79]

The current setting is also in some ways reminiscent of the early stages of European racism or that part of it that focuses on the Aryan race. The sense of belonging to an Aryan race and of the latter's superiority is related to the exposure of Europeans to the peoples of other continents over the eighteenth and ninteenth centuries.[80] Today these cross-cultural encounters take place closer to home as people from the different continents have taken up residence in Western Europe and North America. The outsiders have been brought inside.

It is therefore not completely astonishing that a movement active on both sides of the Atlantic has sought to heighten an awareness of a common "Aryan" identity for "kinsmen" whose own countries now seem populated by groups with whom they share little affinity. Members of the Euro-American radical right tend to see themselves as dispossessed in their own lands and hope to find solace in expressions of racial solidarity that transcend their now corrupted homelands.

Conclusion

The purpose of this chapter has not been to scare the reader with an account of a powerful radical right conspiracy whose designs constitute a clear and present danger to the Western democracies. Instead, our purpose has been to trace the contours of the Euro-American radical right movement with regard to its leaders, followers, subcultural characteristics, channels of communication and organizational ties.

We did this largely from the point of view of the observer, from the outside looking in. In the chapters to follow we change lenses. We offer the reader a close-up, an opportunity to meet leaders of the movement on their own ground. Now let us read what they have to say or write about themselves.

Part Two   The Trees

Chapter 5

The Postwar Years
Through the 1970s

An Internal History

A View from Within

IN CHAPTERS 2, 3, and 4, we concentrated on presenting a macrocosmic view of the historical development and political import of the Euro-American connection in the world of the radical right. The presentation was roughly chronological, and was designed to provide the reader with a broad interpretive framework. With this chapter and the two that follow, we move to a microcosmic view. That is, we seek to take the reader from the position of an outside observer looking into the milieu of the Euro-American radical right to a more intimate portrait of the movement as seen from within. Through interviews, movement documents, and private correspondence, we hope to offer the reader something of the emotive quality of the transatlantic connection.

To do so however, it will be necessary to go back to that period when the contemporary transatlantic racialist movement took shape under the leadership of George Lincoln Rockwell and his European contemporaries. In point of fact, just as every radical right winger today must come to terms with the legacy of Adolf Hitler and German National Socialism, so too must every American National Socialist grapple with the ambiguous legacy of Rockwell and the American Nazi party, for it is in the dissolution of Rockwell's party in the last year of his life and the inability of his putative successor, Mattias Koehl, to don the "Commander's" mantle of leadership that is at the root of the movement's current fragmentation.

Finally, a word of caution is in order. In order to hope to translate the dreams and aspirations of the Euro-American race movement into generally accessible terms, we seek to the greatest extent possible to present the reader with a picture of the world as seen through the eyes of the adherents themselves. Thus, figures such as Rockwell who are despised, even demonized, by the mainstream culture may be presented in this context in comparatively positive terms. Indeed, when frequent recourse is made to the words of the far right faithful themselves, the presentation may be laudatory. We believe that if one is to understand the movement it is necessary for a moment to take the intuitive leap that will allow us, for a moment, to see the world as they do.

With this introduction, then, it is clear that the 1967 assassination of the American Nazi party (ANP) leader George Lincoln Rockwell had a tremendous impact on the evolving Euro-American radical right. At a stroke, the primary candidate for transatlantic movement leadership was removed from the scene, not only leaving the ANP in turmoil with no obvious successor to the Commander, but also returning the World Union of National Socialists to its original essence: a quarrelsome band of radical nationalists with no central focus to their interminable arguments and utopian scheming. In assessing the seismic impact of the loss of Rockwell, we recall the Swedish National Socialist leader Göran Assar Oredsson's ambivalent remarks. He declared Rockwell the man as quite admirable, but Rockwell the American as an unacceptable choice for the leadership of an international NS movement due to his nation's sins in the war that defeated Hitler's Germany. Yet this same Oredsson was devastated upon learning of Rockwell's death:

> I was on my way down south [when] . . . I stopped to pick up the evening papers. The headlines cried out to me:
> "He wanted to be America's Hitler" (*Aftonbladet*); "[A] Sniper killed America's Hitler" (*Kvallsposten*); "He wanted to be a new Hitler . . . His dream ended here" (*Expressen*).
> At that movement I wanted to believe—yes wish—that I was dreaming, that I had read wrong. BUT NO, It came clear to me that George Lincoln Rockwell, the USA's National Socialist leader, was no more among us. Again I had to face how a friend, an ideological companion and battle comrade had fallen in our united battlefield in the struggle against our united enemy.
> In movements like this . . . there are no barriers and distances between the different continents. The distance to a friend and battle companion is never more far away then the distance to your own hearth. It was sometime during 1957 that I first came into contact with Rockwell. It was from letters. Rockwell's letters were many and long. My English was surely not what it should be, but with a friend's help our correspondence was the best you could ask for. Rockwell's letters revealed a brain as sharp as a knife. . . . He gave in his letters almost philosophical explanations and had the most interesting

explanations . . . regarding National Socialism and its ideologists. Why
he had the swastika as a symbol, why he called his party Nazi etc. etc.
. . . I first judged him as a deskfighter. Yes even as a fruitless
theoretician. But I was soon to change my mind. It was when his papers;
The Rockwell Report, National Socialist Bulletin and *Stormtrooper* arrived.
From pictures and articles, his movement proved to be the most brave
and hard fighting Stormtroopers as any one could ask for. And every-
where in these pictures of the struggle, the leader Rockwell was in the
front, as the leader, the speaker, the organizer and the hero, when it
comes to courage and fighting spirit.[1]

Although the truth of ANP numbers and effectiveness was considerably
more prosaic than Oredsson's estimation would have it,[2] his eulogy reveals much
of what would bring the American groups to a position of increasing influence
on the European movement scene. Before examining the various ideologies and
theologies which would play key roles in setting the stage for the current convergence of the Euro-American radical right, it might be well to pause a moment and to consider both the context and the implications of Göran Assar
Oredsson's eulogy to the Commander.

First of all, it is important to consider the aspect of position.[3] Despite occasional quixotic efforts to take part in the political life of the nation through such
unlikely third party efforts as the Populist party or more covertly through such
outsider GOP candidacies as those of Pat Buchanan and Pat Robertson, the
American radical right wing in the 1990s finds itself banished to the most distant reaches of the cultural life of the nation. The European nonparliamentary
movements fare little better. In the 1960s, with the energy in the realm of radical political action so concentrated on movements of the left, the far right was
not as culturally distant as it is today. They did, after all, share in a robust anticommunism that did not conflict with the Western Alliance's emphasis on the
policy of containment of Soviet expansionism. Thus, in the U.S., the émigré
politics on which Russ Bellant has written with such alarm were, at the time,
hardly inimical to U.S. interests.[4] What is more, it was only natural that the
unquestioned U.S. leadership of NATO would be reflected in the readiness of
the European movement to, however reluctantly, accept some form of American leadership.

The U.S. had other advantages as well. The First Amendment to the U.S.
Constitution provided the American groups with the political space to export
published materials forbidden by European governments, thus the impact of the
American Nazi party's publications, and thus too the impact of materials emanating from a variety of other ideological and theological appeals. Faced with
this profusion of literature, and impressed by the relative impunity with which
the Americans could produce and disseminate such forbidden knowledge, it was

little wonder that the tiny and fractious community of the American radical right appeared from the vantage point of Europe to be immensely stronger, wealthier, and more numerous than was actually the case.

The Americans benefited as well from greater geographic space. America is a vast nation blessed with wilderness areas where one could to a considerable degree withdraw from the culture which by the 1960s was becoming inimical to the movement. In the Mountain West, in the Pacific Northwest, in the mountains of West Virginia, a man could leave behind much of American society, drop out of its economic culture, cease his relationship with the Internal Revenue Service, and live in sparsely populated lands in which the governing ethos is one of live and let live. Hippies, cultivators of illegal marijuana crops, survivalists, Christian Identity adherents, millenarians anxiously awaiting the End of Days—all of these and many more came to inhabit these fringes in relative equanimity. Hated symbols of federal and state authority could be ignored, intimidated, or occasionally dealt with using much harsher measures with relative impunity in the 1960s and early 1970s.[5] For those of a less independent bent, rural enclaves could be created with living patterns ranging from the open community model of a Dan Gayman and his Church of Israel in rural Missouri to armed compounds such as the Aryan Nations in Idaho or the Covenant, Sword and Arm of the Lord, in rural Missouri.[6] The European activists had no such luxury. The reality of government control and the presence of watchdogs ranging from Jewish groups to the young anarchists who would later coalesce as the Antifa or antifascist movement was for the European movements an everyday fact of life. They could and certainly did repair to the forests for "training sessions," but these were more holiday jaunts than life-style choices.[7] European nations simply lack the geographic depth to allow for physical withdrawal.

Finally, as alluded to throughout this book, the U.S. Constitution provides protection for the expression of unpopular social and political views that is unmatched in contemporary Europe.

What small use the American movement made of its advantages relative to the European movements becomes clear from an examination of recent history as seen from within the milieu of the radical right.

A Revised Look at History

The Depression-era demagogues considered in chapter 2 had, with the exception of the anti-Semitic populist orator Gerald L. K. Smith, faded from the scene. The one right-wing anticommunist organization which had a large national following, the John Birch Society, was an intensely nationalistic group which after 1963 explicitly refused to condone expressions of racism or anti-Semitism from within its ranks.[8] Many figures who would later be influential in the establishment of the transatlantic radical right, men such as Revillo P. Oliver, Jack Mohr, and Tom Metzger to name a few, passed through Birch Society ranks only to leave or be expelled for their expressions of blatant anti-Semitism.[9]

The Birch Society however, required few overseas contacts to spread the good word of Americanism and anticommunism. The U.S. government through the State Department and its intelligence agencies filled this role more than adequately. Thus, until the rise of Rockwell and the WUNS, the once-thriving transatlantic fascist movement was sundered and the potential for transatlantic radical right-wing contacts seemed small at best.

In the U.S. however, there were stirrings under the surface of what would later emerge as a transnational radical right. These stirrings could be detected in the farthest margins of American political and religious life. They came less from "movements" than from loose amalgamations of like-minded individuals whose ideas would contribute to the formation of a far right-wing orthodoxy and, by the 1980s, the birth of the ZOG (Zionist Occupation Government) discourse that would become the hallmark of the modern movement. These early stirrings could be found in the world of explicit National Socialism, in the activities of various Ku Klux Klan groups, and in the world of Identity Christianity. These movements were noted in historical context in chapter 2. Here, it is time to take a closer look at their leaders and their contributions to the creation of the modern transatlantic radical right.

One early stirring of the postwar effort to reestablish links between the American and European movements may be seen in the work of the author of an important text that hit the market in 1948. The book offered interpretations of history that combined elements of such anti-Semitic classics as *The Protocols of the Elders of Zion* with the sweeping historical analysis of Spengler's *Decline of the West*. This book, *Imperium*, was written by Francis Parker Yockey under the pseudonym Ulick Varange. Yockey, a former assistant with the American delegation to the Nuremberg trials, subsequently resigned this position to begin a series of mysterious journeys to Europe where he reportedly was involved in organizing a neo-Nazi movement known as the European Liberation Front.[10] The ELF remained a shadowy organization about which little is known. The name did turn up occasionally through the years, however. In the late 1950s for example, an American adherent wrote an angry letter to George Lincoln Rockwell decrying Rockwell's attacks on America. His words would prove prophetic for much of the movement view of the 1990s:

> Europe is a tired old man—more like a tired old lady—and if Western
> culture is to be saved, it will be saved by the last Western barbarians, the
> American barbarians I love. . . . You and your egghead gang of dandies
> are in love with what is gone and insist on ignoring what is here. Rome
> is no more. You keep trying to resurrect it, but you can't, because there

are no more noble Romans over there, at least not enough to make a real fight of it. Europe is like one big France—all empty shell, fine words, pretty songs, *and dead men*.[11]

Yockey committed suicide in his San Francisco jail cell in 1960 where he was charged with violating passport laws, but his book would live on to contribute much to the ideological framework of the Euro-American radical right. Moreover, the circle of followers he attracted would figure prominently in this rebirth. Among them were Willis Carto, the last man to see the imprisoned Yockey alive, who wrote a fawning introduction to *Imperium* (published by his own Noontide Press), and Else Christensen, a founder of the racialist wing of the Odinist movement. Carto, a cantankerous and highly eccentric publisher whose Liberty Lobby would go on to be an influential player in international movement politics, primarily through its regular *Spotlight* newspaper and through his founding of the influential Holocaust revisionist organization, the Institute for Historical Review.[12] Christensen, who with her husband Alex founded the Odinist Fellowship in 1971, was much influenced by *Imperium* and introduced Yockey's ideas to the international Odinist community through a series of articles in her publication, *The Odinist*.[13]

This apparent resurgence of native fascism alarmed Congress sufficiently to move the House Un-American Activities Committee in 1954 to reopen hearings specifically focused on the subject for the first time since the 1938 examination of the German American Bund. Congressional reasoning continued to equate fascism with communism; a belief which the 1954 report succinctly summarized:

> Both totalitarian doctrines [fascism and communism] are basically incompatible with the principles of our Republic. Both seek to destroy our constitutional government and supplant it with a godless dictatorship in which the individual is deprived of his rights and liberties to become an abject slave of the state. Both derive strength by dividing the opposition—communism choosing to set class against class, while fascism incites racial and religious discord. . . . Furthermore, the appearance of neo-fascist organizations and methods in the postwar period serves only to impede the intelligent, united effort necessary in the current life or death struggle with communism.[14]

National Socialist Linkages—James Hartung Madole

With this formulation, the HUAC neatly dismissed the radical right self-image as the "watchmen on the wall" in the nation's battle against international communism. This settled, the Committee quickly set its sites on James Hartung Madole and the National Renaissance party as the prime exemplar of contemporary American neo-fascism. Thus, it is with Madole that we begin this chapter's examination of explicitly National Socialist figures whose ideas would contribute to the building of the transatlantic movement. Madole, a great admirer of Francis Parker Yockey's *Imperium*, retained a strong interest in events in Europe, as well as the emerging third world liberation struggles, but his true legacy to the movement was his later efforts to link National Socialist doctrine to the occult, and in particular, to the worlds of theosophy and of explicit Satanism in the 1960s. Madole was largely an isolated figure in this stage of his life—communicating his highly eclectic message through the pages of his *National Renaissance Bulletin* until his death from cancer at the age of only fifty-one.

After his death, Madole was largely forgotten by the movement to which he contributed so much. Today however, Madole is experiencing something of a renaissance in the writings of movement figures on both sides of the Atlantic as a visionary whose thought was decades ahead of his time.[15] Moreover, Madole helped to plant the seeds for renewed transatlantic cooperation through his European contacts, especially in Sweden.

Yet at the same time, Madole's National Renaissance party endorsed a strongly nativist platform that contrasted sharply with the borderless racial nationalism that the NRP held equally dear. It is a split that afflicts the movement to this day. It would therefore be valuable to consider the NRP's original nine-point platform that appears to hold two central, and utterly contradictory tenets: racial nationalism for which identification is based on race rather than national origin, and its antithesis, nativist Americanism. Published in the October 1953 issue of the *National Renaissance Bulletin*, the platform's preamble affirms a dedication to the welfare of the racial collective over the interests of any individual, and states that the current political parties serve "the interests of international Jewry." The preamble reveals a constellation of beliefs that would later become ubiquitous in the movement; a fear of declining white birthrates, fear of intermarriage (especially with Jews), but of greatest resonance, a preoccupation with purity and disease, both in its metaphorical and clinical senses. This said, the NRP's nine point platform reads as follows:

> (1) To encourage racial nationalism among the people's [sic] of Europe, Africa, and Asia as an antidote to the spread of international communism . . . We must also repudiate the operetta-state of Israel unless we wish to drive the entire Middle East into the open arms of Soviet Russia in order that our political windbags in Washington may appease a howling pack of New York kikes, whose sole contributions to American culture have been syphilis and usury.
>
> (2) To enforce a strict policy of racial segregation in America in order to preserve and advance the culturally dominant White Aryan Race which brought the cultural and social benefits of Western Civilization to our

shores in 1492. (By the "Aryan Race" we refer to the Nordic, Celtic, Anglo-Saxon, Latin, and Slavic peoples.)

(3) To bring about a gradual deportation of those racial elements which cannot be assimilated with the culturally predominant White Race. Laws must be passed to prevent racial intermarriage. (Those racial elements which cannot be assimilated in the Aryan racial community are the Puerto Ricans, Negroes, Jews, and Asiatics.)

(4) The Jewish race which constitutes the motivating financial and intellectual force behind Communism, shall be deprived of their American citizenship and hence barred from all political and professional posts. Marriage between Jews and the dominant White Race will be forbidden. (During the past 20 years the Jews have managed to obtain a tremendous hold on American politics, art, culture and commerce. No people on earth with a vestige of pride in itself and national honor will tolerate such a domination of the KEY professions by members of a completely ALIEN race. At the same time, the Jews are a determining factor in those political parties which have sought to undermine the last vestiges of racial and national pride in America. The Jew constitutes an Alien virus in our national bloodstream and as such must be purged from our cultural, economic and political life.)

(5) To bring about the withdrawal of the United States from the United Nations in order to prevent further exploitation of American resources and manpower by foreign parasites. (In regard to foreign trade, America must develop a policy of preserving the American market for the American farmer and manufacturer. America must "Buy American" and subsidize, if necessary, American scientific ingenuity toward the end of producing chemically many of those products which are not found here in America but upon which the nation is dependent.)

(6) The alliance of German scientific and military genius combined with American technology, mass production technique, and manpower could dominate both the American and European continents. Therefore our foreign policy must have the three fold objective of realizing a German-American alliance in Europe, a Moslem-American alliance in the Middle East, and a Japanese-American alliance in Asia.

(7) The Creation of an American Corporate Economy wherein labor and management will be equally represented in an Economic Dept. of the Federal Government . . .

(8) The abolition of parliamentary government [in favor of a] national minded elite.

(9) The use of all educational facilities to imbue the American youth with an intense feeling of racial and national pride as a sure antidote to the international poison of World Communism.[16]

The NRP's 1953 program document is a remarkable encapsulation of the dilemmas which the movement has yet to resolve. Save for the somewhat archaic references to the menace of "international Communism," the same themes that are endlessly rehashed in contemporary movement discourse are set forth. There are in these nine points a number of remarkable juxtapositions. Point one, the exhortation to racial nationalism, remains a staple of movement discourse. It is written so as to embrace the Christian Identity doctrine of all creation being returned to its original place and status as based on the Identity hermeneutic of Genesis, but it fits as easily the contemporaneous pattern of the rise of the Non-Aligned Movement on the world stage, or the later convergence of interests between American black nationalists such as the Nation of Islam and the white separatist movements of the 1980s. Indeed, Madole would have a number of successful conclaves with black nationalist organizations.[17] Finally, the reference to Jews having assumed control in Washington presaged the ZOG discourse just as the reference to Jews as bearers of disease linked Madole to a far older tradition of anti-Semitic discourse. Yet it is significant that the NRP's platform as an avowedly white nationalist party would be centered on world affairs first, with American concerns added almost as an afterthought. The second point, while ostensibly demanding racial segregation, is of greater modern import for its controversial definition of the "Aryan Race" as including Slavs. While Hitler's race eugenists would surely have taken issue with this view, here in 1953 are the seeds for the creation of a transnational racial consciousness.

Points three and four are standard fare for the time, and have aged not at all, dealing as they do with the forced separation of the races and the Jew as an "alien virus" in the pure bloodstream of America.

Of greater interest are points five and six. Here in stark juxtaposition lies the central contradiction of the postwar movement. Point five is a purely nativist exhortation to look inward, to "buy American" and to utilize science to produce artificially whatever resources cannot be obtained domestically. The sentiment could have been drawn from any number of Depression-era demagogues as easily as it could echo the most fanatically suspicious member of the militia movement of the 1990s. Yet how to reconcile this jingoistic ideal with the international alliance structure mandated by point six, demanding regional alliances with, unsurprisingly, each of the defeated Axis powers?

In this riddle lie two important observations which hold true of the radical right throughout its modern history. First, anti-Semitism and its concomitant elements of conspiratorial thinking, an intense quest for "purity" (be it of blood or of the natural environment), and a sense of vulnerability—of a race under siege and in imminent peril of extinction, is the movement's driving force. All else is of secondary import, and it is under the banner of anti-Semitism that any number of contradictory statements and actions can be rationalized by a milieu that is otherwise highly resistant to accepting contradictory information.[18]

Second, for all of its seeming isolation, the radical right is well aware of world events, and in fact, is on the whole probably better read and more thoroughly informed on current events than are most citizens. This stems from the ceaseless search for "hidden truths," the bits and pieces of data that are assembled from an eclectic and wide-ranging corpus of sources to assemble in jigsaw puzzle fashion a picture of the hidden hand underlying the seemingly random course of everyday events. In the process, however, the denizens of the radical right-wing come to unconsciously mirror the world they so despise. Thus, point one's unintended encapsulation of the rise of third world nationalism that would culminate only two years later in the Bandung Conference and the formal creation of the third path of the Non-Aligned Movement. And so too point six's suggested alliance pattern at a time when NATO would soon be joined by a series of U.S.-led regional alliances in Asia and Latin America. In many ways, the radical right serves as a kind of caged canary—the bird that miners take into coal mines to warn of hidden dangers long before they reach the level of consciousness. The study of this esoteric subculture can foretell national controversies yet to take place.[19]

The final points merely seek to institute the practices of the German National Socialist government in 1950s America. Point seven is little more than a lionization of the German National Socialist economic model while point eight has much the same intent in the political sphere. Point nine completes the trilogy in the area of education.

Like all American radical right-wing groups, the National Renaissance party never amounted to much in terms of numbers, with estimates running as high as 700 or as low as 50.[20] Madole, an inveterate streetcorner orator, attracted small coteries of like-minded followers, a larger group who attended the meetings to heckle or disrupt the proceedings, and a shifting group of curious onlookers amused by the spectacle presented by both factions. Yet the group's importance transcends mere numbers. Through its ranks or in the pages of the *National Renaissance Bulletin* passed a number of key figures in the American radical right. The head of the NRP's Nazi-uniformed bodyguards for the diminutive Madole for example was Matt Koehl, later to take his uniform into the service of George Lincoln Rockwell and the American Nazi party—an organization he would inherit and through his inept leadership would fragment on the death of the commander.[21] Eustace Mullins, an acolyte of Ezra Pound and later an influential conspiracy theorist, found his early voice in the *National Renaissance Bulletin*, as did such intellectual fascists as Fredrick Charles Weiss and another key figure in the later American Nazi party, Dan Burros, the author of the ANP's *Stormtrooper Manual*, and some-time Klansman and Odinist. The Jewish Burros, who once seemed headed for a career as a cantor, proved the greatest embarrassment, however, committing suicide when newspaper revelations of his Orthodox Jewish childhood effectively ended his movement career.[22]

Of greater interest to the genesis of a postwar transatlantic movement how-ever, was the NRP's creation of a grandiosely named Overseas Office under the command of Mana Truhill, whose real name was from a movement standpoint less attractive—Emmanuel Trujillo.[23] The NRP's primary overseas contact, ac-cording to the HUAC report, was the Swedish father of Holocaust denial, Einar Åberg.[24] Åberg was indeed a key figure in reforging international movement link-ages, and so we must leave for the moment the fascinating adventures of James Madole and his NRP and turn to Åberg's story. It is important to note however, that at this point in history, the flow of materials and ideas remained as they were before the war, from Europe to America. Madole received and disseminated English language materials from Åberg. It is likely that Åberg was sent copies of the *National Renaissance Bulletin*, but there is no evidence that he distributed the journal.

National Socialist Linkages—Einar Åberg

Einar Åberg is often credited with doing much to keep alive the flame of post-war anti-Semitism in Sweden. A single-minded anti-Semitic fanatic, he was con-verted to the cause by his reading of *The Protocols of the Elders of Zion* circa 1922. His life would never again be the same. During the war, he formed the viru-lently anti-Semitic Sveriges Antijudiska Kampförbund (Sweden's Anti-Semitic Battlefront). Among the first to realize the obstacles that the public perception of the enormity of the Holocaust would present for the reformation of an inter-national anti-Semitic movement, Åberg began his denial activities in 1944. This was a full three years before the texts that are most commonly considered to be the first works of Holocaust revisionism would appear: those of Maurice Bardèche (1947) and Paul Rassiner (1948), making Åberg arguably the father of Holo-caust denial.[25] Clearly, Åberg, like Madole, was a man well ahead of his time. As a result, in a career which lasted more than four decades, his was usually a one-man organization. Yet like Madole, Åberg's contributions to the movement far transcend his limited following. His materials were translated into several languages, and his contacts ranged from the U.S. to other Scandinavian coun-tries, Germany, England, and South Africa. Indeed, no less an anti-Semitic po-lemicist than the Englishman Arnold Leese who is best remembered today in movement circles for his revival of the ancient blood libel of Jewish ritual mur-der, spent a year in prison in 1947 for distributing Åberg's materials![26]

Einar Åberg did indeed seem to have undergone a sudden and radical trans-formation upon reading the *Protocols*. One young Jewish activist in Stockholm recalls that an uncle of his mother, the famous Swedish artist Isaac Grunewald, was a high school classmate of Einar Åberg. This however, was not the same Åberg as he would become following his post-*Protocols* conversion. Appalled to find his old classmate walking up and down the Kungsgaten in Central Stockholm around 1942 peddling anti-Semitic tracts, a heated argument ensued that almost culminated in the two coming to blows.[27] It was undoubtedly not the first nor the last time that Åberg's efforts would draw the violent ire of the Swedish public, but like a true believer, angry words or physical beatings did nothing to dissuade him from his course.

This less than artistic street confrontation followed nearly a decade of tireless anti-Semitic pamphleteering by Åberg. The 1930s was indeed a busy period, with Åberg working by day in a Stockholm book shop owned by Carl Ernfrid Carlberg whose economic support was of key importance to the Swedish National Socialist movement. By 1934, Åberg's day job would be augmented by his association with a violently anti-Semitic newspaper, Nationen (The Nation), a position he would retain for two years.[28]

These positions did little to slow Einar Åberg's passion for writing and disseminating anti-Semitic propaganda under his own imprimatur. His productive "literary" period began in 1933 and included literally scores of pamphlets and several full-length books, including his own translation of The Protocols of the Learned Elders of Zion (Israels Vises Hemliga Protokoll), and An Accusation (En Anklagelse). In addition to his own prolific output, Åberg spent the war years distributing Nazi anti-Semitic propaganda which he received gratis from Germany. In 1944, he paraded around the streets of Stockholm in a sandwich sign reading: "The Jews are the cause of the war and the aggressors," which caused a fair share of disturbances and encouraged further police action.[29] After the war, Åberg was equally tireless in attempting to rebuild international National Socialist and anti-Semitic ties,[30] which by the 1950s had brought him into contact with, among others, James Hartung Madole.

The American clown prince of the 1960s New Left, Abbie Hoffman, once joked that the mark of the successful agitator was to irritate the state sufficiently to stir it from its habitual lethargy to induce it to legislate the miscreant out of existence.[31] By this measure of success, Einar Åberg seized the brass ring in 1956 with the passage of the Åberg Law against incitement to racial hatred. Åberg was further "honored" by being the first to be prosecuted and jailed under the eponymous statute.[32] This law, however, proved no more effective at curbing Åberg's enthusiasm than had the existing 1948 law against incitement under which he had been convicted no less than nine times between the years 1941 and 1945 for distributing anti-Semitic material.[33] Åberg's conviction and year-long incarceration under the same charges are particularly noteworthy from the perspective of this book, as great pressure was exerted on Swedish authorities to file charges they knew from long experience would not deter Åberg for long by the American Jewish Committee in New York.[34] Undaunted, by 1960 he had been indicted no less than sixteen times under the law! But by then, he was in the twilight of a long and extraordinarily active career. Old and ailing, Einar Åberg announced his retirement in 1964, capping four decades of singleminded anti-Semitic agitation.[35]

Einar Åberg' s legacy to the movement is immense, and unlike James Hartung Madole, he would not suffer the indignity of being forgotten by his numerous spiritual progeny. The Swedish movement well remembers him. His pioneering postwar efforts to keep together an international network of National Socialist-oriented anti-Semites paved the road for Rockwell and the World Union of National Socialists. Moreover, again unlike Madole, Åberg was succeeded by a younger acolyte, Dietlieb Felderer, who proved as untiring in his own Holocaust-denial activities and as committed to internationalism as was Åberg himself.[36] Moreover, according to the leading Swedish historian of the movement, Dr. Heléne Lööw:

> The Swedish racial ideologists of the 1990s look to Einar Åberg as a source of inspiration. He is an amalgam of nearly everything the contemporary militant-race-revolutionaries stand for: a strong orientation toward the international struggle for the white race, militant methods, European National Socialist inspiration blended with ideology from the American Ku Klux Klan and South African White Supremacists.[37]

Einar Åberg died in 1970, and once again it was left to Göran Oredsson to offer a eulogy for a good friend whose name had become synonymous with anti-Semitism in Sweden:

> Einar Åberg—the internationally known Swede, the man who couldn't be broken by threats, hatred or harassment, the man who despite illness, prison sentences, fines and legislation (lex Åberg) kept on telling the truth—is gone. . . . The legacy Einar Åberg left makes it necessary for all us fighters for the truth around the world to follow. It is our duty to carry on his struggle.
>
> Einar Åberg's political activities are beyond comparison (on a Swedish basis). And the memory of Einar Åberg has during recent years been carried on by the modern generation of activists, and in 1993 the Einar Åberg memorial foundation was founded, by Rev. Tommy Rydén.[38]

The Einar Åberg Foundation was an idea that never got off the ground. Tommy Rydén, who is the subject of chapter 8, so admired Åberg that he proposed the Foundation and briefly considered adding Åberg's birthday to the calendar of official celebrations of the Swedish Church of the Creator that Rydén then headed. The idea died for lack of response. Worse, when Rydén contacted Åberg's son in a quest to learn more of the man who had died when Rydén was only four years of age, he was told that the tireless anti-Semitic propagandist never spoke of his obsession in his home and the son professed to know nothing whatever of his notorious father's activities.[39]

National Socialism and the Occult

James Madole and his National Renaissance party would not enjoy the movement's accolades as did Einar Åberg, but he too left behind a remarkable, if remarkably different, legacy. The NRP, too, played an important role in paving the way for the more flamboyant and charismatic Rockwell and the WUNS. But of greater import, by the 1960s Madole's occult explorations began to open new pathways from the occult and neopagan revival into the world of anti-Semitism and explicit National Socialism. In truth, an examination of the *National Renaissance Bulletin* over the nearly three decades of its existence reveals little to recommend it to the movement or to historians of the period in any sense other than its mystical quest along the path first blazed by William Dudley Pelley in the 1930s. Madole's writing style was uninspired,[40] his support for the Soviet Union under the banner of world anti-Semitism was, to be charitable, naïve, and his anti-Semitic screeds and coverage of world and local events added new dimensions of tedium to the term "superficiality."

Moreover, his predictions of American economic and political collapse and the ascendance of world totalitarianism of both the left and the right which he repeated with all the imagination of the grayest Stalinist aparatchik imaginable read today as the stuff of farce rather than serious propaganda. But Madole's occultism was of another order altogether. Here, Madole's florid imagination both reflects the occultist currents of the cultic milieu of his day and serves as a kind of archetype of imagined history in which the white race is credited with every achievement of human civilization, real and imagined. Best stated in his ongoing "New Atlantis" series in the 1970s-era *National Renaissance Bulletin*, Madole outlines his conception of the past glories of the race and the chiliastic world to come. In his own words, Madole states that the series' purpose is to "impart to ARYAN MAN both his immense racial heritage stretching back over ONE MILLION YEARS into prehistoric times and his forthcoming Divine Mission to create a higher type of humanity beside which mankind of the 20th century will appear as mental and physical anachronisms."[41] Built of an idiosyncratic reading of history and such spiritualist sources as Madam Blavatsky and the Theosophist channelers, Madole writes:

> The subhuman elements in our society, dominated by the accursed Jew,
> can only intimidate and govern Aryan Man while he remains in abject
> ignorance of his glorious racial heritage derived from the hoary archives

of Lost Atlantis, Tibet and Mother India. In short, as long as Aryan man remains Christian he will inevitably remain a slave to the Jew who imposed his Semitic heresy upon the Aryan mind![42]

This formulation was not new, and it would be a recurrent theme in the writings of Odinists, National Socialists, the Church of the Creator, and with the cosmetic change of the adjective "Jewish," in the Christian Identity polemic against "Jewish" Christianity.[43]

Quite unlike other racialists of his generation, the occult explosion of the late 1960s did not catch James Madole unawares. Rather, he was a man ahead of his time for whom the proliferation of religious experimentation of the day was tailor made. Pushing ever further into these strange realms, Madole was quickly aware of the formation of the Anton LaVey's Church of Satan, and maintained an active and friendly correspondence with LaVey himself. Moreover, such explicitly racialist satanic organization as the Detroit-based Order of the Black Ram, formed by the Michigan State organizer of the National Renaissance party Seth Klippoth, may be traced to Madole's early influence, and maintained close contacts with him and his NRP throughout the 1970s.[44]

Interestingly, the Order of the Black Ram did not choose to make its connections to Madole or its racialist origins and intent part of its own official history, emphasizing instead only its connection to the Church of Satan.[45] The Church of Satan's internal correspondence however, is much more enlightening on the matter. This material well illustrates both the intertwining of occult and racialist belief systems and the transnational appeal of racialism's occult path. The material is reproduced in Michael Aquino's unpublished history of the Church of Satan in which he got his own start in the world of Satanism and where, before his break with Anton LaVey, he was a member of the COS's governing Council of Nine. LaVey's attitude to Madole is instructive:

> The NRP headed by Madole, is composed largely of acned, bucolic types transplanted to New York. They spend their time getting jeered at in street demonstrations. Yes, the Nazis did it too, but they had a fresh approach. Nowadays swastikas sell books and movies. . . . I know Madole personally, and have been to NRP headquarters. Even have a card. They would do anything for us. So would [the] Klan for that matter. I do not endorse either, but acknowledge camaraderie from any source. Madole is actually a nice chap who is doing his thing. No need to fret over Hell's Angel's types. They will come in handy one day, whether they be American Nazi Party or Jewish Defense League.[46]

LaVey's genial tolerance of Madole and the NRP was typical enough of the COS and of the wider cultic milieu, but at the same time internal efforts were begun to both coopt the NRP and at the same time to distance the Church of Satan from overt associations with National Socialism. The latter undertaking in Aquino's account involved both LaVey and Aquino. The immediate source of their concern was the activities of Seth Klippoth in Detroit. LaVey had been apprised of the news that, soon after his resignation from the COS, Klippoth and other NRP activists brought their newly formed Order of the Black Ram to an Odinist gathering in Toronto which included representatives of Canada's Western Guard and the National Socialist White People's party. Moreover, Madole had made subsequent efforts through Klippoth and others to recruit COS members into their organizations.[47] The result was an intensive round of internal correspondence that would define the Church of Satan's, as well as the later Temple of Set's, official position on Nazism.

It is important to note that to both Aquino and LaVey, German National Socialism and the figure of Adolf Hitler is not seen in a negative light. To Aquino, *Mein Kampf*, if read with the mental resolve to eliminate its references to anti-Semitism as a mere personality quirk of the Führer, is an unrivaled political textbook whose efficacy meets the primary satanic criteria for excellence: it and the governmental doctrines that were propounded under its blueprint, work, for they "are the true essence of political power."[48] It is with anti-Semitism however, that the COS parts company with Nazis:

> Now you may understand why all avowed neo-Nazi groups are pariahs in the eyes of the Church of Satan. First, they know nothing of the true keys of power employed by Hitler. Instead, they glorify the anti-Semitism and the more ostentatious attributes of Nazi Germany which have been glamorized by Hollywood. Secondly, they openly champion Nazi Germany by name, setting themselves up publicly against the Auschwitz taboo. Thirdly, they propose 1930s solutions to 1970s problems.[49]

Aquino concludes with the accurate observation that these "Hollywood Nazis" are regarded by most Americans as "refugees from a loony bin" and that if their longed-for right-wing backlash did occur in the U.S., they would be the first to be eliminated, as an American Führer would appear in a business suit rather than a swastika armband and would be touting the values of America in 1776 rather than Germany in the 1930s.[50] This truism is yet another seemingly unbridgeable contradiction of the transatlantic movement of the present day.

LaVey himself endorses these sentiments, but reveals a more Machiavellian turn of mind. Based on his own experience with the NRP and its leader, LaVey sets out the foundation for much of the later interaction between the satanic and the National Socialist worlds which would be so prominent a feature of the 1990s movement:

> The NRP is enamored with the Church of Satan. Their racist ideals are

also worn on their sleeves and, I believe, are as removable as their armbands . . . symbolism and symbolism alone supplied their identity. That is how it is with most outlaw groups. There are only two ingredients necessary for their existence: a symbol and a scapegoat. The NRP already has the swastika, but obviously is drawn to our sigil. They have the "Jews and Niggers," but if properly propagandized could transfer their wrath to our enemies. How? Through just such extensions of propaganda as [The] Occult [and the Third] Reich which have emerged from *Satanic Rituals.* . . . [Their belief patterns are simple and we] are dealing with intelligence levels on which ideals and imagery are easily interchangeable . . . [thus they think] All my life I've been the weakling, but with my swastika I am strong. My Satanic amulet gives me power. I'm not a misfit anymore, with pimples and a heart murmur and flat feet. What does it matter if I can't play baseball or spell too good? So what if I can't get a girl—I got my armband. . . . Maybe we can get the C/S to help us defeat the kikes and niggers so America can be pure again.[51]

It is this desperate search for allies and acceptance in the face in nearly universal hostility and scorn which makes the National Socialist enthusiasts under Madole such ideal candidates for recruitment into the Satanist churches. In the event, LaVey proved prophetic, for this would be a major pattern in the milieu of the transnational radical right of the 1990s.

This would do little enough for Madole in his lifetime. James Hartung Madole died on 6 May 1971. His mother, Grace, tried to keep the already nearly defunct National Renaissance party alive for the last two years of her life, to little effect. Then in an irony that perfectly symbolized Madole's life's work, the last leader of the NRP died in a common street mugging and the organization's records were scattered to the winds over the blood-spattered highway.[52] Madole, and the NRP, soon faded from memory.

Yet it was Madole who did much to establish transatlantic contacts, open new paths to National Socialist beliefs, and would through his tireless activism keep the flame of National Socialism alive in the bitterly hostile postwar years. His organizational model, not to mention the use of uniformed activists, predated Rockwell's own American Nazi party, and it is likely that much of Rockwell's early organizational structure was borrowed in toto from the NRP through the defection of Matt Koehl among others from the NRP to the ANP. It is true that National Socialist occultism is not for everyone, and even today is a minority trend in the world movement. But where in the 1990s this is a vital and much traveled path, in the 1950s and early 1960s, it was virtually unheard of—especially in America. Madole was simply decades ahead of his time, and his current obscurity is very much a product of this isolation.

National Socialism—The Commander

Far more successful was George Lincoln Rockwell and his American Nazi party. Of course, success in this milieu is a relative term. Rockwell's ANP at its height hardly numbered more than Madole's National Renaissance party. Estimates range from around 500 hard-core followers to a more realistic 150, of whom only a few dozen could long manage the rigors of Rockwell's impoverished party headquarters in Virginia. Perhaps a dozen others lived in a fractious state of tension on the West Coast. By the early 1960s, even the most biased watchdog sources agreed with movement insiders that the Party had shrunk to perhaps fifty or sixty.[53] Yet it was Rockwell and not Madole who would have the greatest success on the international stage through the World Union of National Socialists. It was under Rockwell, too, that the tide of movement leadership began to shift from Europe to America. Of even greater contemporary import, America began to serve as an important center for the publication and distribution of National Socialist propaganda materials.

Moreover, where Madole's followers (with the exception of a few soon-to-be ANP members such as Matt Koehl) were hardly to go on to movement stardom, Rockwell's alumni serves as a virtual who's who of the contemporary racist right. We have considered Rockwell and WUNS elsewhere, but in the self-view of the movement, his contribution to the creation of a transnational racialist movement are such that some further discussion is in order.

Rockwell's primary interest in his overseas activities was to gather together the scattered faithful of the anti-Semitic and racialist right under the banner of explicit National Socialism. The World Union of National Socialists was built to unify these highly disparate activists so as to fulfill the slogan immortalized by the title of Rockwell's first book: *This Time the World!*[54] In this aim he would be disappointed. As we have seen, even committed National Socialists and Rockwell admirers such as Göran Oredsson for a variety of reasons chose to stay aloof from WUNS. Others who could ally with National Socialists over the Jewish question or over matters of race too shied away from membership, fearing the stigma attached to the swastika symbol. Rockwell's frustration over this state of affairs is reflected in his correspondence of the period. Typical of this frustration is a 1958 letter from Rockwell to Einar Åberg. It is reproduced in full below to offer an insider's view of the difficulty of establishing alliance relationships in the postwar transnational radical right. In reading this, it is important to keep in mind that Åberg was not himself a National Socialist, although it was from the N.S. camp that much of his support was drawn. Rather, Åberg's fanaticism was centered wholly on the Jews, and through this obsession, with the Holocaust.

Dear Mr. Åberg,
Thanks for the two envelopes of materials on the Jewish question. They

are all superb—particularly the piece about the poor six million Jews "gassed" by Hitler. That one is a beautiful piece of factual work. But I am drowned,—steeped, soaked and deluged with such material. My basement is full of it. Not much of it is of a quality to compare with yours,—but to be perfectly honest,—what I hoped for, from you, was not education in a matter in which I am already a tragically aware master, but a reaction concerning my request for a UNION of all of us to FIGHT, under a REAL master, Adolf Hitler.

Perhaps it was filched from the envelopes, but I found no personal letter at all. Am I to conclude that even YOU are scared to communicate with me? I have openly declared my allegiance,—and more,—to Adolf Hitler here in the Jewish center of the earth,—and so far I am still alive and kicking,—altho [sic] I am aware that they are desperately scrambling to for a way to make me out a cheap criminal or madman,—as they have you. What is your reaction to a WORLD UNION of National Socialists?—

Will you please write and let me know,—in a sealed envelope, your own ideas of what we are going to DO about the approaching Jewish seizure of OPEN mastery, to complete their present conquest of the world in secret. I am not interested in any more EDUCATING.—Here in the U. S.,—and I imagine in your country too,—millions of people already KNOW the score,—but will NEVER do anything to change the situation because they are AFRAID. SOMEBODY has to stand up and fight,—and STAY standing up in spite of all the Jews can do,—then we can expect to see millions crawling out from under their beds to join us.

You surely have proved your incredible courage and determination,—and I cannot imagine you will be content to "tell on" the Jews forever. What satisfaction is there, for a brave man, in showing his chains to his fellow slaves? How long are we going to keep whimpering about being cheated and aggressed and outraged,—and DO something about it?

Let's hear from you, and get GOING. Damn the Jews, full speed ahead,—as one of our Naval heroes once said about torpedoes.
Heil Hitler![55]

Rockwell's plea however, fell on deaf ears. Einar Åberg had no interest in joining WUNS, nor for that matter in fighting anybody. His was the "prophetic voice" seeking to awaken the world to an esoteric "truth" apprehended by him and a bare handful of others. Rockwell's obvious haste, however, is important. It is notable that in 1958, Rockwell did not see the Jewish conquest of the nations of the earth as yet accomplished. Such was the tenor of the radical right of the 1950s and 1960s. It was felt that if only people could be awakened, there was still time to reclaim the nations of the earth from the dread machinations of the "International Jew." But how? WUNS was a dream and for Rockwell and his associates around the world, the ideal vehicle for the realization of the Führer's vision. But failing this, how to awaken the sleeping masses before it was too late?

The answer occurred to key Rockwell associates early on, but the Commander was reluctant until it was made clear that the religious strategy was a mere Trojan horse. James Madole had embraced the religious strategy without dissimulation already, but his path was too esoteric for most to follow. Why not link National Socialism to religion—and in particular, to Christianity? For Rockwell, National Socialism was already his religion in every sense of the word, and he revered the figure of Adolf Hitler in clearly soteriological terms.[56] In his autobiography, *This Time the World!*, and even more openly in the writings of two generations of movement hagiographers, Rockwell describes his own conversion to National Socialism in explicitly religious terms.[57]

First, there was the motif of the spiritual quest—in this case in the San Diego public library in a frantic search for the truth underlying the dross of everyday events. Then there was the fortuitous discovery on a back shelf of a musty book shop of *Mein Kampf*. This was a truly life-changing experience, and William Pierce's description of Rockwell's fascination with the book eerily presages the scene in his influential apocalyptic novel *The Turner Diaries* in which the protagonist, Earl Turner, is allowed to read the Organization's Holy Book which, like Rockwell's reading of *Mein Kampf*, suddenly drew away the veil of illusion which masked the luminous realities of the world. In Pierce's accounts, neither Rockwell nor the fictional Turner would ever again see the world in the same way following this deeply mystical experience.[58] But there was more. In his confidences to intimate comrades, Rockwell confessed to having a series of extraordinarily vivid and nearly identical prophetic dreams in which, in a variety of everyday contexts, he was called aside from crowded commonplace situations to a private room where standing before him was his newfound god, Adolf Hitler.[59] It was not long before Rockwell was moved to build a literal altar to his deity, hanging a Nazi flag that covered an entire wall of home, under which he placed a table containing a bust of Hitler, three candles, and candle holders, and:

> I closed the blinds and lit the candles, and stood before my new altar.
> For the first time since I had lost my Christian religion, I experienced
> the soul thrilling upsurge of emotion which is denied to our modern,
> sterile, atheist "intellectuals" but which literally moved the earth for
> countless centuries: "religious experience." I stood there in the flickering
> candlelight, not a sound in the house, not a soul aware of what I was
> doing—or caring.[60]

William Pierce, an intimate of Rockwell and the publisher of the ANP's party organs, waxes lyrical over this experience. Describing it in terms familiar to any student of mysticism, East or West, Pierce writes:

It was a religious experience that was more than religious. As he stood there he felt an indescribable torrent of emotions surging through his being, reaching higher and higher in a crescendo with a peak of unbearable intensity. He felt the awe inspiring awareness for a few moments, or a few minutes, of being more than himself, of being in communion with that which is beyond description and beyond comprehension. Something with the cool vast feeling of eternity and of infinity—of long ages spanning the birth and death of suns, and of immense, starry vistas—filled his soul to the bursting point. One may call that Something by different names—the Great Spirit perhaps, or Destiny, or the Soul of the universe, or God—but once it has brushed the soul of a man, that man can never again be wholly what he was before. It changes him spiritually the same way a mighty earthquake or a cataclysmic eruption, the subsidence of a continent or the bursting forth of a new mountain range, changes forever the face of the earth.[61]

Having come face to face with the ineffable, little wonder that Rockwell would be dubious of linking National Socialism with any other religion. But America is a deeply religious nation,[62] and to build a mass movement in the U.S., it is essential that this reality be addressed. As a competitor in the religious marketplace, National Socialism clearly had little mass appeal. While far more secular in orientation than America, Europe, too, evinced a spiritual void that some of Rockwell's closest domestic allies as well as influential voices within the World Union of National Socialists hoped to fill. Finding a way to graft National Socialism onto Christianity was one option. The established racialist doctrine of Christian Identity suggested yet other possibilities.

The syncretic melding of National Socialism with Christianity was an obvious nonstarter on both sides of the Atlantic. In America, the intensely negative association of the term "Nazi" had a certain utility to Rockwell in gaining attention for his fledgling movement, but to seek to link the much demonized figure of Hitler to Christ, even obliquely, would surely have aroused outrage greater than even Rockwell was prepared to contemplate while at the same time risking alienating his base of N.S. true believers.

Prospects for success in such an endeavor in Europe were little better. Besides the predictable public outrage, there was the problem of the tightly controlled state churches to deal with. It was a problem that was never fully solved in Hitler's Germany, despite the terrifying power at the disposal of the state to enforce compliance with its will.[63] Thus today it is the figure of Dietrich Bonhoeffer who is remembered and revered today, while those in the churches who compromised or collaborated are long forgotten. But if not the dogma of Christianity, at least its organizational structure—particularly in its Catholic form—could serve as a model for a National Socialist church structure that one day, after the "great awakening" of the European masses to the Führer's clarion call, would supplant "Jewish Christianity." And what a "delicious irony" it would be for the Jews (and no doubt for most Christians) to wake up one day to find "thousands of priests and monks suddenly throw off their habits and robes . . . and reveal the full glory of their National Socialist organization?"[64]

The prime mover in this plan seems to have been the German WUNS leader, Bruno Ludke, although as early as 1957 Rockwell seems to have toyed with the idea of creating some sort of National Socialist Christian front group.[65] The Ludke/Rockwell discussions began in 1962 when Ludke, the German translator of *This Time the World!*, suggested that passages critical of Christianity be softened. For Ludke, the Catholic Church presented a marvelous model in which Rockwell could speak with "political authority of the Führer and the moral authority of the Pope."[66]

This unlikely aggregation was to be called the Christian Naturalist Church whose primary dogma appeared to center on stressing the similarities which they perceived between Hitler and Jesus. In this, the historic role of Christianity in persecuting the Jews made the proposition of creating a false flag form of "Christianity" to accomplish this purpose doubly attractive. Ironically, the WUNS member most skeptical of the enterprise was England's Colin Jordan, who in the 1990s would devote much of his writing in his journal *Gothic Ripples* to strongly religious themes of a decidedly Odinist flavor.[67]

Of course, the Christian Naturalist Church, like so many of Rockwell's stratagems, went nowhere. The press of events, the rush of ideas, the constant pressures of leading an organization boasting a bare handful of capable followers, and the incessant street confrontations, allowed Rockwell little time to see any idea through to fruition.

Other Avatars—Åberg Redux

A chapter on the early transatlantic contacts of the radical right would not be complete, however, without a brief look at the panache enjoyed by the Ku Klux Klan among some European activists. Klan activity in Europe may reliably be traced to the 1920s—precisely the era when the Ku Klux Klan was enjoying a significant resurgence in the northern American states. At first glance, the attraction of the Klan, born of America's traumatic Reconstruction era and rooted as it is in the American experience of race and immigration, may be somewhat puzzling. However, even in this early period the Klan was creating significant continental linkages—especially in Germany and Sweden. That Germany would be a primary Klan "mission" field is somewhat ironic in that German immigrants were something of a bête noire for the Ku Klux Klan, particularly in the American Midwest, due to their dual sins of being immigrants in a period of massive immigration, and being largely Catholic in a period when Klan animosity toward Catholics was almost as intense as it was toward native blacks.[68]

Be this as it may, we have already noted the formation of a secret society, the Order of the Fiery Cross, by the Reverend Otto Stroschein in 1923. It was an organization which would be dissolved by Hitler in the 1940s, but which would nonetheless be the trailblazer for a long and fruitful relationship between American Klansmen and German fascists, and would be manifest in the cordiality of the German American Bund's meeting with the Ku Klux Klan.[69]

Why would the Klan have a particular appeal in 1920s Germany? The answer to this must be somewhat speculative, but it is highly probable that dissemination of Klan ideas and materials took place on two levels; personal contact as with Reverend Stroschein, and through the mass media. In the latter context, it is important to note that D. W. Griffith's epic film *Birth of a Nation* was released in 1914. It had a major impact on the rebirth of the American Ku Klux Klan, but in a postwar Germany for which, having suffered the humiliation of defeat and occupation, and crippled by reparation debt, the film's themes of selfless vigilante resistance to an unjust occupation and the humiliation of the white population of the American South may easily be imagined to have taken on a universality undreamed of by Griffith when he made his film. Moreover, Germany had a long history of secret societies in which the Klan, with its Masonic inspired hierarchy and imagery, would not have been as alien as might at first be presumed.

Nonetheless, Klan contacts in Germany never involved more than a handful of adherents, and was easily swept aside by the rising energy of National Socialism. These contacts however, are an important milestone in the reversal of the traditional pattern of east to west diffusion of right-wing ideology.

Swedish anti-Semites were less enamored of Americana than were such Germans as could be influenced by Reverend Stroschein. However, again for the earliest contacts with American Klan groups, and other American racist groups as well, one need look no further than the inexhaustible Einar Åberg. Åberg's Klan contacts in fact date back to the 1920s,[70] and these contacts expanded his own horizons on the dimension of the "Jewish problem." Thus, to his already prolific output of anti-Semitic materials, Åberg added such American racist staples as "A Hidden Hand in the War Between the States" which was a gift of one Hal Stearley of Brazil, Indiana, and "Whose Is the Hidden Hand?" a tract that purports to be an extract from "British Communist spokesman" Israel Cohen's 1912 book *A Racial Programme for the Twentieth Century* which was read into the *U.S. Congressional Record* on 7 June 1957. The key sentences in this passage, long a Klan staple, read:

In America, we [Jews] will aim for subtle victory. While inflaming the
Negro minority against the Whites, we will endeavor to instill in the
Whites a guilt complex for their exploitation of the Negroes. We will
aid the Negroes to rise to prominence in every walk of life, in the
professions, and in the world of sports and entertainment. With this
prestige the Negro will be able to intermarry with Whites and begin a
process which will deliver America to our cause.[71]

This flair for Americanisms brought Åberg a wide range of North American correspondents beyond the Klan and the world of National Socialism en-
compassing the famous and the obscure. It mattered not to Åberg. He happily
reprinted and redistributed to the Americas whatever interested him and would
advance the cause, stamping it with his own imprimatur and his trademark quotation from Edmund Burke: "All that is necessary for the triumph of evil is that
good men do nothing." Thus, in 1968 one Thomas J. Devane of Peotone, Illinois, submitted a page of exceedingly bad poetry titled "Apocalyptic" which
Åberg duly reprinted in quantity. Slightly better known was another American
contact, Joseph Dilys of Chicago who contributed the "secret Jewish document"
"Protocol for World Conquest 1956: Confidential Notice to All Jews (Orthodox, Reform, Non-Religious, and 'Christian')."[72]

Einar Åberg's best-known American correspondent, however, was in fact a
national figure of considerable standing on the far right: Gerald L. K. Smith. In
addition to sharing such materials as Smith's "What the Jews Say about Themselves," Åberg's tale of international Jewish persecution was presented to Smith's
American readers in a 1962 issue of *The Cross and the Flag*. In this article, a
capsule biography of Åberg is presented as a prelude to the story of the 1947
attempt by the American Jewish Committee to have Åberg declared insane by
Swedish medical authorities and incarcerated in a mental institution.[73] The per-
tinent documents, including Dr. Hans Nystrom's finding that he was perfectly
sane, are translated by Åberg and appended to a copy of *The Cross and the Flag*
article.

With this introduction to the postwar linkages which were being forged between activists on both sides of the Atlantic, we now proceed to the contemporary transatlantic scene for which such pioneers as Åberg, Madole, Rockwell
and many more paved the way.

	The Transatlantic Race
Chapter 6	Movement Today

At the Vanguard

THE PREVIOUS CHAPTER introduced the postwar avatars of the contemporary transatlantic radical right. Its cast of major characters, men like Einar Åberg, James Madole, George Lincoln Rockwell et al., were essentially street agitators in search of a following. Åberg was a one-man band, tireless in his quest to awaken the public to the machinations of the "International Jew." Rockwell and Madole were in their own ways masters of street theater. Others, activists like the Oredssons in Sweden, Colin Jordan, Savitri Devi, and Bruno Ludke from the World Union of National Socialists (WUNS) were National Socialist true believers, organization people eager to keep the flame of Hitler's dream alive. While to most observers their successes were few—their respective "movements" never amounted to more than a handful of the faithful and a fistful of infiltrators from state and private watchdog agencies—they nonetheless did succeed in keeping alive the utopian dreams of the radical right. Moreover, they laid the groundwork for the thriving transatlantic linkages we see today. They did this in two ways. For the National Socialists, the dream of an organized international movement—a kind of centralized fascist mirror image of the Socialist International—made transnational linkages a necessity. For the street toughs and radical individualists of the movement however—activists representing a number of ideological and theological perspectives—the motivation for establishing international contacts was more elemental: the need for community, for any sign of support in a lonely and often violent quest to awaken the sleeping population to an esoteric truth of alien domination perceived only by the chosen few.

The world of the 1980s and 1990s was a very different place than that experienced by the movement's fallen martyrs and surviving elders of the 1940s through the 1970s. By the late 1980s, several overlapping revolutions had quietly taken place that made the path of the modern radical right wing at once easier though far more complex than that of the idiosyncratic activists whom we introduced in the previous chapter. Specifically, on an instrumental level, the world of the 1980s introduced an era of mass communications undreamed of by the previous generation. Concomitantly, the easy assumptions of the cold war faded as the Soviet empire collapsed. In its place a world system is emerging based on interdependence and increasing globalization as regional structures—particularly in Europe—begin to usurp the once jealously guarded perquisites of the nation state. A new nationalism is being born, and once again, the radical right is nothing if not a mirror of its surrounding environment.

Thus, emanating from the level of its core adherents, a new movement is coming into being that eerily resembles the new world system it so heartily loathes. From this vanguard a new view of nationalism has begun to emerge that, utilizing some form of the Zionist Occupation Government discourse, endeavors to establish linkages beyond the nation state based on concepts of race and shared history that transcend the bounds of narrow nationalism so as to offer the faithful the movement's own version of globalism: a transnational ideology of race and place that despairs of reclaiming their individual nations and seeks instead to establish new forms of community while longing for the day when these dreams can be brought to fruition in a particular geographic setting.

What distinguishes the contemporary movement from its predecessors is an unceasing search for community under conditions that are even less favorable than those faced by their immediate postwar predecessors. This chapter will take into account the traditional forms of "community" within the radical right; those involving loosely knit transnational organizations based on the mails and supported by such media as published materials, music, rallies, and rock concerts, and occasional face-to-face visits. Chapter 8 will then consider both the prospects for the creation of actual communal societies located in both urban and rural enclaves and the fascinating implications of virtual communities based on the expansion of computer technology.

First, however, it might be well to add a word contextualizing the modern transnational racialist subculture's search for community. In a crowning irony for a movement whose chief tenet is anti-Semitism, the core adherents of today's radical right resemble nothing so much as pre-Holocaust Zionism where an elite cadre of the international Jewish community—a group that represented no more than a tiny minority of the assimilated Western Jewish population—sought its own national refuge. This comparison might strike both the Jewish and the movement worlds as exceedingly distasteful, but it is offered to provide a context in which the nonspecialist reader may better understand the importance of the minority of core movement adherents whose postnationalist outlook is at the heart of this study. The similarities between pre-Holocaust Zionism in Western Europe and North America and this elite core of the modern radical right are, on the surface, striking.[1]

At root, both groups sought above all the formation of a community that would link disparate peoples through the creation of a form of national identification based on factors beyond the simple fact of having been born within the borders of a given country. This quest for separation was in both cases born of a perception of dispossession; the Jews from their biblical land of origin and the modern right-wing movement from nations that they see as at once familiar and yet utterly hostile—nations that have fallen under the control of ZOG and its cosmopolitan minions. According to the ZOG discourse, the ultimate goal of this conspiratorial elite is the genocide of the white race through the assimilation of foreign communities within national borders and ultimately through a long-term program of miscegenation. Assimilation, too, was and is one of the great fears of the Jewish community, making the American experience of acceptance ironically threatening in a way that some have dubbed "the silent holocaust." In both cases, the faithful feel as strangers in the lands of their birth. From this flows a marked perception of "chosenness" or "otherness," and from this too is born a sense of mission of almost messianic proportions in which the activist must seemingly act alone with every hand turned against him or her.

This isolation, be it based on rejection *by* the national community as perceived by the Zionists or upon rejection *of* the national community by the contemporary race activists has much the same effect. That is, a desperate search for alternate forms of association capable of both sustaining the dream and a drive for space—ideological, religious, and ultimately physical—in which the true believers may withdraw to live their lives in accordance with their beliefs.

Here the analogy ends, however. The early Zionists worked both with and within governments to achieve their ends while the movement is oppositional by definition and sees little hope of reaching accommodation with governments which they are certain are under the thumb of an alien cabal. This hostility is fully reciprocated by the states and by nonstate watchdog groups, thus creating the potential for violent confrontations that Western Zionists did not have to face. Moreover, the television age and the contemporary use of computer communications technology does not afford the right-wing movement the same luxury of self-delusion which allowed the earlier Zionists to see Mandatory Palestine as "a land without people for a people without land."

Today, communal experiments exist on the sufferance of their host states, and in a postcolonial world of states, state power is an omnipresent reality in the lives of all movement activists. There are no longer empty spaces on the map that can serve as a national homeland for the dispossessed white race warriors. Lacking this space, the current transnational radical right is unlikely to enjoy the success of the Zionists in achieving an enclave in which they may live their dreams. It is, parenthetically, the movement's conscious awareness of the similarity of their own predicament with that of the early Zionists that may be a factor in both the centrality of Holocaust denial to the contemporary ideology of the radical right and to the prevalence in movement literature of the imagery of the racial and cultural genocide of the white race. These ideological factors, as well as the search for space in a world environment that has little to cede, will provide a continuous subtext throughout this chapter.

With this introduction then, we turn to the forms of community sought by the transnational racialist movement. The contemporary movement is far more diverse in ideological and theological terms than were the activists of the postwar era. Yet they are more interdependent too. This chapter will examine some of these movements and consider the appeal of a postnationalist zeitgeist to the activists who compose the movement in the mid-1990s.

Traditional Forms of Radical Right-Wing Community

"The Allies won the war,
But Hitler won our hearts."
  —Varg Quisling Vigernes[2]

For all of the technical advances made in recent years, and despite the timeless dream of a separatist utopian racialist community, the primary form of organization within the radical right remains the "mail order" membership in a variety of radical right-wing belief systems. This is very much the tradition in this milieu—as ubiquitous in Rockwell's day as it is in our own. At the cutting edge of the movement, however, there have been some significant changes. The most striking of these involves the increasingly open mysticism, and indeed religiosity, which has always been the hidden face of the radical right. Today, the occult paths are well trodden. Where Rockwell's mystical experience of unity with the Führer had to be hidden and shared with only his most trusted comrades, the occult has now become a ubiquitous part of the modern race movement. With the trend toward an increasingly open racial mysticism, there has been a concomitant drift toward syncretism. That is, such seemingly incompatible ideological mixtures as Christian Identity and National Socialism or National Socialism and explicit Satanism are becoming increasingly more common.

Thus, the minority of adherents of explicit National Socialism in the 1990s who adhere to a postnationalist ideology may well be dubbed the "children of Madole," so prevalent have currents of National Socialist (N.S.) mysticism ranging from Satanism to Odinism become within their ranks. But while the Rockwell generation has gradually faded from the scene, a few of the movement elders remain active and influential. Colin Jordan in England continues to publish at irregular intervals his newsletter, *Gothic Ripples*. William Pierce, author of *The Turner Diaries*, has through his writings and his short wave radio program *American Dissident Voices* had a considerable impact on the transatlantic movement that transcends the meager number of adherents of National Socialism. Nonetheless, the Rockwell generation is fast fading from the scene. Göran Assar Oredsson announced his "retirement" from active politics and sold his archives to a Swedish academic research institution. The "old fighters" who remain on the scene are simply that—old. With rare exceptions, they are no longer fighters, although one notable exception is the ebullient Finnish expatriate activist Nils Mandel. Mandel's role is to link the movement's Eastern and Western European activists with their source of stickers and published propaganda in London. He is a fixture at the annual skinhead celebration cum riots that mark Rudolf Hess's birthday in Belgium.[3]

Before introducing this youthful community of activists, however, a word need be said about the importance of their immediate elders in the ranks of the National Socialist faithful. Of these, none has had a greater impact on the nurturing of the transnational dream of a National Socialist revival than has Gary (Gerhard) Lauck. Until his arrest in Denmark in 1995 and subsequent extradition to Germany, Lauck, a Hitler cultist of the first magnitude, was the primary source of supply of N.S. materials to the German movement. Lauck was found guilty and sentenced to four years in a German prison, despite the insistence of local prosecutors that his actions—fully legal in America but a serious offense under German law—deserved the maximum term of fifteen years which is allowed under the German legal system.[4]

The fate of a Lauck-less NSDAP/AO is uncertain. The NSDAP/AO is a perfect example of the mail order movement, with the American "organization" never amounting to much more than a post office box and shifting cast of a few "subordinates." The *New Order* continues to appear under the editorship of Michael Storm and Michael Hansen, but each issue carries as well pleas for patience as the curious and the committed from around the world continue to write in for the NSDAP/AO's propaganda packets.[5]

The National Socialist Liberation Front

Whatever the ultimate fate of Gary Lauck and his organization, it is incontestable that he is a figure of considerable standing in movement circles, particularly on the European side of the Atlantic. More controversial is another American activist of the immediate post-Rockwell generation, James Mason of the Universal Order. Mason, currently incarcerated in Colorado, is a survivor whose National Socialist pedigree should hold considerable allure for the younger generation of N.S. activists. His long history with the movement, his current international following, and the syncretic appeal of the Universal Order make Mason worthy of some further consideration.

James Mason's biography is typical of the National Socialist faithful of his generation.[6] Born in 1952 in Chillicothe, Ohio, Mason's awakening to the world of radical political activism took place with the onset of puberty. It was, moreover, primarily oppositional rather than racial. Mason despised the status quo, and in those days the primary opponents of the values of the American middle class were black. The civil rights movement of the mid-1960s was in full swing, and Mason recalls being on the whole rather admiring of his black classmates.[7] A common thread running through the biographies of many current movement activists is a perception of always being oppositional, always different. In this, it is the availability of an oppositional milieu rather than the persuasiveness of a particular ideology that will often first draw the activist to the movement. Mason is no exception:

> My interests always diverged from the mainstream. I rather don't like competition, preferring to have a field more or less to myself. If necessary, I'll always invent one of my own. I've seen it that what I pick out early often has a way of catching on. Not surprising that when that happens I usually move on. When just beginning in this [National Socialism] about 1966 or 1967, I felt absolutely confident I'd make some mark, if only through sheer default.[8]

His epiphany came from a viewing of a news report of an American Nazi party march in Chicago. Here was a movement that was both oppositional and universally despised by Americans. Better, it was led by a charismatic and fearless fighter of his own race. Here was a movement to which Mason could belong, and here too was a form of political activism that, under the swastika banner, could strike fear into the hearts of its opponents in a way that Klan robes no longer could. At the age of fourteen, a life-long National Socialist was born.

Determined to be a Nazi, what could a poor boy from backwater Ohio do to contact these distant urban heroes? Showing the same remarkable ingenuity that many another fledgling race activist would demonstrate in establishing his first tenuous link to the movement,[9] Mason made contact with a classmate who had a reputation for being something of a "Hitler Youth," and thus was given a book, *Extremism U.S.A.*, that contained a picture of ANP West Coast activist Allen Vincent in front of a truck emblazoned with the address of the Berkeley, California, party headquarters.[10] A letter to Vincent quickly produced the Arlington, Virginia, address of Rockwell's ANP. James Mason became a dues paying member at the age of fourteen.

Soon finding himself in trouble for chronic truancy, Mason saw the opportunity to leave Chillicothe behind for the more exciting world of ANP headquarters in Arlington, Virginia. A call to ANP central resulted in a conversation with Mason's hero, William Pierce, who told him (perhaps unwisely given his age) to hop a bus and come on down. Mason was then still a minor at sixteen. Pierce for his part was indeed concerned about Mason's age, thus nothing was at first kept in writing and Pierce paid Mason's expenses out of his own pocket.[11]

Mason loved the life of the party activist. Indeed, his enthusiasm for doing "whatever needed to be done" was less than universally popular with older and less daring adherents. It would be the first, but hardly the last, conflict Mason would have with the movement's conservative majority. Nonetheless, when Mason reached eighteen, he was sworn in as a full-fledged member of the National Socialist White People's party by Matt Koehl, the successor to the martyred Rockwell. But Koehl's leadership fragmented the movement, a development that ironically brought a small portion the National Socialist movement into the revolutionary direction that would be adopted by many of the younger adherents on both sides of the Atlantic who today are creating the groundwork for a postnationalist racialist movement.[12]

The ideological basis of this split centered on the competing theories of mass action versus the creation of a revolutionary vanguard,[13] although personality played at least as great a role in the movement's atomization. At the core of the split was the conflict between Pierce and Matt Koehl.[14] Fueling this split was, on the one hand, the generational shift between the younger activists and the older leaders. But more fundamentally, the roiled period of the late 1960s with the primacy of left-wing radicalism deeply effected the younger National Socialists. The key figure to arise from this group of youthful revolutionaries was Joseph Tommasi.

> Joseph Tommasi, as founder of the NSLF [National Socialist Liberation Front], was the first of a new breed. A hero and a martyr to the Cause. What he wanted most was to provide the movement with its much overdue HIT TEAM and not to set himself up as some sort of cheap, tin horn demi-god like the rest. Tommasi personified the kind of man we MUST have: those desiring to serve the movement— and do so with great facility—not pose around in gaudy uniforms as "Hollywood Nazis."[15]

Tommasi is little remembered today, but he was nonetheless a seminal figure in creating the groundwork for the current Euro-American convergence. This is ironic for a leader who forthrightly declared his faith in American exceptionalism:

> White people in America are not like those who participated in past European struggles. Americans tend to go against the "grain" on

practically everything. We are not Europeans and won't respond as Europeans.[16]

Yet Tommasi's thought, as is true of so many chronicled in these pages, was far ahead of its time. Joseph Tommasi emerged from the fractious California cadre of Rockwell's American Nazi party. A deeply committed National Socialist, Tommasi held out for some years after the Commander's assassination before he too fell victim to Matt Koehl's ongoing purge of the party. But where so many others similarly disgusted with Koehl and company departed for other belief systems throughout the radical right, Tommasi was an NS true believer who, until his expulsion from the Party, believed in Koehl to the end.[17] His analysis of the sad state of affairs of the post-Rockwell movement marked the first attempt to adapt the stereotypical Nazi subculture of the 1950s to the youth culture of the late 1960s and early 1970s. The results were intended to be revolutionary, and they were.

The National Socialist Liberation Front (NSLF) was founded in 1969, but unknown to most, the real inspiration from (well) behind the scenes was William Pierce. This was odd in that, according to James Mason's recollection, Pierce and Tommasi could not abide one another. Yet from the late 1960s to date, whenever talk of violence in NS circles is seriously contemplated, Pierce is usually involved, albeit always at a safe distance. Thus, Pierce conceived the NSLF as a front group to compete with the radical left on the college campuses and Tommasi, whose speech at the Second Party Congress in 1970 electrified some and appalled most with his denunciation of the conservative majority of the party by chance coincided with Pierce's split with Koehl. Tommasi was thus the ideal candidate to lead the NSLF.[18]

The NSLF concept did not really go anywhere until 1973 however, when Tommasi was unceremoniously booted out of the National Socialist White People's party by Matt Koehl for his un-National Socialist behavior of smoking marijuana in Party headquarters, entertaining young women within those hallowed precincts, leading unauthorized armed paramilitary maneuvers, and, it was rumored, misusing the scant Party funds.[19]

In 1973 or 1974, Tommasi's slogan—which remains current to this day in N.S. circles—became known to such East Coast Nazis as James Mason, and in that year too the NSLF held its foundational meeting. Tommasi's dictum, "THE FUTURE BELONGS TO THE FEW OF US WILLING TO GET OUR HANDS DIRTY. POLITICAL TERROR: It's the only thing they understand," appeared on a poster featuring a .38 caliber pistol and a swastika. It would not be the last time Tommasi would borrow slogans, style, and eventually even dress and physical appearance from the New Left of the 1960s. Even more striking in this vein was the slogan that opened Tommasi's *Building the Revolutionary Party* pamphlet, the Maoist truism: "POLITICAL POWER STEMS FROM THE BAR-REL OF A GUN." [20] Indeed, even the group's name is strongly reminiscent of the Vietnamese National Liberation Front while the name of the group's journal, *Siege!*, was borrowed from the Weather Underground.[21]

The NSLF's revolutionary ideology was based on the rejection of the "conservative" theory of mass action that Tommasi correctly believed was paralyzing the NS movement. Under the mass action doctrine, no serious antistate actions were contemplated until the party could build up a coalition of supporters which would, in aggregate, form a mass movement capable of mounting a popular revolution. By 1969, it was clear that if any mass movement was capable of building a revolutionary mass, it would be a movement of the left rather than the right. By 1974, even this hope was dashed. Clearly, to delay the revolution until the slumbering American masses could be awakened was tantamount to a vow of permanent ineffectuality. So, based on the model of the Weather Underground and other leftist guerrilla formations of the day, the NSLF would "seize the moment," regardless of how unpromising that moment might appear to the uninitiated.

Certainly, 1974 was a decidedly unpromising moment to seize. Thus, of necessity, Tommasi formulated an early version of leaderless resistance or lone wolf tactics that would not come into vogue in the movement until the late 1980s. The credo of the NSLF was violent revolutionary action, and its propaganda in the pages of its original journal, *Defiance*, and the more well-known successor to that publication, *Siege!*, suggested that the NSLF had formed armed cells and had already launched the "first blows against the empire."[22]

According to NSLF propaganda, the group's foundational meeting held on 2 March 1974—a full five years after Tommasi created the group—hosted "forty-three National Socialist revolutionaries" in El Monte, California.[23] It was at this meeting that the mass action strategy was officially put to rest in favor of revolution now. The NSLF was conceived as an activist, and thus violent, revolutionary organization. It was structured in a manner reminiscent of David Lane's current theories of organization, with an above-ground membership that may have numbered perhaps forty or more, and a tiny underground contingent of lone wolf revolutionaries.[24] The underground core of the NSLF never numbered more than four, including Karl Hand and David Rust:

> Yes, the N.S.L.F. of Tommasi had four persons who carried out the illegal activities. The remainder, the majority, weren't that much different from the N.S.W.P.P. members except they were a lot more forward thinking.[25]

James Mason was a close friend and collaborator with Tommasi and the group, but he never officially joined the NSLF. However, within a year, Tommasi was dead, and it was not long thereafter that Hand and Rust were imprisoned for their acts of leaderless resistance. The NSLF underground died with Tommasi.[26] The legacy of the tiny movement however, is far greater than its meager victories would suggest.

The primary accomplishment of the NSLF was that it was the first NS group in the postwar period to attempt to adapt to the times. Tommasi had no qualms about taking lessons from the radical left, and he had no interest in the puritanical outlook of the postwar radical right. Nor was Tommasi a man to deceive himself that the world of explicit National Socialism would ever be able to attract a significant enough following in the U.S. to justify the movement's mass action theory. Clearly, mass action was synonymous with ineffectuality. If the time to seize the gun was not the chaotic year 1969, when would it be? Thus, the credo of the NSLF was one of action, and action now!

Yet the NSLF could not escape the reality of its minuscule numbers. It was fine for Tommasi to borrow the communist belief in a cell structure, but the grim truth was that had the NSLF's combatant core formed a fighting cell, it would have had to put all its eggs in one basket! On an ideological level however, it was not difficult to find a rationale, and a hope, for ultimate victory in the face of overwhelming odds. For one, the National Socialist faith has always been at heart religious and deeply millenarian. Ultimate victory was assured to the faithful simply by virtue of their faith and of their ultimate "rightness."

On a more immediate level, Tommasi believed with Rockwell and Evola and Hitler too that the masses were in essence female, waiting to be swept off their collective feet by a leader whose daring and charisma would guide them into the timeless racialist dream.[27] Thus the suicidal audacity of the NSLF's "operations." Thus, too, the ease with which the organization was smashed and surviving members jailed. David Rust, Tommasi's first successor, went down on firearms charges. Karl Hand, Tommasi's final successor, was imprisoned briefly in 1980 for firing a gun into the home of a black neighbor, and then received a fifteen-year sentence for other weapons violations and attempted murder.[28]

The shell of the organization carried on, at least in name, for several years after Tommasi's 1975 death. By then, James Mason was something of a full-fledged member by virtue of his having been sent a membership card by Karl Hand, and a few other activists soldiered on as well. By 1978, the NSLF's mantle fell by default to Mason, with the same Allen Vincent whose picture in *Extremism USA* had so impressed a young Mason handling party propaganda.[29] Like many another right-wing group whose nonexistent cadres are filled out by the deeds of others, the NSLF's journal, *Siege!*, which went on under the editorship of James Mason until 1986, was not reticent about claiming any act of white racial violence.[30] The truth was, however, that the NSLF as a combat group was dead, but its influence did not end there. Indeed, in something of an emotional farewell to Tommasi, Mason noted that:

. . . it were now as if Tommasi never went away. He'd have admired Oklahoma City. "Pray for Victory and not an end to slaughter."[31]

Charles Manson and the Universal Order

James Mason continued for some time to publish *Siege!* as a journal, and to head his own one-man band, the short-lived National Socialist Movement, which by Mason's own admission soon foundered.[32] Then came Mason's discovery of the teachings of Charles Manson. This association ended Mason's connection with his old comrades. Manson urged Mason to jettison the NSLF in favor of a new grouping, the Universal Order, and as a result Mason and Karl Hand amicably agreed to part ways, with Mason holding *Siege!* as the organ of the Universal Order and Hand keeping *Defiance* as publication of the NSLF.[33]

Despite Mason's earlier contention that he was not among the movement's "religionists,"[34] his adulation of the Manson Family and his tireless efforts through his current vehicle, the Universal Order, to present Manson to the international movement as an avatar on the level of a Rockwell or a Tommasi, and perhaps even of Hitler himself, of the coming National Socialist revolution is a religious quest par excellence! From 1982 until the journal's demise, *Siege!* became the primary vehicle for the glorification of Charles Manson.

Mason himself was no stranger to the occult aspects of National Socialism, and like so many of the movement's 1960s generation, he was drawn for a time to the teachings of Anton LaVey and the Church of Satan. Mason notes that in 1969, he purchased a copy of Anton LaVey's LP *The Satanic Mass* from a fellow ANP trooper, and has "cherished it ever since."[35] But while Satanism, particularly in its Church of Satan guise, was no stranger to the world of National Socialism, the figure of Charles Manson was quite something else. The selection of Charles Manson and his largely female following as NS heroes seems as unlikely on first glance as was the elevation of Horst Wessel from dissolute street fighter to the selfless martyr of the original NSDP.

Certainly, the Universal Order's insistence on this recognition of the role and leadership of Charles Manson has not met with much success among the conservative majority of National Socialists. It has also encountered significant criticism among the young fighters of the skinhead movement—men who for the most part were not born until after the sensational capture and trial of the Manson Family.[36] The reaction to this thesis by the young readers of *Resistance* magazine was so overwhelming that the editor, George Eric Hawthorne, presented in the next issue a full-fledged debate on the proposition from two of his magazine's readers. His introduction to this debate is a fair representation of the "resistance" the Universal Order has faced in its quest to promote the thought and example of Charles Manson:

In the last issue of RESISTANCE Magazine, James Mason, author of Siege, took a fairly unpopular platform and proceeded upon a difficult thesis: although few people in the pro-White movement realize it, Charles Manson is actually ideally suited to be "the" leader of our generation, and for us to win, we must recognize it. We were literally flooded with letters and phone calls from irate readers who firmly disagree with this concept, stating that any connection to Manson is pointless and dangerous to our credibility. One distributor even clipped out the Manson article from the issue before distributing it.

But on the other side of the subject, there is a growing body of Manson supporters that see the public view of Manson as a late 20th Century icon who carries weight and influence with his name, so much so that it may be the tool we need to sway the youth of our generation.[37]

But there is more here than meets the eye, and the Universal Order's fealty to the legacy of the Manson Family deserves some attention both for what it has to teach of the state of the contemporary movement and, of more pressing import, for the key adherents this movement has gathered in both the U.S. and Europe. The appeal of Manson is well summed up by one of these younger activists, Michael Moynahan, whose Storm Publications brought James Mason's early writings to a considerably wider audience through the publication of Mason's book, *Siege!*:

> Manson is extremely important, as he one of those rare individuals capable of operating on many levels at once. This applies equally to his life, message, and actions. I am less interested in the murders he allegedly directed, and I don't think anyone will ever know exactly what really happened and what lead up to them. I am much more compelled by Manson's mind and what he has to say. For whatever reasons (and it is made even more puzzling by his criminal background) he often verbalizes incredibly erudite and obscure concepts which can be traced back to much earlier native European spirituality. There is no doubt that he expresses some very deep, subconscious thoughts which very few people are aware of or even understand in the present day and age. The fact that he is able to instinctively convey these things is unique among any modern man of public renown.[38]

In an interesting exploration of the mystique of radical individualism—and indeed the aura of evil—as a cultural phenomenon, art historian Stoddard Martin sees Manson as but one of a long line of figures whom he dubs the artist-manqué.[39] For Martin, the artist-manqué is a man out of time. He is an artist burning for recognition, but one who is all too well aware that he has yet to fully realize on the canvas of his own cultural reality the full implications of his vision. Unable to achieve the glory the artist-manqué feels his due, and driven by a quest for expression that he can never fully transform from the ether of ideas to the physical world, "the phenomenon of artistic frustration is likely to exacerbate tendencies to shock . . . challenge conventional morality, explore areas of decay, parade the ego, cast one's personae as messiahs, and sensationalize crime."[40]

With this conception, Martin offers a long line of contemporary artist-manqués. Two of these, Hitler and Manson, abandoned their art to become men of action. Others, Herbert Marcuse, the Marquis de Sade, and Nietzsche, for example, would remain men of ideas—often with great success—but would never realize the level of recognition that they believed was their due, and would always live in an adversarial relationship with their respective societies.

Yet for all of the long history of this personality type, there was something special about the 1960s, and particularly the pivotal year of 1969. The 1960s was a time of instant gratification. Manson could never display the patience or doggedness of an Adolf Hitler in achieving his ends. Moreover, 1969 was the year of the Rolling Stones' Altamont concert, the success of the Beatles' *White Album* and their subsequent break-up, and the beginning of the Manson Family's apocalyptic Helter Skelter plan for race war which foresaw the imminent emergence of the Family to assume ultimate terrestrial power. If ever a life was lived as an art statement, it was Manson's in the late 1960s. Not surprisingly, those most susceptible to the appeal of Manson's leadership today are drawn from the occult fringes of the movement. Many are artists in their own right, and the National Socialist life in the present day is nothing if not a particularly theatrical public performance.

The Universal Order thus has been able to gather only a relative handful of adherents and hangers on in the U.S. and in Europe. It is in any case a "state of mind" movement rather than an organization with a membership, per se.[41] But its primary mission, to create around the aura of Charles Manson a kind of soteriological cult has met with some success. Manson is indeed more of a ubiquitous cult figure today than ever before. From the playful "Charlie Don't Surf" T-shirts that became something of a fad in California to the recording of Manson's songs by such popular rock bands as Guns and Roses to the proliferation of Manson-related World Wide web sites, the visage of Charles Manson has become well known to a new youth generation. Indeed, a profitable cottage industry has sprung up around Manson, with CDs of Manson's music and words becoming available again, with articles about Manson proliferating throughout the underground, and with publishing houses bringing a number of Manson-related books back into print.[42]

This apparent disparity between the lack of success of the Universal Order's championing of Charles Manson as a prototype of the successful modern National Socialist leader and Manson's current cult status throughout the international underground calls for a moment's reflection. What is it about the Manson persona that attracts James Mason and his NS comrades on the one hand, and the decidedly non-National Socialist youth culture on the other? Here, several observations may be in order. In terms of the wider youth culture, the Manson message does have a resonance. Manson's primary message of rebellion and the nation's betrayal of its young is rooted in the 1960s, but resonates again all the more strongly in the rapidly changing environment of the 1990s. Consider in this regard a tale, perhaps factual, perhaps apocryphal, that Manson relates on *Manson Speaks* and that was adapted on a cut from Michael Moynahan's Blood Axis CD, *The Gospel of Inhumanity*.[43] In the Blood Axis cut "Herr, nun laß in Frieden," Manson intones a monologue over the funereal tones of a Bach organ cantata that relates a story told to him by his grandmother of his grandfather's experience in World War I in which, standing atop the body of an enemy soldier, Manson's grandfather finds a Bible in the pocket of his fallen foe, and inside the Bible, a picture of the man with his wife and daughters. In a flash, the realization dawns that beneath the differences of uniform and language, both men were alike, and he wonders what kind of a government would send out a man to kill his brother over nothing.[44] Prefacing this, Manson alludes to the Vietnam experience—and perhaps both to the charges against him and the recent betrayal of the Family by Tex Watson as well, when he states:

> He lost his brotherhood. . . . He lost his swastika and he lost his brotherhood. For lying. Cause he thought it was a big joke to stab somebody in the back who just took a life for him. If somebody's giving their life for you and they're going into the battlefield for you, you can't very well laugh at 'em when they come back. If a man's over there in Vietnam and he's over they're in the mud and the blood and he's over there fighting and dying for you and then you spit in his face, what kind of fucking country can that be? You see what I'm saying? Does that make sense? So it's the same way all the way down the line.[45]

Here, Manson sounds many of the themes underlying the current search for a postnationalist community based on race and culture: the sense of betrayal by a nation that, for the profit of "others" would set racial brother to kill racial brother, the small thanks that the returning warrior can expect upon his return "home," and the swastika as the badge of honor that the race activist must strive with each new day to prove himself worthy of bearing. From a wider perspective, if one eliminates the imagery of the swastika, Manson sums up in its totality the anomie that is so well described among the Vietnam—and the post-Vietnam—generation of American men by James William Gibson in *Warrior Dreams*.[46]

To James Mason, the Manson allure as the prototypical NS Führer however, goes much deeper. In the pages of *Siege!* when the journal became in effect the organ of the Universal Order after 1982, the case for Manson as a movement archetype is put forth in depth. This appeal goes beyond the Manson family's chiliastic dreams of race war—a fantasy that has never lost its allure to the American movement. On a deeper level, Mason points out the painful fact that Charles Manson's following was primarily female. In a movement that manages to attract very few women, this is no small matter.[47] James Mason's view is simple and to the point:

> [G]ood as it now poses is limp prick at best and people who are still alive
> sense this. Hence, the fascination with "evil" which at least has some
> life to it. Hitler being the best example. Manson being another. Women
> flocked to them both.[48]

More, Manson and his women were no mere armchair revolutionaries. Like Tommasi before them, they seized the moment and acted. The Manson murders are thus of little consequence to Mason given the apocalyptic intent of the crimes. Manson in this conception emerges as the ultimate realist. The leader who like Hitler and Rockwell had torn aside the veils of illusory sentiment and the blinders of "system lies" to reach true freedom on that Nietzchean plateau that transcends mundane considerations of good and evil. It is a detachment that Mason himself aspires to, but even such repugnant apologias as the dismissal of the murder of Sharon Tate's unborn baby with the contemptuous: "With regard to the eight-month-old fetus Tate was carrying, it was, after all, a Jew"[49] falls far short of Manson's amoral example.

Thus when Mason took his case for the consecration of Charles Manson as movement leader to the aficionados of white noise music in the pages of *Resistance* magazine, it was a kinder, gentler Führer that was on offer. Accompanied by a photograph of a smiling, bespectacled Manson who looks uncannily like a grandfatherly version of Alan Berg, the Jewish radio talk show host who was murdered by the Order in Denver, this Manson is presented as the logical successor to Rockwell's mantle of leadership. After all, not only did Manson carve the swastika into his own flesh, announcing to the world his irrevocable allegiance to the National Socialist dream, but the motto of the Family, ATWA (Air, Trees, Water, and Animals) is presented, dovetailing well with the current movement's emphasis on ecology as a natural outgrowth of the movement's obsession with purity in every form.[50] Mason concludes with this exhortation:

> White man, now is the time to use your secret weapon, your *brain*, and
> see and embrace your leader: Charles Manson. Then and only then can
> you effectively use your renowned weapon, fury and skill in battle,
> without being undone by the scheming Jew and his filthy, ZOG
> system.[51]

The plea for Manson's accession to Rockwell's role as leader is unlikely to be widely heeded. The Universal Order remains a tiny band of dreamers, although the Universal Order's minuscule size is not atypical of the explicitly National Socialist groups in both Europe and the United States. Each is numerically insignificant, but a few have had an impact far beyond their numbers. Previous chapters have considered the impact of such small National Socialist groups as Gary Lauck's NSDP/AO and the National Renaissance party of James Madole. Indeed, even Rockwell's American Nazi party and the international movement it helped to spawn, the World Union of National Socialists, was not much bigger. The same can be said for the European movements such as the Swedish party under Göran Oredsson. Yet each left a legacy to the movement which successor groups have built upon. Mason and the Universal Order have had such an impact, and as we have seen, their ideas, if not their prescription for the universal acceptance of Manson's leadership, have filtered out beyond the world of explicit National Socialism.

Keeping Hope Alive: Other Transatlantic Connections

While National Socialism has the advantage of enjoying considerable resonance on both sides of the Atlantic, it is far from the only belief system to seek to establish a mail order membership here and in Europe. Christian Identity, too, has enjoyed some success in this respect. Identity is a particularly important case to take up in the context of this study in that its current racialist leadership is invariably American and the foreign following it has managed to attain are centered primarily in Europe, Southern Africa, Australia, and New Zealand. Even here, however, the picture is far from monolithic. Pastor Dan Gayman has for years sought to expand the operations of his Church of Israel to Europe and South Africa, and has enjoyed some success in this respect. Pastor Pete Peters by contrast, a younger and more radical figure in the Identity world, has done much the same, and in some cases has "poached" some of Gayman's flock as the Church of Israel's message has become increasingly withdrawn from the world of action, retreating instead into a Romans 13-centered obedience to secular authority.

Before looking briefly at these ministries, however, a word of caution is in order. Dan Gayman has both a mail order ministry and a residential center. Gayman's community is an open one, with adherents, who so choose, buying property around his rural Missouri Church and becoming part of the Church of Israel community on a daily basis. This is in stark contrast to, for example, Richard Butler's Aryan Nations which is headquartered on a closed compound containing barracks-style accommodation for his followers. Pete Peters, while eschewing communitarian living, has been active in the area of technology, reaching out to a global following via the Internet in a far more sophisticated way than Butler's Aryan Nations (Gayman, by 1996, has taken only tentative steps into Internet technology).

With this proviso, then, we will consider the international outreach of Dan Gayman's Church of Israel.[52] In the 1970s, Dan Gayman was at the heart of the Christian Identity world. The Church of Israel's journal, the *Watchman*, was a stridently racialist publication enthusiastically holding forth on the "two seeds" doctrine that sees Jews as the satanic offspring of Eve in the Garden and pastor Gayman held the *Dearborn Independent's* "International Jew" series as a literal statement of fact.[53] Indeed, at the height of the Order aka the Silent Brotherhood's revolutionary activism, Pastor Gayman was accused of having received $10,000 of Order funds—money, which at FBI insistence, was surrendered when Gayman agreed to testify for the prosecution at the Fort Smith sedition trial.

Since then, the Church of Israel has become increasingly withdrawn from political involvement. This withdrawal has continued into the mid-1990s. Church of Israel publications almost never mention politics beyond exhortations based on Romans 13 to obey civil authorities. Indeed, in the last two years, only one article dealing explicitly with race has appeared in these pages.[54] Indeed, from its own point of view, and from that of the wider Identity movement, the Church of Israel is no longer considered part of Christian Identity, based on its adherence to submission to civil government. This withdrawal, according to Pastor Gayman, was not a sudden break but an evolutionary process that began in the late 1970s and took on major form and substance by the mid- to late 1980s.[55]

From its inception, the Church of Israel has had a global vision involving the ingathering of the remnant peoples—that is, the racial progeny of the tribes of Israel as seen through the lens of Identity hermeneutics. These include the Anglo-Saxon and kindred peoples of Europe. As originally configured, the Church was divided into twelve dioceses, each named for one of the tribes of Israel. Pastor Gayman heads the Diocese of Manasseh, named for the son of Joseph and covering the United States. Other branches of the Church were located in Europe and South Africa. For a time, England had a particularly active mail order congregation, and Sweden, too, hosted a branch, thanks to the efforts of the ubiquitous Tommy Rydén before his discovery of the Church of the Creator. The South African branch of the movement stems from a trip made by Rydén who, at Pastor Gayman's request, brought along Church of Israel tapes and literature for distribution.[56]

This international outreach has, if anything, intensified in the 1990s. The Church is once again active in Sweden (Diocese of Asher) through an adherent in Sollentuna, while of greater import, Pastor Gayman made a tour of Australia and New Zealand in the summer of 1996. He had toured the British Isles and Europe before, in 1978 and 1982. Letters from the faithful throughout the world, as well as news of the Church's global outreach, is reprinted in the various issues of the *Watchman* from 1994 to 1996. However, while the Church mails its publications to most European countries, the recipients of this literature are described by Pastor Gayman as passive readers who form no congregations as such.[57]

Pastor Pete Peters is considerably younger than Dan Gayman (although a relative youth before the aged Richard Butler). Peters, as we have seen, has picked up much of the more militant Church of Israel following abandoned by Dan Gayman's post-Fort Smith withdrawal from militant activism. Pastor Peters and his Scriptures for America ministry's following combines an active mail order ministry with a pioneering use of technology (radio, satellite television, short wave radio, and the Internet) to attract a following of the more militant of Identity adherents.[58]

The mail order ministry came first, however, and Scriptures for America's newsletter and tape ministry are among the most active in the Identity world. Pastor Peters preaches an unbending, racialist two-seed Identity message whose condemnation of Jews, blacks, and homosexuals has attracted a wide following in the Christian Identity camp here and in Europe. Peters, however, does not offer his church grounds as a home to the disaffected. For one thing, LaPorte, Colorado, a small town a few miles south of Fort Collins, is hardly the rural redoubt that would appeal to the survivalist instincts of Identity's radical fringe. More to the point, however, is the fact that the state of Colorado seized Peters's church to settle an unpaid fine for a minor election law violation.[59]

Like Dan Gayman, Peters mails his Scriptures for America materials throughout Europe and receives in return letters which are duly printed in the newsletter. To increase the circulation of the newsletter and Pastor Peters' voluminous output of pamphlets and books, Scriptures for America was an early proponent of the Internet. In late 1996 Peters established a page on the World Wide Web, while Scriptures for America materials have long been available for download to a worldwide audience at an FTP (File Transfer protocol) site.

Going beyond Identity, mail order ministries have been the order of the day on the occult fringes of the movement. These groups tend to liberally blend National Socialist ideology with such religious creeds as Odinism and Satanism. It is among this vanguard of the movement that the dream of a postnationalist racial homeland is the strongest, and it is among this group, too, that the dream of separation from a surrounding world seen as irredeemably hostile is the most distant. The reasons for the chasm between separatist longings and the more mundane realities of urban life among these groups is elemental—lack of funds to buy land and establish centers of their own. Moreover, in Europe where these occult-oriented groups have had their greatest proliferation, the lack of space and the aggressiveness of the antiracist watchdog community have both worked to make this dream more distant than ever.[60]

One prominent mail order ministry with dreams of communal separation in Britain is that which loosely combines the outreach of David Myatt and his occult National Socialist organization Reichsfolk and that of Anton Long and Christos Beest who are the moving forces behind the National Socialist-oriented Satanist group the Order of the Nine Angles. Myatt, an avid and compelling writer, has published extensive treatises on various aspects of National Socialism, racial nationalism, and various occult themes. The primary dogma of Reichsfolk is that National Socialism is in itself a religion, and Adolf Hitler is seen as the head of that faith in explicitly soteriological terms.[61]

The Order of the Nine Angles is closely associated with Reichfolk—so much so that many in the milieu believe that all are run by the same person using a variety of pseudonyms. While this is not true, the waters in the world of NS-oriented Satanism are exceedingly murky, with groups borrowing (or expropriating) materials and sharing names despite having little or no connection to each other. The Order of the Nine Angles compounds this confusion by allowing their voluminous materials to be rather freely reproduced by other groups. The key point here, however, is that the Order of the Nine Angles is very much a mail order ministry whose numbers are infinitesimally small but whose goals are world changing.[62] They cooperate closely with Reichsfolk—at times even sharing a post office box—based on mutual agreements in some areas and an agreement to disagree on other areas. Both however, would like to withdraw to a rural communitarian existence to which like-minded adherents from around the world would be invited to join. The problem with realizing this goal, however, is money—a problem that seems at the moment insoluble.[63]

The final N.S.-oriented Satanist mail order ministry to consider is by far the most confusing to document: the Black Order. All agree that the Black Order was founded by Kerry Bolton in New Zealand as a successor to his Order of the Left Hand Path.[64] The group met with some success in attracting an international following, but like many of Bolton's projects, it was eventually supplanted by fresher inspiration and the Black Order was turned over to a group in England. From there, it grew to have adherents throughout the world, with the first U.S. group founded only in 1996.[65]

All of this is clear enough, but the name Black Order has been taken up by an array of groups around the world without any formal linkages being established. Thus, Göran Gullwang's Swedish Black Order, which has become notorious in Sweden for the convictions of its leader and a number of its members for murders of Gothenberg homosexuals,[66] was unknown to the British group until they read of Gullwang in a manuscript copy of one of Kaplan's articles! Gullwang's membership application is identical to that of the Black Order save that it has been translated into Swedish (although respondents are asked to reply in English!). In any case, the Black Order is, like the Order of the Nine

Angles, a remarkably influential purveyor of NS-oriented occultism throughout the world.

What is clear from this brief survey of contemporary mail order movements is that the transnational movement today is characterized by an eclectic and evolving ideology that does not hesitate to blend elements of National Socialism, religious ideas drawn from such unlikely bedfellows as Christian Identity, Odinism, and even Satanism and the occult (with occult ideas ranging from UFOs to various strands of spiritualism and health faddism), and a strong commitment to ecology. This heady ideological stew is composed of a powerful sense of apocalypticism, persecution, and a vision of the movement and its tiny band of adherents as a vanguard of a doomed and besieged race.

Little wonder then that, with a zeitgeist so radically at variance with that of the mainstream culture, many in this milieu would seek to withdraw and to create a communal environment free from the contamination of the outside world. This dream, however, has proven elusive to the European side of the movement. America, with its long history of communal experiments, has proven somewhat more fertile ground. Even in America however, these efforts have been hampered by problems both internal and external to the movement. The following chapter will examine three such communal movements in an effort to illustrate the variety of efforts that have been undertaken in separating from a society deemed as irretrievably under the domination of the malign cabal of ZOG. These test cases are the Aryan Nations compound in Idaho, Elohim City in Oklahoma, and the abortive efforts of the National Socialist Kindred to form a community in rural northern California.

Chapter 7   The Communal Dream

THE ANNALS of the far right wing are filled with utopian attempts at building remnant communities. Almost all have failed miserably. Most disappeared of their own accord. A few, such as the Covenant, Sword, and the Arm of the Lord in rural Missouri and the Rulo, Nebraska, fief of Michael Ryan fell to the power of the state, despite their empty promises of resisting ZOG to the bitter end. More recent is the extended standoff at the compound of Rodney Skurdal's so-called Freemen in Montana in 1996. This too ended, albeit months later, without a shot being fired.[1] While these communal attempts are instructive on a number of levels, they represent purely American groups confronting the American government. What interests us here, conversely, are rural communal experiments that either feature transatlantic connections or that have the potential to attract an international group of adherents.

Similarly, scant attention will be given to urban communalism which is much more a feature of the European than the American scene. Here for example, skinheads simply followed the example of left-wing youth groups of the 1960s and 1970s and occupied abandoned urban structures as squatters. Thus, in European cities from Amsterdam to Berlin to Stockholm, groups of right-wing youth simply occupied and fortified structures that, as often as not, had them living as neighbors to the most committed antiracist groups and representatives of radical youth appeals from militant feminism to deep ecology.[2]

One of the more interesting recent American communal experiments is Almost Heaven, a profitable venture in which Bo Gritz sold adjacent parcels of land in Idaho to upscale apocalyptists. Envisioned as something of a cross between a 1950s-style suburban development and an End Time enclave, Almost Heaven features such decidedly unconventional accouterments as mandatory paramilitary training conducted by Gritz, a highly decorated Vietnam-era Green Beret.[3] Almost Heaven represents the perfect marriage of marketing and millennial fears, but it is hardly the norm in American right-wing communalism.

Of greater interest is evidence of European involvement in two of the better-known American rural enclaves and one less successful utopian dream. The relative success stories are Richard Butler's Aryan Nations property at Hayden Lake, Idaho, and Elohim City, the lesser-known settlement on the Oklahoma side of the Arkansas-Oklahoma border. The grand failure was the abortive National Socialist Kindred effort in northern California. We will then consider the implications of the Internet as both a recruiting and communications tool in building what we term a 'virtual community' on both sides of the Atlantic.

The Rise and Fall of the Aryan Nations

The Aryan Nations (A.N.) compound has been in existence since the 1970s. Founded by Richard Butler, the Aryan Nations is, like Pastor Butler's health, in a period of considerable decline today. As Butler's age and infirmity catch up with him, the daily life of the A.N. community is a sad shadow of what it had been in its 1980s heyday. Then, it was the public (and much publicized) face of the Christian Identity movement. The compound itself, adorned with twelve flags representing each of the "Nordic" or kindred nations, spoke eloquently to the Aryan Nations' global aspirations. From its ranks came a virtual who's who of the American racist right. Robert Mathews and the core members of the Order were residents of the Aryan Nations at one time, and unbeknownst to Pastor Butler, it was the printing equipment of the Aryan Nations movement that gave the Order its first entrée into the perilous but profitable world of counterfeiting.

From Aryan Nations ranks, too, came such as James Ellison, the idiosyncratic polygamist who founded the Covenant, Sword, and the Arm of the Lord compound before his ignominious surrender to federal officers and his eventual star turn as the chief prosecution witness at the Fort Smith sedition trial in 1988. Following a prison term, Ellison today resides at Elohim City. Butler's compound, too, has been the reluctant host to a number of agents for the federal government and such private watchdog groups as the ADL. It was one of the former whose clumsy efforts to entrap Randy Weaver contributed to the disastrous federal siege at Ruby Ridge in which Weaver's wife and son, as well as a federal agent, were killed.[4]

From its highly publicized inception, Butler's compound has been well known in European racialist circles. Sometime visitor and frequent contributor to the various Aryan Nations journals Manfred Roeder, a German National Socialist figure, was considered in chapter 1. Butler and the Aryan Nations have in fact hosted at their annual gatherings a number of European activists ranging from skinheads to more serious neo-Nazi activists. They have, moreover, carried on a lively correspondence both published and unpublished with movement activists throughout the world.[5]

Indeed, from its inception, the Aryan Nations through the vehicle of its annual congresses have made solid alliances with activists in Germany.[6] With its remarkable ideological synthesis of National Socialism and Christian Identity, Richard Butler's organization in the 1970s seemed for a brief, shining moment poised to assume leadership of the American racialist movement. But this was not to be.

The most complete program of the Aryan Nations is found in the eponymous premier edition of the organization's newsletter.[7] This foundational creed provides a remarkable insight into the mindset of the separatist aspirations of the movement in the 1980s, and is thus worthy of some attention. Opening with a detailed explanation of the symbolism of the swastika-like Aryan Nations emblem which is redolent with the arcane beliefs of the Identity creed, the document then segues into a detailed political manifesto that begins, fittingly enough, with the question of "population and race." Here, Identity's emphasis on the descent of Caucasian man from Adam is blended with the "science" of eugenics. In particular, miscegenation is expressly forbidden.[8]

Next the Aryan Nations turns to the problem of private property. Here, what is demanded is a utopian socialism in which the nation's productive capacity in the forms of agriculture and industry will be placed under communal control to be administered "in the national and racial interest." This is followed by a brief section on industry and finance in which the "financial system of International Jewish Capitalism" is to be abolished, all adults are expected to be productive contributors to society, and loaning money at interest is to be abandoned.

The subject of Aryan youth follows. Here the model is Platonic by way of National Socialist Germany. Youth movements for both boys and girls are mandated:

> In young men the Aryan ideal is of physical and athletic fitness,
> reliability and determination of character, proficiency in chosen
> livelihood-occupation, and general usefulness to the community.
>   In young women the accent is primarily on fitness for mother-hood
> and home-making, but also on athletics and arts.[9]

For the rest, the Aryan warrior ideal is touted, as is a call for discipline, race consciousness, and obedience to the laws of God.

The role of women is of particular concern to the Aryan Nations. Here, an Aryan woman's primary duty is clear:

> Every child that an Aryan mother brings into the world is a battle waged
> for the existence of her people.

The program of the National Aryan Women's Movement has a truly a single point—the child.[10]

Then, among idealized calls for feminine purity and paeans to the complementary nature of the separate roles for the Aryan male and female, the manifesto cannot resist the passing observation that it is far better to be "the mother of healthy Aryan children than to be a clever woman lawyer."

When the document turns to more global questions, much of the specificity found in discussions of social relations vanishes. In a formulation that would appall the narrowly legalistic militia movement of the 1990s, Aryan law is described as something that is to be followed more in spirit than in the letter, and judges are given wide latitude to apply the law in the racial and national interest. Much the same applies to the formation of the Aryan armed forces. Here, the central concept is the motto: "At the beginning of our struggle there stood a people; at the end of our struggle there will once more stand a people." The underlying concept here would be of importance to the later transnational movement—the key consideration in battle is race and not territory! The Aryan army is to defend "Aryan freedom" and the "whole of the Aryan state."

But what constitutes the Aryan state? What are its borders? The following section "Constitution and World Outlook," the longest in the document, seeks to elaborate. First, the primacy of the leadership principle is affirmed. The putative Aryan state will be explicitly National Socialist in structure. Thus, the constitution will reflect the divinely ordained interests of the Aryan people, and will brook no dissent, for: "Intolerance of opposing ideas is necessary to strength." But in 1979, the movement's vision had yet to disengage from the central paradigm of the nation-state. World leadership in the cold war world was vested in the U.S., and thus leadership of the world to come would rest with the Aryan United States. But the seeds of something greater are nonetheless present:

> The Aryan views not only his State and nation, but his race throughout
> the earth; and he works for "understanding and union between the
> different language groups of the one ordained ruling race." Against the
> international organization of Jewry, he sets his World Aryan Christian
> Union.[11]

The sections which follow, on culture and education respectively, are both of a piece. On the one hand, they contemptuously reject "intellectualism" in favor of spirit. On the other hand, culture (which remains largely undefined), is seen as the genetic possession of the Aryan people. No other racial group is capable of possessing this priceless gift from God to the Aryan folk. The education system is geared primarily towards inculcating the young with this amorphous, divinely mandated Aryan culture.

Surprisingly, the only section dealing explicitly with religion is one of the document's briefest. The entire exposition is neatly summed up in the opening sentences, for which little follow-up is needed: "Christianity for the Aryan is Race; and Race is Christianity. Race is Soul seen from without; and Christianity is Soul seen from within." With this genetic vision of religion, all that need be added is the rather contradictory assertion that to be truly Aryan, Christianity "must be purged of all remnants of Jewish thought."

The penultimate section reprises economics, stating again that agriculture is to be the foundation of the Aryan state, while the document closes with the standard assertion that communism is Jewish and thus a contemporary mask of Satan.

What is perhaps most important in the Aryan Nations' foundational document is its generic nature. There is little in it that is so specifically Christian Identity that other sectors of the race movement would be put off from becoming associated with the organization. If anything, National Socialism rather than Identity Christianity provides the document's primary thrust.

The appeal thus attracted many of the disaffected. Most were content to attend the annual Aryan Nations Congress, although a few of the most committed donned Pastor Butler's snappy imitation Nazi uniforms and became full-time residents of the compound. It was here that men like Robert Mathews, Gary Yarbrough, and Frank Silva talked late into the night of their hopes and dreams, and thus gave birth to the Silent Brotherhood. But the Order's emergence and brief but violent revolutionary career owed much to the frustration of Aryan Nations residents with the steady diet of dreamy promises of impending apocalypse and white renaissance that contrasted so sharply from Richard Butler's cautious disinclination to go beyond words to the propaganda of the deed.[12]

Other contradictions ate away at the Aryan Nations' base of support among its resident faithful, making the outlook for the movements following Butler's demise all but hopeless. There has been, for example, in recent years a fruitless search for a successor to Butler which has not accidentally coincided with the defection of several senior followers. The most interesting of these defections is arguably that of Floyd Cochrane, to whom the implications of the Aryan Nations' fixation with race eugenics was graphically driven home in bunk house conversation when a fellow race warrior casually noted that Cochrane's own son, born with a cleft palate, would probably have to be eliminated under the New Order! This seems to have brought home the practical implications of the ideology for the first time and Cochrane not only left the movement, he renounced his racialist beliefs as well.[13]

Throughout the 1980s, not only did the Aryan Nations' residential population decline, but the attendance at the Annual Congress dropped precipitously as well. Part of the problem was that in the wake of the successful efforts of the Anti-Defamation League to outlaw paramilitary training at such gatherings,[14] it simply wasn't much fun anymore. Moreover, acutely aware of the presence of federal agents and private spies working for groups like the ADL, the ever-cautious Butler had allowed little of the kind of fiery rhetoric that once typified the Congress.

It was probably something of pleasant surprise, therefore, when Butler, searching for new ways in the late 1980s to make his organization relevant, hit upon the then novel approach of inviting skinheads and, more important, skinhead rock bands to perform at these gatherings. While the Aryan Nations regulars were hardly thrilled by the musical efforts of the white noise bands, the ploy did for a time bring a much welcomed jolt of new life to the movement. Thus it must have seemed like old times in 1986 when a young skinhead named Gregory Withrow, founder of the White Students' Union, mounted the podium to make a brief four-minute speech calling for the "total extermination of all subhuman, non-Aryan peoples from the face of the North American continent: men, women, and children, without exception or appeal."[15] The skinhead youth culture however, has done little to halt the Aryan Nations' slide into oblivion. Efforts by such movement luminaries as Louis Beam, Tom Metzger (who was primarily responsible for bringing in the skinhead contingent), and Don Black of Stormfront web page fame all appear to be too little and too late to save the Aryan Nations' dream.

Although the Aryan Nations appears to be in permanent eclipse, it is none-theless of considerable importance. It provided a relatively stable communal ex-periment that outlived more radical contemporaries such as the Covenant, Sword, and Arm of the Lord. Pastor Butler established important connections with European movement activists, especially in Germany, that will continue to flourish long after the Hayden Lake compound is but a memory. Perhaps of greatest importance, the Aryan Nations spawned the Order, whose martyred leader Bob Mathews is lionized in Europe in song and story and whose mem-bers, men such as Gary Yarbrough and David Lane, have become icons of the European race movement.[16]

The Enigmatic Tale of Elohim City

Far less is known of Elohim City, a community that came to public light only after the discovery that convicted Oklahoma City bomber Timothy McVeigh had apparently visited several times and made some phone calls to the com-pound shortly before the bombing.

Elohim City was founded in the mid-1980s high point of separatist rural enclaves by an expatriate Canadian, Robert Millar. From its inception, Elohim City became a crucial link in the world of rural Christian Identity compounds which included the Aryan Nations and the Covenant, Sword, and Arm of the

Lord. Internally, Elohim City is a highly patriarchal organization, deeply imbued with the Identity faith and run in an autocratic fashion by Millar and a handful of "elders"—nearly all of them blood relations, not coincidentally—who often present the public face of the group in place of the reclusive Millar. Millar's connections to the world of white separatism run deep and his loyalty, once given, appears to be unconditional—a remarkable rarity in the world of the radical right.

For example, Millar was one of the few not to abandon Richard Snell during his time of tribulation as he sat on death row in Arkansas for two racially motivated killings. Millar not only appeared in court as a character witness for Snell, but provided Snell's body with its final resting place following his 19 April 1995 execution.[17] The execution took place the very day of the Oklahoma City bombing and on the anniversary of the Waco tragedy. Even more remarkable, when James Ellison, who is today almost universally reviled throughout the movement for his appearance as chief prosecution witness at Fort Smith, was released from prison, Millar alone stood by him and gave him a place to live at Elohim City.[18]

Elohim City exists to this day, and much of its survival may be credited to the consistently low public profile adopted by Millar and the remarkably isolated rural enclave he created. Unfortunately for Elohim City, the Oklahoma City bombing brought an end to this relative obscurity, and in so doing, brought to light a fascinating transatlantic connection: Andy Strasssmeir, a German citizen and, more intriguing yet, the son of prominent Berlin politician Guenter Strassmeir.[19] The elder Strassmeir is a former Berlin Secretary General of the ruling Christian Democratic Union (CDU), while an uncle currently serves in the regional parliament from a district in Berlin.[20]

It is not our purpose to establish or disprove the unlikely thesis of Strassmeir's connection to the Oklahoma City bombing. What is important from our perspective is the attraction of this rural racialist redoubt in one of the most distant corners of the U.S. to European movement activists. Certainly, in the normally cautious and closed atmosphere of Elohim City, Strassmeir was welcomed. He did get to know Timothy McVeigh (albeit he claims that the connection was peripheral at best), and of greater import, he became close to more important American movement figures such as former Klansman and current member of Tom Metzger's White Aryan Resistance (WAR) organization, Dennis Mahon.[21] Strassmeir, when his name came to light, wisely returned to Germany. Elohim City remains a largely closed enclave, although realizing the value of getting their side of the story to the public in the wake of the post-Oklahoma City paranoia about all deviant political and religious sects, they have cautiously begun to talk to selected academics and journalists.[22] Finally, in a bizarre twist, CNN reported on 13 November 1995 that three men, Ray Willey Lampley, his wife Cecilia, and John Daire Baird were arrested while building a fertilizer bomb intended to level the Elohim City compound. No reason for the plot was given.[23]

Despite these conspiratorial suspicions, the fact remains that Elohim City and Aryan Nations are atypical in that they have survived for a reasonable period of time. This is unusual in the milieu of racialist rural enclaves. This staying power may be attributed on the surface to circumspect relations with local and federal authorities on the part of the leaders of both movements. As the episode with the Order and Richard Butler amply demonstrates, violent rhetoric is simply not to be matched with violent actions if a movement hopes to be permitted to survive in a hostile political environment. One need point only to the Justus Freemen in rural Montana or to the ill-starred faction of the Republic of Texas militia headed by the Michigan-born Richard McLaren for evidence that this hostility is often directed at such enclaves not only by the government and the watchdog community, but often, by neighbors and estranged family members as well.[24]

Of greater importance, the internal cohesion of the group seems a key factor in the relative success of Elohim City and the Aryan Nations. Elohim City offers a radical version of the Identity doctrine under an authoritarian leader. The rules are clear, and anyone not in agreement is free to leave (or not join at all). Moreover, the majority of residents of Elohim City are members of the large Millar family.

Richard Butler and his Aryan Nations kingdom offers a version of Christian Identity designed to appeal to as eclectic a cross-section of the radical right-wing as possible. National Socialists and Odinists may partake in the dream as residents, and skinheads may bring their beer and guitars and visit during an annual open house.[25] But like Elohim City, Butler is an authoritarian figure and decision making is very much retained in his own hands. These factors seem to be of key import for the survival of a separatist racialist enclave. Moreover, it may well be that it is precisely this success at creating, at least on the surface, a racialist enclave that is so appealing to segments of the European movement for whom such rural communal opportunities are not so readily available.

The achievements of Elohim City and the Aryan Nations simply in weathering the test of time is not to be underestimated. Most such attempts die stillborn. It is to one such grand failure that we now turn.

National Socialist Kindred: A Dream Stillborn

In the 1980s and early 1990s Jost[26] led a group known as the National Socialist Kindred that sought to meld National Socialism and racialist Odinism into an ideology that would attract similarly disaffected individuals dedicated to the creation of a separatist community in the mountains of Northern California. The idea of a National Socialist haven was hardly new. Donald Clerkin of the Euro-

American Alliance had dreamed of such a National Socialist enclave before the formation of the Aryan Nations.[27] The dream has been shared by such high-profile figures as Rick Cooper of the National Socialist Vanguard whose vision of a community known as Wolfstadt is the stated reason for the group's existence.[28] And most recently, we have seen the efforts in Britain involving the Reichsfolk, the Order of the Nine Angles and the Order of Balder to form communal separatist groups that would adhere to National Socialist ideals. Jost tried to bring these dreams into reality.

It was not to be. Jost died of a heart attack in late 1996, while still in his early fifties.[29] By then, he had already abandoned the National Socialist Kindred and the communal dream in favor of a remarkable theology that brought New Age ideas into the already heady mix of Odinism and National Socialism to form Arya Kriya—a holistic belief system combining health faddism, meditation techniques, and racialist ideology into a kind of correspondence course. At the time of his death, Arya Kriya had subscribers throughout the U.S. and was being translated into Swedish for distribution in Scandinavia.[30]

What follows then, will be a history of Jost's efforts, told primarily in his own words. Through this medium, we hope to convey not only the substance of the white nationalist dream, but much of its emotional appeal as well. Jost was married to the sister of Maddy Hutter, the ex-wife of the founder of the American Ásatrú movement, Steve McNallen, and he lived near McNallen, with whom he remained very close. His ideas, like those of so many others in these pages, were ahead of their time, and thus the successes and the failures of Jost's endeavors are in a very real sense transitional. It remains to be seen whether his ideas will be carried forward by others. Of particular import to this chapter, however, is the fate of his communal efforts and the reasons that, in the end, the dream had to be abandoned. It is a lesson that others before him have learned to their cost. Moreover, Jost's unhappy experiences make the survival of the Aryan Nations and Elohim City all the more remarkable.

No better introduction to Jost's life and mission may be offered than that penned by Jost himself. Within this extended quotation, several mysteries are revealed to the curious—press, public, and government officials alike—who in the wake of the Oklahoma City bombing have lavished intensive scrutiny upon the denizens of America's hinterlands and wondered at the intensity of their antipathy for the federal government. What is remarkable in Jost's simple prose is the candid picture of the transition from two cultures, the hippie ruralists of the 1960s and the right-wing paramilitary and survivalist rural migrants of the 1980s and 1990s.[31]

As Jost explains, what unites these vastly different cultures is a shared ethos of live and let live and a powerful oppositional mindset against all forms of government authority. Moreover, Jost documents the destructive impact of the rising price of marijuana in the 1980s that turned many a hippie cultivator first into a "hip businessman" and then into a successful criminal entrepreneur. With this transformation, the idyllic ruralism of Jost's early days became a setting for armed violence as each cultivator took up arms to protect his investment. While this had the effect of making the countryside a less pleasant place of refuge for the fleeing right-wingers, it did increase the level of armaments available and it increased too the level of violence which the residents of these areas were willing to employ to discourage federal incursions. Thus from a neighborly milieu was born an unlikely alliance of armed hippie cultivators and armed right-wing revolutionaries equally determined to resist the government's attempts to project its authority into "their" areas.

Listen then to the words of Jost. No corrections or changes have been made to the original text:

> In the late 1960's I had just returned from two consecutive tours of combat duty in the rugged mountain highlands of South Vietnam. California had become a very different place from the one I had left, and two years of isolation in the Asian jungles had not prepared me for that to which I had returned.
>
> I was suddenly in an alien world of long hair and beards, drugs and sexual promiscuity, civil disobedience and racial color blindness. It was the day of the "Hippy," "do your own thing," and the encouragement to "drop out" of society.
>
> For a while I was in a state of shock, but as I adjusted, I began listening and observing. I dismissed most of this "new age" philosophy as childish nonsense. However, two years in the jungles had given me a different outlook on life. I could now see the selfishness and materialism into which the White race had sunk, and I had some sympathy for my hairy co-racialists. I especially liked their idea of destroying the system by non-participation, and it has always remained in the back of my mind.
>
> By the early 1970's there was a growing movement among these social drop-outs to go "back to the land", advocating self-sufficiency on the land, free from modern society's support, living simply like our ancestors. Their pioneering in this area has done our Folk an invaluable service.
>
> By the mid 1970's I had given up trying to be part of the urban social and economic system. Already I could see the growing political power of non-whites, and the indifference and growing materialism of the white majority. Seeing no real alternative, I packed up my family and headed back to the land. There, I discovered a whole new world, a much better and more natural way of life, and an Aryan destiny!
>
> In the isolated mountains of Northern California, there were already a number of individuals and families, many college educated,

who had fled the cities and begun a new life of homesteading. They were all permeated with an anti establishment idealism which was directly descended from the hey-day of the hippy movement. Their philosophy of life was a combination of left-wing politics, oriental religion, Robin Hood and brotherhood, as well as a tolerance for drugs which ultimately led to an early destruction of the movement.

Nevertheless, these urban refugees had done a staggering amount of research, and a great deal of practical application in the field of self-sufficient homesteading. They learned to build their own simple shelters, everything from log cabins to yurts. They learned the skills of organic gardening, animal husbandry, and home processing of foods. They revived the arts of midwifery, herbal medicine, and such skills of self-sufficiency as spinning, weaving, and leather craft. In the spirit of being anti-establishment, they put great effort into supporting themselves off the system, and made some great progress into the area of cottage industries. They spurned corporations and conducted their business exclusively with thrift shops and small businesses. They made great progress in pioneering alternative education for their children. As their numbers grew, they began manifesting a real spirit of community and Folk.

These modern-day pioneers were happy to help any newcomer, and I spent the next couple of years learning the many skills of homesteading and self-sufficiency. For the first few years our family lived in crude octagon cabins, barns and even teepees. We cut firewood with antique handsaws, used herbal medicines, raised organic gardens, and learned to process our own food. Our lives were simple, yet fuller than ever before. Summer work was hard, but there was always ample recreation at the river swimming hole where numbers of locals from all over the mountain ridges would congregate to relax and cool off. Like our pre-christian ancestors of old, they were not burdened by christian puritanism. They saw nothing evil or dirty about the human body, and they swam and sun-bathed quite naturally unadorned by swimsuits or cutoffs. Winter was the time for enjoying the fruits of summer labor. We joined other modern-day homesteaders in rough-hewn cabins all over the mountains, sitting around the wood stove, repairing tools, watching the rain and snow, and planning the next season's chores.

But these pioneers did not understand the importance of discipline to their own idealism and homesteading success. They generally failed to pass anything on to their children. They opted for Jewish permissiveness. The heirs of the movement can be seen here and there throughout the area—purposeless, undisciplined, drug-using youth.

The end really came with the rise of marijuana cultivation. Ideals began to vanish with the temptation of large amounts of easily acquired cash. Materialism and the greater supply of drugs destroyed both the

community spirit and idealism. Today, the mountains are waiting for a
new back-to-the-land movement, one imbued with a true idealism, and
a sound spiritual philosophy. This time it will not be the pressures of
White middle class materialism that will spur a back-to-the-land
movement. This time it will be the awesome pressure of mass non-white
immigration, and White second-class citizenship.

All of the elements for building an Aryan Folk community are here.
The time is now ripe. There is little future for White youth in any city.
The cities are becoming more and more non-white. Economically, it is
getting more and more difficult to survive in the city. The social welfare
system is becoming more and more anti-white. The schools are sorely
anti-white. Today, the disenfranchised Aryan youth are beginning to
stir. The Skinhead movement is a reaction to the growing non-white
terrorism, and White indifference. It pains me to see our youth sitting in
government prisons for smashing a few degenerate heads in a futile
attempt to fight back against overwhelming oppression. How much
more useful it would be to put their energy into hewing themselves a
homestead, and ultimately an Aryan community, out of the unsettled
rugged mountains. There is still a great deal of open land in this country,
and although it is not as easy as it used to be, it is still possible to live
there simply, inexpensively, and reasonably independently. It is also
quite possible to establish communities which are largely independent of
the established system. Why not take up the old hippy slogan to "drop
out", and begin destroying this anti-white system by non-participation?

Just as Adolf Hitler advocated the "Drang nach Osten" (the
acquisition and settlement of the vast, unsettled lands in east Europe),
we advocate a new Aryan back to the land movement. We hope that
Volksberg, our family homestead in the secluded mountains of Northern
California, will serve as an example, a viable alternative for the responsible and self-reliant of our Folk, to begin a new life, a simple, joyful,
Aryan life, close to nature, and away from the degeneracy of the urban
cesspools. As our Folk grows and grows, we hope to provide a viable
destiny for Aryans: Back to the Land![32]

As Jost and his family patiently laid the foundation for the Volksberg community, he published a large number of tracts under the imprimatur of the National Socialist Kindred. The NS Kindred, too, republished the work of such
foreign neo-Nazis as the Aryan Nations' regular Manfred Roeder as well as pieces
by imprisoned veterans of the Order such as David Lane.[33]

Jost's writings can be divided roughly into three categories: National Socialism and particularly on the person of Adolf Hitler who in Jost's formulation
is raised to the level of the gods themselves, religious tracts on racialist Odinism,
and increasingly through the 1990s, earnest exhortations towards self-improve-
ment that would point the way towards Arya Kriya. One point should be noted

before continuing however. Jost's Odinism was deeply felt and quite sincere. But the NS Kindred was very much apart from the organized Ásatrú community.[34] This isolation may have contributed in large measure to Jost's drift out of Odinism into Arya Kriya.

Given his isolation in Odinist circles, Jost's National Socialism provides the primary point of entrée for the creation of a physical community. For Jost, National Socialism is, like Christianity in its most idealized form, a religion of love par excellence:

> Adolf Hitler was literally an evangelist of love. His words, his actions, his entire existence is testimony to his selfless love of his Folk. Anyone who takes the time to honestly examine Adolf Hitler's speeches and writings can readily see the great love he had for his Folk. His actions proved his words. Everything that he did was done for the benefit of the Folk. The welfare and higher evolution of the Folk is the only reason for the existence of National Socialism. Every aspect of National Socialism, no matter how small or insignificant, is for the present and future benefit of the Folk. Every decision was based on the answer to one question: Is it good for the Folk?[35]
>
> . . . With the flowering of our heart's natural love, we can clearly see the enemy. We can see that our enemy is not the Negro. It is not the Asian or Latin. Our enemy is not International Finance, or World Jewry. They are all just symptoms of a deadly disease of selfishness.[36]

For Jost, the failure of National Socialist Germany and the dismal condition of the contemporary Aryan race may be traced to the failings of the Aryan rather than the seemingly superhuman guile of the Jews. In a remarkably literal sense, Jost posits Hitler as a Christlike martyr who "was destined to be overcome by the forces of selfishness and materialism," in order to awaken the white man to the evil of this world and to prepare him for the apocalyptic battle to come. In Jost's terms: "There is no other way except for Aryans to experience the horrors which await them, "*and these horrors are coming soon!*"[37]

Like many other visionaries in the race movement, Jost soon came to despair of the lamentable quality of many of those attracted to his message. It is thus little wonder that Jost would fold the National Socialist Kindred in 1995 and turn inward to something of a New Age teacher of a racialist form of yoga known as Arya Kriya. Moreover, the communal dream of Volksberg died with the N.S. Kindred. In a letter to Tommy Rydén in Sweden, Jost candidly explains what had gone wrong.

> We stopped using the name NS Kindred for three reasons: first, our scope is so much different now that the name is misleading; second, legally, the NS Kindred is considered a business name, and this requires bi-annual fees and bureaucratic paperwork which we no longer wanted

to deal with; third, Arya Kriya training and our whole program is unique and it requires a much more personal relationship than any organization could afford. So, we decided to drop NS Kindred and publish and correspond simply under Jost, which eliminates the bureaucratic BS, is more personal, and has no connotation which might be misleading.

Yes, we had some problems with . . . Nazis . . . They destroyed years of hard work. We found the Folk-community concept was very alluring, but few people were willing to forsake job, home, friends, family, etc., to move here. We found that more often than not, those who were willing to pull up stakes and move here were willing to do so because [they] had no job, no home, no family, no friends, nor anything else. They were looking for somebody to take care of them! Most were psychopaths and dangerous.

We learned (the hard way) that a Folk-community must be organic, that is, it must spring from those who are already established in the area. So, now that we are working with our neighbors, who we know and who are already established, to build an organic Folk-community here, and this is working much better. However, for fear of attracting psychopaths (the racial movement is full of them) we decided not to publicize it anymore. We publish the ideas so that others can form Folk-communities in their own areas, but are quiet about our work here.

We had hesitated for many years about introducing Arya Kriya. We didn't want to "cast pearls before swine" (pardon my paraphrasing of the dead Jew.) But realizing its awesome potential, we finally . . . decided to give it a try. To our surprise, there has been lots of interest, even though we have not really advertised it. Also, since it requires some Aryan discipline, it doesn't attract the psychos. We have a number of prisoners taking the course, but they are of higher intelligence than most, and the Kriya seems to be really helping them. Meanwhile, our Folk-community here is becoming a Kriya community as well. Interest is growing in all quarters.[38]

Arya Kriya itself barely had time to get off the ground before Jost's early death. It is too soon to judge the post-Jost fate of Arya Kriya. Tommy Rydén continues the work of translating Arya Kriya materials into Swedish for distribution throughout Scandinavia under the imprimatur of his DeVries Institute, although he does not plan to himself carry the work forward.[39] It is likely that Arya Kriya, like the Volksberg community, will remain a dream unrealized.

Virtual Communities

The popularity of computer technology as a medium of communications has, by the mid-1990s, brought the transnational movement on line and into constant communication with each other and, to a degree, with the dominant culture as well. While it is still far too early to predict with any certainty the impact this technology will ultimately have on the future direction of the race movement, the availability of a mode of communication that connects the continents instantaneously opens a number of fascinating possibilities undreamed of by the movement's elders but a scant few years ago. For some time now, the various watchdog organizations have warned of the dangers of the "networks of hate," but the question of most concern in this chapter is how this technology will affect the movement's quest for community. Here some fascinating possibilities—and a number of pitfalls—are already apparent.[40]

First, it is clear that this transnational connection is likely to result in a degree of homogenization which goes well beyond the already marked degree of ideological and theological syncretism that has always characterized the radical right.[41] To an ever increasing degree, the movement's medium of exchange is English, and the ideas that characterize a particular belief system have become the common property of all. Moreover, no longer do even the most isolated individuals, whether in a geographic or a social sense, need to feel alone. Today, they may become an interactive part of a seemingly vast community of adherents that, from the vantage point of the computer screen, appears to grow stronger and more numerous by the day. It would appear to be the watchdogs' darkest fears come to life.

Yet appearances in this regard may be deceiving. There remains a disjunction between the worlds of virtual reality and the arena of political action that may never be bridged. Thus, as the Internet becomes ever more crowded with movement e-mail discussion groups, web sites, and vitriolic USENET exchanges with antiracists, the adherent risks becoming drawn ever deeper into the virtual world, losing touch with events beyond the purview of his or her computer screen. This allows the adherent to ignore the more mundane realities of the movement's isolation and minuscule size. In this conception, the comforts of a virtual transnational community of like-minded individuals and the interactive confrontations with antiracists may be a process in which both sides become increasingly insular, so absorbed by the technology, that the computer becomes for many the real world and the movement merely an absorbing computer game.

Should this prophesy prove prescient, an argument could be made that the much feared "networks of hate" may in the long run act to inhibit rather than to facilitate radical right-wing violence. If so, this certainly was not the intent of the European and American movement pioneers of the use of computer technology.

On the American side, the rapidity with which the movement has gone from the mimeographed newsletter to the World Wide Web is stunning. By the time the alarm was sounded by the Anti-Defamation League in 1985, the movement had begun with limited success to take up the possibilities offered by the computer and modem through the construction of two national computer BBS (Bulletin Board) sites. Of these, the most influential BBS was sponsored by the Aryan Nations under the tutelage of Louis R. Beam. Beam is a Texas Klansman whose primary mission in life at one point was to revitalize the Ku Klux Klan, and thus to bring it into what he referred to as its "Fifth Era." He is as well a charismatic leader whose adventures include Vietnam service, fugitive life on the run in Mexico with his now ex-wife (whose killing of Mexican *federale* in a gun battle that allowed Beam to escape is the stuff of movement legend),[42] and an acquittal at the Fort Smith trial where, among other charges, he was accused of using his BBS to target enemies and informers for death through a game that assigned point values to each target, depending on their importance and vulnerability.[43] Described variously as a movement hero or a gun-toting psychopath, Beam was a guiding force in bringing the American movement from the age of the Xerox to the computer age.[44]

Beam for his part is more modest than the ADL, noting that the existence of movement BBS sites dates back to 1964.[45] The reference, however, is to telephone-based rather than computer-based technology. Indeed, when Beam began to publicize the Aryan Nations' leap into the world of hi tech in the early 1980s, he was constrained not only to explain what a computer is, but to urge on his fellow patriots with the assurance that the technology is so simple that, of the approximately forty active BBS sites throughout the U.S.: "One of the forty is run by a thirteen-year-old child!"[46] It was indicative of the movement's adaptability to the new technology however, that nearly a decade later, Beam would still feel the need to explain again the basics of the computer—in even simpler terms than before.[47] Rather than wait for the movement to adapt to the new technology, the Aryan Net BBS was forced to operate a telephone-based message system that allowed the non-computer literate to listen to menu of recorded messages, albeit at the price of an expensive long-distance phone call.

With these unpromising beginnings, the explosion of Internet technology in the mid-1990s caught everyone, not least the movement, by surprise. A good measure of the credit for this rapid assimilation is due to the influx of younger people—often university undergraduates—into the movement. These young adherents brought with them a vision of the new medium as one open to all ideas—even theirs—that effectively spelled the end of the strategy of restricted access to sites. Rather, new strategies were being considered that hoped to use the new technology as a powerful recruitment tool, as well as an opportunity to establish new forms of global community.

The advantage these younger adherents enjoyed was their access to the Internet via university accounts. Yet the early attempts at utilizing the Internet for the movement were halting at best until the 1995 advent of the Stormfront web page. Before the explosion of html-based technology which made the World

Wide Web (WWW) possible, movement activity was confined to simple e-mail exchanges and the creation of several pioneering FTP (File Transfer Protocol) sites by such organizations as Pete Peters' Christian Identity Scriptures for America and William Pierce's National Alliance. FTP technology is a comparatively primitive affair, allowing the visitor to view long lists of files that are marked by coded names allowing the receiving party to have only the most rudimentary idea of what the file contains. There is no possibility for on-line reading. However, a pattern was already emerging in which well-established racialist organizations were able to utilize the services of younger adherents to create and maintain computer sites in order to archive and disseminate a group's writings. All of this changed radically in 1995 when Don Black, a former Klansman heretofore best known for his involvement in a quixotic attempt to overthrow the government of the tiny island nation of Dominica, created Stormfront, the first racialist web site.[48]

The advent of WWW technology began a spiraling growth of the movement's use of the net which shows no sign of abating. Today (1997), the primary activity of the American movement is concentrated in three major areas of the net: e-mail lists, USENET news groups, and of greatest import, World Wide Web sites.[49]

You Have Mail!

The e-mail lists are many and various. They serve at once as the most personal form of communication and the most exclusive. Subscription is comparatively easy, and the lists serve a variety of purposes. Don Black runs several lists through Stormfront, which allow the white nationalist community to discuss issues of interest. Black moderates these so as to prevent the risk of threats of violence that could result in action being taken against the list by its service provider, the government, or the various watchdog groups, all of whom monitor the discussion. Harold Covington, a loquacious National Socialist figure, disseminates his views through his own list. Ernst Zundel, a Canadian Holocaust revisionist figure whose virtual adventures on the net lifted him from obscurity to fame, runs his own list with the aid of Ingrid Rimland. Zundel's Zgram list promises that the subscriber the dubious pleasure of a fresh from the computer breakfast greeting from Zundel every morning.

Other lists are more specialized. Milton John Kleim, Jr. created the ANA (Aryan News Agency) service which trolls the net for news stories of interest to the community. Such mainstream publications as the *New York Times*, the *Washington Post*, the Associated Press, Reuters, and many others would no doubt be less than delighted to know that their material has been downloaded and redistributed in this way. When Kleim graduated from college in May 1995, the list was taken over by a Canadian, Rick Knight. Someone styling himself Anton88 then took over in 1996, apparently with the help of Don Black.[50] Resistance Records based in Detroit under former Church of the Creator and music impresario George Eric Hawthorne sent out a biweekly newsletter which is meant to publicize Resistance products and recycle ANA stories.[51]

These email lists constitute primary building blocks of the emergent transnational movement. They provide the faithful with a sense of community, the lonely with a source of companionship, and the true believer with an interactive confirmation of faith. E-mail however, has shown few signs of utility in bringing new believers into the fold. Indeed, efforts, covert and overt, to use e-mail to spread the word beyond the confines of the subscription list have proved counterproductive. For example, when Jeff Vos who was associated with the CNG Homepage sent out a mass mailing of propaganda for the National Alliance under an assumed address, the reaction of the recipients was so intense that the National Alliance was suspended briefly by its Internet provider.[52] Thus, while e-mail lists provide the most tangible form of virtual community available, they remain at the same time the forum least likely to provide a viable recruiting tool.

USENET: *Dialogue of the Deaf*

USENET groups have provided the unlikely cutting edge of the battle between racists and antiracists, and are looked to by the former as a prime venue for potential recruits. This at first glance would seem curious, given the highly specialized nature of discussion groups and the insularity of this virtual realm. Yet it was precisely here that the greatest push for recruitment has taken place, and it is in this realm the younger adherents were able to step out of the shadow of movement elders and take the lead in the assault on the USENET groups.

The USENET controversy began with the observation by several of these youthful adherents that the racialist discussion groups formed a virtual ghetto in the sea of USENET groups. Such movement outposts as alt.skinheads, alt.nationalism.white, alt.politics.white-power, and alt.revisionism had become the site of regular and predictable flame wars (vituperative exchanges) that were succeeding in changing no one's minds and were taking up valuable time that could be better spent in other endeavors. It was in this context that a young adherent from Minnesota, Milton Kleim, wrote his lengthy essay, "On Strategy and Tactics for Usenet."[53] Kleim's suggestions here were simple enough:

> We MUST move out beyond our present domain, and take up positions on "main-stream" groups . . .
>
> Find groups that require "tailored" messages: rec. groups concerning food would be suitable for our "kosher tax" message; alt., soc., and talk.

groups concerning politics and American society would be suitable for our message about the Jewish-controlled media.

Find groups that are suitable for organizational and literature advertisements: talk.politics.guns should have regular posts explaining how to order The Turner Diaries and Hunter; rec.radio.shortwave should have regular posts of the American Dissident Voices schedule; alt.music. groups should have regular posts about Resistance Records.

* Create posts that are succinct and self-sustaining. By "self-sustaining," I mean the post should be ideologically clear, with adequate information to assist the curious to find the "proof" they seek. An example is in the "kosher tax" issue: DON'T post something complaining about paying more so Jews can keep kosher. Post something that directs the curious to their cupboard to "prove" our contentions, with reasons why they should be concerned about the issue.[54]

These ideas were aimed at recruitment, particularly for the National Alliance. They grew out of the "success" experienced by Kleim, WAR's Wyatt Kaldenberg, and George Eric Hawthorne of Resistance Records among others, who found something of a second home on the alt.fan.oj-simpson newsgroup following Simpson's acquittal.[55] Soon racialist postings began cropping up in the most unlikely of places—often without the subtlety suggested by Kleim. So in addition to posting to groups which might have an affinity for a racialist message, any number of USENET groups ranging from alt.support.lonliness to alt.sex.stories became the venue for often crude racialist messages.[56] This was the diametric opposite of Kleim's cautionary suggestions.

How effective has the USENET recruiting drive been? Given the ephemeral nature of the web, it is impossible to tell for certain. It may be indicative however, that such leading lights of the young racialists engaged in the USENET offensive as Milton Kleim, Colin Cooper, and Ray Hourigan have themselves publicly renounced the movement.[57] Kleim's exit is particularly instructive.

Kleim's resignation was announced through the vehicle of the USENET, and his successive follow-up letters were posted as well. He began with some standard denunciations of the movement's elders:

I am here to tell those young ones, the "cannon-fodder" for the money-idolizing maniacs of the "movement," to stand down.

Your lives mean more to me than earning yourselves prison for [William] Pierce or a bullet for Burdi [George Eric Hawthorne]. To me, you are young Aryans with a future; to them, you are an instrument in a personal political quest. Expendable. Replaceable. You are pawns in a game played by small men with large egos. You are tools for the fulfillment of power trips, grandiose schemes, lunatic, unrealizable designs on America and the world.[58]

Of greater interest are the paragraphs which follow, in that they illustrate two vital points that reveal much of the difficulties faced by the movement in trying to establish any form of community in the real world. First, there are the contradictions faced by a movement dedicated to the tenets of race purity and preservation that is unable to attract to its ranks more than a handful of women. Indeed, it is arguably for a woman's love that many of the younger adherents have left the movement.[59] Second, it is notable that physical withdrawal from the movement is considerably easier than psychological withdrawal from its core beliefs. In the case of Kleim, his resignation letter and a number of follow-up texts noted that he would stay true to his racialist beliefs, even if he would have nothing more to do with the movement itself. Within a matter of months, this would change to a rejection of racism altogether and ultimately, at the urging of his new girlfriend, the destruction of all movement-related materials in his possession.[60] With this introduction then, the heart of Kleim's resignation letter is worth considering at some length:

> I feel as you do. I understand the frustration of our generation about the radical transformation of America in our lifetimes. I share your despair, your dreams—shattered, in most cases—your hopes, unfulfilled. Of course I do, because that's why my works have been received so warmly by so many.
>
> Much has been said about the failure of the "movement" to attract White women to its ranks. The misogynists declare women inherently corrupt, and more prone to "race-treason." I declare, rather, we must examine not what fails to attract the ladies, but what actually attracts the males.
>
> Deep down, every Aryan male within the "movement" feels an unmistakable sexual frustration. Especially so unattached males, but nearly all males in general. It's a matter of "darkie getting blondie."
>
> He who denies this is a liar.
>
> The "movement's" entertaining aspects serve as a diversion and a release for the sexual tension all racially-conscious Aryan males experience each and every day multi-culturalism is encountered. In a short-sighted yet gratifying manner, cussing "niggers" and bitching about "the ZOG," listening to the latest pseudo-revolutionary idiocy the drunkards have screeched out, or reading the latest moronic missive by a self-serving, money-grubbing guru are imagined to be "fighting for the Race." Reality, however, is that it's a cop-out, a feel-good recipe to soothe hyperactive hormones.
>
> Young Aryan males need to stop whining like those they condemn and start acting like men. Never mind that Tyrone and Juan are "getting some" with Stacy and Heather—they'll find their fate by their own choosing. Concern yourselves with acting like real men, gentlemen, and

present our racial sisters with something they'd be attracted to. No more cowardly bullshit—no more excuses. Most women want men—not just males—who are wise, successful (at least to a reasonable degree), and strong spiritually and physically. The simple reason the "movement" "lacks" women is because the ladies see it at best [as] a joke, full of losers and cry-babies (despite the delusionary "successes" I and others have "accomplished"); at worst, a social menace around which a family should never be raised. Most Aryan women are not born "race-traitors." But, neither are they drawn to the shameful imbecility which is the "movement."

Throughout my "movement" career, I made countless excuses for the debauchery, the decadence, the dishonesty within its ranks. I told myself the "movement" was a holy cause, a just association, but with a few corrupt elements within it.

However, today, I hold a more honest—and accurate—view. The "movement" is not an association of good, noble people working for a great cause, containing a few corrupt elements. Rather, it is, in reality, a corrupt "movement" of ignoble aims with a few idealistic but misguided souls within its ranks. . . .

The "movement," with its shallow lip-service to ideals, and lack of honor and wisdom does not and can not offer a sound alternative to what the System offers. Both the "movement" and the System operate with materialistic premises, upon a base plane of the visible world. Righteousness is not a precept founded in the material world, but one of a higher plane, a spiritual plane.

We Aryans are, and always have been, our own worst enemy. In fact, there is NO "enemy" besides ourselves. The cowards, frauds and losers blame all Jews, all Blacks, and all other non-Whites for our own failings. WE, not they, lack the character to advance ourselves. WE, not they, refuse to accept responsibility for our shortcomings. In infantile jealousy "movement" leaders put forth hateful orgasmic fantasies of conquest and nuclear revenge against those peoples who have the stamina, the insight, the COURAGE, to advance themselves where we have abdicated.[61]

The World Wide Web

If the USENET recruiting drive may have resulted in more conversions out of than into movement ranks, the use of the World Wide Web may be more promising. Certainly, it is here that the watchdog community has concentrated their greatest firepower. Indeed, the debate among watchdogs engendered by the rapid proliferation of the web has created an unusual split in their ranks that has resulted in three very different approaches. The most interesting of these is Ken

McVay's international NIZKOR project, which maintains a website archive of Holocaust and other racism-related materials and whose primary thrust is to counter the propaganda of racists in general and Holocaust deniers in particular in whatever virtual forum it may be found. NIZKOR is in fact linked to a number of racialist and Holocaust revisionist sites. NIZKOR's activists however, are strongly opposed to censorship in any form.[62]

Among the established Jewish watchdog groups, a rare public argument over tactics erupted in the aftermath of the 1996 effort by the Simon Wiesenthal Center to "convince" (i.e., force) both university and private Internet providers to refuse service to web users promoting racism or anti-Semitism. To its credit, the Anti-Defamation League has publicly refused to endorse censorship, relying instead on an approach which seeks to expose racism and anti-Semitism, but accepting that First Amendment considerations make actually seeking to shut down these sites counterproductive.[63]

The web is the most difficult aspect of the Internet to analyze in terms of its contribution to the creation of a transnational racialist community. On the one hand, there is a new site appearing almost every day. Many of these, such as the National Socialist-oriented Alpha site, can be accessed through links to Don Black's Stormfront site. Moreover, while English remains the overwhelming language of choice on the net, Stormfront now provides files in Spanish and German, while European sites such as Flashback in Sweden provide links to Scandinavian-language sites as well as English ones. Clearly though, it is the hypertext capability of the web—the ability to surf from site to site—that makes the web such a powerful potential tool in the creation of an interactive transnational movement. And while there has been some effort to make the web multilingual, English is and will remain the dominant contact language.

Yet there remains something terribly ephemeral about the emergent web culture. A site can have a number of hits per day, and a few offer such amenities as chat rooms and bulletin boards where visitors can leave behind messages or engage in real-time discussion. Since the 1995 inception of Stormfront, the most important of the various racialist web sites have become increasingly specialized and technically sophisticated. The Resistance Records web site for example, allows the curious to download music (albeit with download times for a thirty-second excerpt ranging from twenty to thirty minutes) and to order CDs, videos, and other merchandise (on-line Visa and Mastercard transactions welcome). Ernst Zundel's Canadian based website in late 1996 has begun to experiment with live radio broadcasts every Friday, in addition to acting as the usual file repository. In fact, to some degree, virtually every major (and many minor) racialist organization within the past year has acquired a web site. These may range from the Women for Aryan Unity Homepage which is little more than a logo and an address to the extremely crude racism of Tom Metzger's WAR homepage to the more sophisticated offerings of the National Alliance and the Aryan Crusader's Library.[64]

Exactly what impact do these pages have on the creation of a transnational community? It is hard to posit an answer with any certainty. Of course, to the computer literate, the mushrooming of racist web pages have put movement propaganda within the reach of an infinitely larger audience than ever before. Moreover, the effortless ability to link to pages containing such esoterica as bomb-making instructions and weapons manuals does present at least the potential for real as opposed to verbal or virtual violence. Yet evidence that the net is an effective recruiting tool is rather sparse. Rather, reading the postings left at the various sites, one is left with the impression that the sites are rather "preaching to the choir." It would seem that Milton Kleim's observations noted above that the movement has become a form of entertainment is incorrect only in that the youthful Kleim lacks a sense of movement history. No less a figure than George Lincoln Rockwell said much the same in the early 1960s![65]

On the other hand, the very number of these pages, and the hypertext capability that links pages throughout the world, probably does have a positive impact on the creation of a virtual community of like-minded adherents. It is this bonding of the already committed which may prove to be the web's greatest utility to the race movement.

The European movement has approached the Internet in many of the same ways as have the Americans, with one significant exception. Around 1994, the watchdog groups went public with their fears of what appeared to be a terrifying new phenomenon among the European, and particularly, the German groups: a network of computer-based communications posited to be impervious to government or watchdog penetration. The most famous of these systems came to be the German-based Thule Net.

In contrast to the more open nature of the American movement's approach to the Internet, the Germans had from the beginning envisioned the net as an opportunity for internal command, control, and communications that would be free from the prying eyes of antifascists, the media, and especially the German security services. While the suggestion that German intelligence would be unable to monitor movement communications on the net seems optimistic at best, a flood of stories in the press seemed to indicate that the Thule Net was a terrifying new weapon, as well as a powerful tool for coordination with like-minded foreign groups.[66] Meanwhile, while the hue and cry over Thule Net and its sister e-mail-based networks was at its zenith, the German government was evincing considerably more concern over the implications of the net as a conduit for racist and anti-Semitic propaganda that, while perfectly legal in the U.S., was proscribed by German law.

Before the 1990s proliferation of Internet technology, the importation and dissemination of propaganda materials into Germany was no easy task. It was this that made Gary Lauck's NSDP/AO organization so problematic for German authorities. The seeming impunity with which Lauck was able to import materials was a source of considerable German frustration. It is for this reason somewhat ironic that when Lauck was arrested in Denmark and eventually deported, tried, and sentenced in Germany, the Internet had already made his operation passé. Suddenly, unlimited quantities of propaganda, pictures (gif and jpg files), sound (wav files) and even video clips could be obtained from web sites in countries like the U.S. and Canada that have no laws restricting the electronic dissemination of such materials.

This left the German government in a quandary. Their answer, ultimately unsuccessful, was to link neo-Nazi propaganda with pornography and to put pressure on Internet providers to do something to block access to sites carrying either. One target of convenience was the Canadian Holocaust denier Ernst Zundel's Digital Freedom site, which was duly blocked by Deuttsche Telekom AG in January 1996 in a move patterned after an earlier attempt to force Compuserve and other providers to block access to pornographic sites. The move backfired badly, however. Zundel, heretofore a rather marginal figure in movement circles, was suddenly front-page news and was in the process transformed into an unlikely martyr for free speech. Worse, at least ten different mirror sites suddenly sprang up at prestigious American universities. These sites were founded by American students who, while evincing a distaste for Zundel's ideology, found censorship of the net more odious still.[67] The German government was thus faced with the choice of blocking communication between German universities and major research centers abroad in a doomed attempt to keep illegal materials out of Germany or to take the humiliating step of backing down in the face of the opposition of a handful of young free speech activists around the world. In the end, it was the German government that blinked when Minister of Technology Juergen Ruettgers announced that Internet providers would be prosecuted only if they are both aware of and possess the technical means to block the dissemination of illegal materials. The loophole that effectively gutted the law stated that providers would not be required to search their systems for outlawed materials.[68]

With this consideration of the various forms of radical right-wing communitarianism complete, we now turn to the biography of Tommy Rahowa Rydén, an activist whose life may serve as a paradigm for the emergent transatlantic race movement.

Chapter 8

Tommy Rydén

A National Socialist Life

IF ANY ONE FIGURE could be said to personify the transatlantic connection at the heart of the current convergence of the Euro-American radical right, it is the Swedish race activist Tommy Rydén. From the age of fifteen, Rydén has sought to establish linkages with American racialist groups of every description. As we have seen, transnational linkages have been common throughout the postwar years. Einar Åberg, for example, supplied his anti-Semitic writings—in a variety of languages—to activists throughout the world from the 1940s until his death. The World Union of National Socialists under the leadership of George Lincoln Rockwell, following the Cotswolds Conference, sought to formalize these linkages under the aegis of an organizational infrastructure. Moreover, a number of lesser-known activists, by accident as much as by design, formed stronger alliances with foreign movements than they would enjoy with their own compatriots.[1]

Unlike the activists who had come before, Tommy Rydén looked first to the foreign groups and only after having established contact with the American movement did he become active on the Swedish scene. While this remains an unusual introduction to the racialist milieu, it is likely that in the vanguard of the contemporary race movement, this postnationalist vision of race rather than nationality as the primary source of identification will become increasingly prevalent.

The primary thrust of this chapter will be to introduce Tommy Rydén in his own words. It is hoped that by presenting Tommy Rydén thus, it will be possible to gain a greater understanding of the individuals who are drawn to the transatlantic racist right. Much of what follows is thus taken directly from the transcripts of taped interviews with Rydén that took place in Sweden in 1995 and 1997. Letters, faxes, and Rydén's writings will play a large part as well. This approach has been taken for several reasons. First, Tommy Rydén is an articulate advocate of his beliefs, and it was felt that the reader would better understand the transnational movement if given the opportunity to see the world through his eyes. Second, Tommy Rydén is a much feared—and much demonized—figure in Sweden. He thus exists on the fringes of Swedish political life. This formidable aura is in some ways beneficial, drawing to him a steady stream of the alienated and the merely curious, but at the same time this public image has allowed the Swedish antiracist activists to create through the media a caricature of the man and his ideas that has little basis in reality.

In this respect, Rydén's life is in some ways paradigmatic of the racialists of his generation. Indeed, elements of his biography are the common coin of the life stories of a number of activists from a wide variety of oppositional belief systems whom Kaplan has interviewed over the years. But the central focus of the chapter will remain Tommy Rydén and his world.

Early Days

Tommy Rydén was born in Linköping, Sweden, on 5 January 1966. He has a younger brother and sister. His father was a salesman, a profession that Rydén has recently taken up as well. Today he lives with his wife, Maud, and five children (Ronja, age seven; Andrée, age five; Disa, age three; Embla, age eighteen months; and Robin Remir, born 19 June 1997 as this chapter is being written) in the small town of Mullsjö in the Jönköping district of Sweden. From the outside, Rydén's home looks like any other in the middle-class neighborhood in which he resides. Once inside, this air of middle-class conformity is somewhat skewed by the photographs of American and Swedish National Socialists adorning the wall—a wall on which pride of place is given to a photograph of the founder of the American Church of the Creator, Ben Klassen. The living room is lined with bookshelves covered with (so far) child-proof netting. Rydén's small study, which doubles as a bedroom, is decorated with photographs of the Führer and of a Klan cross burning in a bricolage par excellence of the transnational race movement.

Beyond the photographic exotica, however, the Rydéns are hospitable and the atmosphere is relaxed and friendly. It is thus the contradictions between Tommy Rydén's public and private persona that are perhaps most striking. He is in fact bright, well read, and gifted with a sardonic sense of humor. Yet his views are unwaveringly racialist and anti-Semitic. Because of these views, the impression of a comfortable, if idiosyncratic, middle-class existence tends to fade. Both Tommy and Maud are committed racialists, and both are dedicated followers of the strict dietary guidelines of the Church of the Creator.[2] These beliefs and lifestyle obviously isolate them within their community, estrange them from most members of their respective families, and create the constant unspoken fear that at some point the families—or the state—may seek to remove the children from the home. Moreover, the actions of antiracist activists are of some concern, as are the sometimes unsavory individuals who are drawn to the racialist movement and to Tommy Rydén.

With this introduction then, it is time to allow Tommy Rydén to tell his own story.

> TOMMY RYDÉN (HEREAFTER TR): My background is, well, I've been raised in a middle-income, ordinary working family. Nothing special, but from an early age I was very curious, wanting to learn more about things, reading a lot of different books. And that's the way it was. Step by step. . . . I can say that from my beginning [my] conservative philosophy of life was in large part an inheritance from my father who . . . is much older than my mother, so he was the old traditions so to speak. And I think . . . there are probably more similarities between me and him than between me and my mother. There is a big difference in fact. . . . But it seems that I got all the genes from my father who is a little bit of a factor as a personality. He is willing to fight for what he believes in, etc., while my mother is soft actually, in many other ways, more careful.
>
> JK: I'm very curious. Growing up as a fundamentalist in Swedish society is different.
>
> TR: [excited] Yes, this is different, but the reason is of course that I have been raised in a religious environment, and my mother took me to these so-called revival meetings, you know, Pentecostal meetings where they sing "hallelujah" well, like they say, praising the Lord. I have been raised in that environment. Religion has always played a very important role in my life. Always. But of course, different kinds of religion. But that is what I grew up with. But of course, like everyone else, I have had my rebellious time too. Like all teenagers. But I have been different all the time from the others in that my interests have been different . . . [from] the majority so to speak of children and teenagers. I was reading, like I said, I was reading books that perhaps some other people would think were very odd. But all the others were out at discotheques and were playing around and having a good time, I was in fact more interest[ed] in reading antique books . . .
>
> JK: Was your father a conservative Baptist in the American sense, no smoking, no drinking, no dancing?
>
> TR: Yes, yes, oh yes. So in fact he is still the only one who has supported

me morally. He doesn't share my religious views, but he is the only one among the relatives next of kin who have supported me and my family . . . morally, and a couple of times financially too. So I guess when you ask me about these things there is some strong similarities between myself—and my father, but somewhere it stops. I am not a copy of my father, and he is not a copy of his father. Everyone is unique in some ways. And as I said, he was and is a conservative. But I am not a conservative today. I am a racialist. And that puts me on their left-wing side on some issues concerning the environment and some other issues that are not considered to be conservative. But I don't label myself. I am not interested with the labels at all.[3]

This aspect of being a true seeker from a very young age is typical of most racialist activists. Virtually all note among their earliest memories a feeling of being different, of not fitting in to their respective societies. Many have been avid readers, and it would appear that it was more the availability of an oppositional milieu rather than attraction to a particular ideology or theology that would provide many with an entrée to the world of radical politics. As with so much of Tommy Rydén's life, this quest for knowledge would become all-consuming and his commitment would be total.

JK: Did you experiment with other ideas, other than the racial?
TR: Oh yes, oh yes. I was in contact with communist groups in Sweden. And everything between heaven and earth you know [laughs]. I was reading everything. I would read books about the Muslim creed. I mean, I was open![4]

At the age of fifteen, an incident occurred that would have a considerable impact on Tommy Rydén's life. Such events are not uncommon in the recollections of race activists, and serve a variety of functions. Most important, they serve in a sense as bridge-burning events. The activist, faced with the consequences of his or her actions, is forced to make a decision; either to continue along the racialist path or to abandon the belief system and to return to the safety and comfort of the status quo. This decision of course had always been implicit, but the young activist will often be shocked at the negative sanctions that result from acting upon what he or she had perceived to be widely held racist attitudes. The backlash is therefore often interpreted as evidence of the hypocrisy of the dominant culture. In this regard, the young racialist is little different from other seekers who find their way to a wide variety of oppositional belief systems in a quest for the hidden truth that underlies the seemingly chaotic rush of everyday events. The search is for absolutes, and any deviation or compromise will be contemptuously rejected. So it was with Tommy Rydén's bridge-burning event.

TR: There are so many things that influence you as you grow up. But I want to point out that I have never been attacked by any foreigners. I have never been harassed by any foreigners. In any way. So I have no reason to feel any hate toward any minority group. . . . There are no such motivations. But of course one thing that was a turning point in my young life . . . that I have said very little about . . . at age fifteen I and a few other guys got involved in some kind of militant activities . . . I'll tell you it was an all-white community, but a gypsy family, a nonwhite gypsy family moved into the neighborhood and they have a very special style of life. Quite common here in Sweden in various places. Anyway, we, I and a few other guys, we were teenagers at that time, attacked the house where they were living. Crashed some windows and there were some real terrorist activities [laughs] at that young age. And anyway to make a long story short . . . the family moved away from the neighborhood, and there was a lot of publicity in the newspapers of course, on the local level about it, and later they found out, the police found out, the newspapers found out, that I and a few others had been involved. We were young teenagers then. I was fifteen, two who were fifteen and one who was fourteen. And I was interrogated by the police in my home. Not very dramatic but anyway at that age of course, it didn't lead to court. No trial whatsoever because of our age. We were very young. So one could say that we escaped it in the end because of our age. But of course there were some interrogations and some trouble before that. But in any case, this whole thing you know probably meant a lot in my life, because judging from what I have written in my diaries I had to make a decision at that time to give up. Because the other two guys they gave up. Their parents blamed it on me.

JK: So you were the leader?

TR: [laughs] Yes, perhaps I had some leadership abilities at that time [laughs]. I don't know. Anyway I got the blame from them and many people you know started to . . . I don't know what the hell people like to call it. . . . People stopped talking to me. And there were many different reactions to it. Even with the people who liked it of course. In any case, I had to make a decision and I made a decision at that time to continue on the road. That I had taken part in these actions and that I was going to stand for it. Whatever the cost. And I was not supported by my parents. No one supported me whatsoever. I was completely 100 percent alone in that situation. And you know when you are fifteen, barely fifteen years old, you have to go through that and you decide to take up the fight with the whole world. And that changes you as a person. Either you can handle it or you can't. And in some ways I have been able to handle it. And it was a very traumatic experience, because when I came back to school—it all happened during the summer—when I came back to school I could see some reactions from the teachers and so forth. Suddenly they all began to talk about Adolf Hitler and concentration camps [laughs] that no one had mentioned before . . . [laughs] [about how many] were killed and all those things you know, mixture of reality and fantasy. So it was a very difficult situation and this whole incident changed the direction of my life. Until that I had been a young man you know who was just experimenting, reading books and, but I was not, I didn't know very much about it. I didn't have any hardcore views.[5]

For Rydén, the contradiction between the strongly negative feelings in the community about the gypsy family and the universal disapproval of the actions he and his friends undertook to act on the community's views, created an irreconcilable dissonance. All the more so given the tacit approval of the gypsy family's decision to leave. Rydén's reaction was to reject the perceived hypocrisy and compromise of polite society. Yet even then, this quest was not confined to the racialist path. He had in the months before this action begun to contact a variety of groups in the U.S.

His first contacts with the American racist movements show the same remarkable ingenuity which has been noted before in these pages with reference to James Mason's efforts to make contact with the American Nazi Party from small-town Ohio.

JK: It sounds like you always looked to the outside for different things, as you say writing letters at a young age.

TR: Yes, but it is very difficult to give an explanation to that because I don't think one can explain such things. Some people will say it's fate, it's the genes, it could be a hundred reasons to why one is like one is. I don't have any . . . but I can only state as a fact that I've been like that from a very young age. Interested in those kind of things. When I was fifteen years old, that was the first time I got in contact with the first racialist organization, the very first racialist organization, when I saw the Ku Klux Klan in America. That is also fantastic. I mean [laughing] there was no advertisement for the KKK in the town I was living in, but to make a long [story] short, I read a hostile article about the KKK in the United States and in that article one could see where they claim they [were] living, I mean, there was no address, but somewhere in the South. So I wrote down all the facts I could get together about this address. I was hoping that the letter would reach him and it did and I got in contact with the KKK in the United States, and with that I managed to establish some contacts with racialist groups in the United States. I am talking about Bill Wilkinson's small Klan.[6]

I put together some kind of an address and sent a letter and someone was nice at the postal office in America so it reached him. And I got a reply from him, from his organization. And a newspaper and all those things. Bought some audio tapes from them and stayed in touch and subscribed to the magazine. And it was later that I got in touch with organizations here in Sweden. But the first organization was American.

JK: That's amazing. Why so?

TR: I think that I am a curious person. That explains part of it, but you have to realize that at that time there was no well known nationalist organization here in Sweden. It was years later that the BSS, Keep Sweden Swedish movement came. But that was later. So at that time it was, well, you were looking out in the world and that's the organization that I found.[7]

Bill Wilkinson's Klan group, the Invisible Empire Knights of the Ku Klux Klan, was all too typical of the American radical right. The Invisible Empire came into being in reaction to David Duke's mediagenic approach to the Klan. Wilkinson's Klan was positioned as a traditionalist, action-oriented group, and until the 1980s it was moderately successful.[8] Indeed, in Wilkinson's grandiose telling, the Invisible Empire was the only viable Klan organization in the country.[9] Yet in the same time period, it was revealed that Imperial Wizard Wilkinson was an FBI informant, and had been for many years.[10] Such disappointments become the common lot of those who persevere in the racialist milieu for any length of time. In this context, the early shock of the hostile public reaction to the attack on the gypsy family—while hearing few voices bemoan the family's decision to leave the neighborhood—certainly must have served to inoculate Rydén against these future disappointments. Asked precisely this question in 1997, Rydén observed:

TR: It didn't hurt me. No, no way. Because nevertheless, I felt it was far away from me in another part of the world. This was before e-mail [laughs] and fax machines.[11]

This same tolerance would be extended to other American movement figures suffering a similar fall from grace.

This early American connection may also have acted as a sort of solace for the isolation that Rydén suddenly experienced in his home town. Shunned by the community, the Americans appeared to offer a welcoming hand and a vital sense of community in a world infinitely more exciting than small-town Sweden. Unlike the Swedes, the Americans appeared to be active and effective, conferring by association a sense of power on the young Tommy Rydén.[12]

TR: My father was very shocked at the beginning, because I was caught. [laughs] You know the father, well, one could see parents, not only my father but also other parents talk about these gypsies shortly before. And at that time these gypsies were the scum of the earth. But then when their own boys are caught attacking these people and doing something about this problem, they are talking. That's how you know it's very sensitive and at the same time, no afterwards, I could understand his reaction because his opinion at that time was that I should not take all the blame on myself. You know, as I mentioned the other parents blamed it on me and they tried to escape it. And I was the little boy they were writing about in the newspapers. They didn't write one word about the others. The headlines were "Young Racialist" or some kind of commando attack [laughs] on the gypsies. Very sensational. Because of my age of course. And during the interrogation they asked if I had any accomplices in the world? [laughs] And I mentioned the Knights of the Ku Klux Klan. [laughs] And also the group in West Germany . . . the Hoffman National Socialist group. [laughs] Who [laughter] were having [laughs] paramilitary [maneuvers] preparing for the coming war. So of course I said those things and they leaked it to the media. So I could read about it in the newspapers afterwards. [laughs] Of course I put myself into a difficult situation in one way. But I was a young man and you don't know anything about interrogations, police, and trials, newspapers. Everything was new to me.

JK: At the same time, there must have been an element you liked in that, standing alone against the world.

TR: Yes, yes, but I—that's something I had been born with I suppose . . . I don't think that I have that from my family. Of course, my father has been a singer. He has been in the opera, traveling around seeing different places. So of course he has been a public person in one way, but not in the sensational way. So I don't think I have anything in my genes from him when it comes to this. But of course, yes, there was something in it that I liked. To be in the center. To have the spotlight on myself.

JK: Did that spotlight attract other comrades in your immediate circle, the school or the town?

TR: No, [they] fled with all the rest. [laughs] Well, of course, I remember that my . . . schoolmates . . . were all very curious of course, asking me a lot of questions. Anyway, it's far back now. I don't remember all the details, but I know for sure that this incident changed the direction of my life. So after that I became more deeply involved in those things. That is not the same thing as saying that I suddenly . . . knew exactly what to think and say, no not at that age. There was still a lot of development in my life. A lot of things happened after that too. I was involved in Christian, well, I went to a Christian Bible school in the northern part of Sweden for some time. I was a member of a Christian congregation. But all the time I was one could say in the right-wing camp. As a youth, but inside in that camp somewhere. And sometimes in racialist youth also.

JK: Did that search push you out farther and farther, looking farther afield for ideas, for people you could correspond with?

TR: Yes, all my life, even today, I'm constantly writing to new people, and sometimes with success, and sometimes with no success of course. But these new people lead me to other people, to new organizations, for example, I have been corresponding with I don't know how many hundreds of people and organizations during my life. Of course, many of these people and organizations and political parties and whatever . . . have had some . . . kind of influence on my life. You know, I've perhaps learned a few tricks here and there.[13]

Rydén's contacts with the U.S. in this period were wide ranging. On the one hand, he sought to contact as many radical right-wing groups as possible. On the other, his interest in fundamentalist Protestantism brought him into contact with such luminaries as Jerry Falwell of the Moral Majority and radio commentator Cal Thomas. In all cases, Rydén showed great ingenuity in unearthing even the most obscure addresses. And none were more obscure than the American National Socialists that began to occupy more of his curiosity. Here, fate intervened in the form of the ever helpful United States Information Agency.

TR: I grew up with the same stories [about National Socialism] as anyone else. But I think that too changed with . . . the publicity, that attack on the house. Because after that, I went to the library . . . and looked up every book I could find on National Socialism. I read everything I could find. And I wrote to the American embassy and got a list of addresses to National Socialist organizations.

JK: From the American embassy?

TR: Oh yes. [laughs] The NSDAP/AO for example.

JK: Gary Lauck's group?

TR: In Nebraska, yes. I remember their address because they sent me a lot

of material. And Matt Koehl and the World Union of National Socialists. They were still active.[14]

At some point, every committed adherent of a radical right-wing ideology
must confront what Anton LaVey in a previous chapter accurately refers to as
the "Auschwitz taboo." That is, he or she must come to terms with the legacy
of German National Socialism and the person of Adolf Hitler. This by no means
necessitates the acceptance of National Socialism as an ideology or the near-
deification of Hitler that is so common in the U.S. National Socialist movement. But the enormity of this history—and the powerfully negative perceptions
that Hitler and all his works engender in the dominant culture—is simply too
important to be ignored. For Tommy Rydén, this moment of truth came early.

TR: So it's a natural interest that you are involved in these kind of things
you have to, sooner or later, you have to decide where you stand on
National Socialism. Either you are a supporter of Adolf Hitler—that
doesn't mean that you have to support every soldier in the German
army or SS. . . . But one has to decide if one has to support Adolf
Hitler or if one is an enemy of Adolf Hitler. One can never escape
that. There are some people in Sweden who think they can avoid
that question. They call themselves Sweden Democrats and many
other things. And they think they can be racists without calling
themselves racist. And they think they can promote National Socialist policies without giving any tribute to Adolf Hitler without
calling themselves National Socialists. But . . . one has to make a
stand. But for me that hasn't been a problem. But it has been a development like everything else. I mean I am not interested in the
war. It was a world war and it was a stupid thing. A disaster for everyone. But I have been interested in the individual, Adolf Hitler.
The person. So I read many books and material about his life. And
I can see many similarities between his boyhood dreams and his way
of looking at things. Between him and me. There are many similarities in the way we look at the world. But then of course that was
in the thirties and we live in the nineties. Of course there are many
things that have changed. Of course, the situation is much more
complicated today. I have stated on Swedish television that I am
an admirer of Adolf Hitler and I think that he was a great man, etc.
I never backed off from that. But then of course one could discuss
all these other details. There were different personalities around him,
Then . . . well, that's another story.

JK: Following on that you began to get in contact with the American groups
as well. The National Socialist groups?

TR: Yes, I have been in contact with the National Socialists in America . . . I think they, are, well, there are good people in American [NS groups]—I have been corresponding with them, and there are many intelligent people. But for some mysterious reason they have a habit of living in the past you know. They try to be more like Germans than the Germans are themselves you know.

JK: Hitler cultists?

TR: Yes, sectarian perhaps to put it one way. Because the people I have been in contact with in the United States, they are constantly talking about, 'oh, what a great time it was. Adolf Hitler. Göring.' [laughs] The old boys. [laughs]

JK: Keep the uniform in the closet.

TR: Yes. [laughs] . . . That is the problem I think. The past. I know I have been corresponding with a guy in, it's the man who is on the wall out there. We were in contact.

JK: What's his name?

TR: Ron Michaelson, I was corresponding with him for a long time and he was a real nice guy.[15] I sent him some material, and he sent me some. But he is a good example. He would talk all the time about the good old times. As he thought it was. Because there are no real leaders, because if you compare David Duke to Adolf Hitler, well, it was a different year. You just can't do that, but they do it. So it came as a surprise to me. I just think it's sad and unnecessary.

This process of coming to terms with German National Socialism can be traumatic and life changing. For some, such as George Lincoln Rockwell, a true conversion experience may take place. Rockwell's apparently mystical experience of National Socialism and the legacy of the Führer is echoed by one young Swedish activist, who states:

> At first I thought the Nazis were just shit. I hated Germans, everything German, but I was interested in the Second World War. I read everything I could find about it. And it became sort of an awakening. I suddenly woke up. I and my friends went to a meeting where one old National Socialist spoke. He spoke about the democracy, the hypocrisy, the double standard, the lies. It was like something fell from my eyes. I woke up. We walked away as different human beings. . . . But it's hard to be like us. . . . I have asked myself hundreds of times why I'm doing this. Why I'm not doing something else with my life. But I cannot do that. This is my life. There is nothing to do about that.[16]

Similarly, Tommy Rydén would emerge from his own study of German National Socialism a committed, if not uncritical, true believer. On the one hand, he would condemn the Second World War as a disaster for the white race out of which little good could be salvaged.[17] Unlike so many in the American movement—and an older generation of European National Socialists—Hitler is not absolved of responsibility for the war, and the German war machine is not spared Rydén's critical assessments. For Rydén, the root cause of the war was the nationalism of the German National Socialist state. This unchecked nationalism caused the fratricidal conflict between the white nations of Europe and served to benefit only the Jews. Worse, Hitler himself stands accused of never daring to challenge "Jewish Christian society" which serves as the "Jews' best weapon against whites." Yet even with so strongly held a belief as anti-Semitism, Rydén is somewhat equivocal and self-critical: "I have no Jew fixation, but I have to admit that during the years I have been active I am frustrated to encounter again and again so many Jews among our enemies. . . . Many of those who appear on TV and talk stupidly about neo-Nazism and so on . . . are in fact of Jewish descent, so certainly there is a conflict between Jews and whites, so to speak—they say so themselves."[18]

The first Swedish movement that Tommy Rydén would become involved with was Keep Sweden Swedish (Bavara Sverige Svenskt or BSS). BSS was a small antiimmigrant organization that was the beginning of the parliamentary parties formed in the late 1970s to oppose (nonwhite) immigration. The BSS was in essence an interest group formed to push for a national referendum on immigration. It never coalesced into a political party, and was never very large, with an estimated 300 members by 1984.[19] Nonetheless, passing through BSS ranks were a number of adherents destined for careers in both the parliamentary and the extraparliamentary far right. The BSS however, offered little that would hold Tommy Rydén's interest for long.[20] Rather, ironically enough, he had by then begun to think of emigrating himself. His vision was of a white redoubt where the dream of community could be realized in a more concrete fashion than could be achieved through the mails. In the 1980s, South Africa became the destination of choice for a number of young white racialists from Europe and the U.S. Tommy Rydén arrived in South Africa on 2 May 1988.

Travels with Tommy

Rydén was to spend three and a half months in South Africa. There, he would have a number of experiences that in retrospect would be life changing, but none had as dramatic a symbolic impact as his observation of a beautiful white woman whom Rydén describes as the "Aryan ideal" on one side of the street, while on the other side was a "typical African Black woman" walking on the opposite side of the street, weighed down with packages. At once, Rydén knew with absolute certainty that the races were different and ordained to be forever separate, forever unequal.[21]

JK: Why did you decide to go to South Africa?

TR: Because I regarded this country as a lost country. Which is strange today, because we know the facts today about South Africa. But at that time I thought that Sweden is a lost country and I have to go away to the United States or South Africa where people are doing a bit more—trying to do something at least. And so when I came to South Africa I immediately got in touch with the Afrikaner Resistance Movement. And similar groups [like] the Conservative party. And I spent a lot of time with the police officers, the priests (and of course, I am talking about the Christian priests on the conservative side in this case). But all kinds of people. I traveled around and toured South Africa for three and a half months by car, bus, a very intensive time.[22]

Let me first of all point out that I was NEVER EVER a supporter of [the] apartheid-system, using cheap black labor power for all the most silly things—it was obvious to me that it would end with the whites losing all power and control. I told them this over and over again—but in vain. Christ-insanity played a major destructive role here since they actually believed it was their "Christian duty" to give the black man a job—but they did not want him in the same swimming pool! I was in support of an ALL WHITE area—but that was something else!

When I arrived in South Africa on February 5, 1988, I had been an active Christian for five years. In early February, an AWB-member in (Afrikaner Weerstandsbeweging) Bloemfontein took me to Bert Steenkamp who was the leader of a Christian Identity congregation called Israel Vision not far from that town . . .

In February, I also held a short speech at a Conservative party meeting Ladysmith (Natal) where I urged the middle-class audience to fight for a white-governed South Africa. A priest from the Calvinist Church (NG Kerk) took me to that rally. . . . Later that month, I and 7,000 others(!) applauded Eugene TerreBlanche[23] in the Skildpadsaal, Pretoria, when his men burned the ANC flag. I approached him afterward and shook his hand. That was a great moment for me! By the way, another well-known Swedish activist attended the same meeting, but none of us knew that the other was there![24]

On March 31 1988 I wrote in my diary: " . . . I have realized that is my life and destiny to be in battle throughout my whole life. It is like a burning fire within me." . . . In South Africa I also read Hitler's *Mein Kampf for the first time!*[25]

For Tommy Rydén, the South African trip was as much of a religious pilgrimage as it was a political statement. Ever the searcher, at the time he departed for South Africa Rydén was immersed in two contradictory religious traditions, conservative Christianity, which has been documented throughout this chapter, and Christian Identity. Further, he had already begun to make the contacts that would lead him to yet another direction—the American-based Church of the Creator. When he left Sweden, Rydén was already in contact with several American Christian Identity churches, and this would play a large role in his activities in South Africa.

In light of what he saw and experienced in South Africa, Rydén's attachment to Christianity was first eroded and then abandoned entirely.

JK: As you look back . . . what . . . really turned you from this conservative Christian path toward the racialist path? Or was it just a gradual evolution?

TR: It was gradually. . . . It was not just one thing that dropped down on me from the sky, not at all. But in 1988 I really got involved 100 percent. Before that I'd been moving around, but I was not making a name for myself in racialist circles. Not in my opinion at least. The turning point was South Africa and my experiences at that place.

JK: What experiences in particular?

TR: Well, in South Africa I could see that Christianity is a Trojan horse seen from a Christian perspective. I mean, in South Africa I met a lot of people that were telling me that Jesus was going to save them. Well, somehow I found this strange that their Jewish messiah were going to save neo-Nazi-looking white militants in South Africa. [laughs] it was just a little bit too much. Even if I try to be understanding, that's nonsense. So that was, that's the thing I remember strongest. The strongest impression. But then of course in South Africa one could also see the big difference, I mean the racial difference, at that place one really felt that one was completely surrounded by nonwhites, like in the shops—they were talking about apartheid, but I saw very little of apartheid while I was there. In fact . . . to me it looked like a very multicultural society except for a little bit of power. Otherwise it was very multicultural. And it was a very strange situation for me because I several times I had to argue with South Africans, who were telling me "oh we have a chance, but we have to be multicultural. The whole world is against us, etc." And I who came from Sweden was telling them it remained a white nation fighting for their old nation. So there were many things which made me think about religion and politics, and also this fact that if we don't do anything we will be outnumbered. That of course was a strong impression in South Africa. I realized that if the whites in this place give up, then they are really lost for the future. And the same thing will happen to Sweden too. If we are not fighting back, then they [non-white immigrants] will draw in numbers like they are doing right now and will out number us in no time. It's just that I turned from being a Christian fundamentalist hoping for Jesus to save me, I was turning into a social Darwinist with a biological approach to the conflict.[26]

It is hardly a revelation that Tommy Rydén would be attracted to Christian Identity. Identity is, after all, a racial religion. Better, in it's current formulation it is an *American* racial religion. And for an adherent coming from a conservative Christian background, Identity's peculiar hermeneutics and intense biblical focus would be particularly amenable. Moreover, just as British Israelism, Identity's genteel nineteenth-century British predecessor, would have an attraction to the imperial endeavors of Great Britain, racialist Identity had a ready audience in the waning days of South African apartheid. By 1988, Rydén had established contacts with a number of the American Identity ministries which have passed through these pages, including such luminaries as Richard Butler of the Aryan Nations, Pete Peters of Scriptures for America and Dan Gayman of the Church of Israel to name but a few.[27]

Tommy Rydén today is somewhat loath to accept that he was once a Christian Identity believer. This may be attributed in large part to the strongly negative view that the Church of the Creator takes of Christian Identity. As his South African days drew to a close, Rydén was alienated from the Identity creed's Jewish roots and yet more convinced than ever that the answer to what he believes to be the disastrous situation facing the white race is a racial religion. The obvious place to turn when he returned to Sweden was to the United States, and to the small but growing Church of the Creator (COTC) under the leadership of the self-styled "Pontifex Maximus," Ben Klassen.

The Church of the Creator

The COTC is a fascinating study in itself. Written off as moribund after the 6 August 1994 suicide of its founder and Pontifex Maximus Emeritus, the church began to reunite in 1995 under the leadership of Matt Hale in Wisconsin and today is showing signs of vibrancy which was sorely lacking in Klassen's final years.[28] A COTC comeback is by no means assured, but given the distinctly unpromising history of the COTC, the strides that the group has made in the last two years under Reverend Hale are remarkable.

The COTC has roots in the early 1970s, but in its own official history was founded in North Carolina on 10 March 1982 by Ben Klassen.[29] The Church of the Creator propounded an extreme antitheology that combined a violent abhorrence of Jews and nonwhite races with a complete rejection of Christianity as a conscious Jewish plot to subjugate the white race. In place of Christianity, Klassen offered a religion that replaced worship of God with the veneration of the white race itself. The essence of Creativity as propounded in its credal statement, the Sixteen Commandments of Creativity, is a blend of secularized Christianity, health faddism, conspiritorialism, and extreme racism.[30] Klassen was a prolific writer, producing lengthy, albeit repetitive, texts that were disseminated to the small band of faithful. Klassen's dream for his church is encapsulated in the title of one of these tomes, RaHoWa, The Planet is Ours, which is an acronym for Racial Holy War and spells out the Pontifex Maximus' vision of, in COTC terms, "a whiter, brighter world."

From its earliest beginnings, Klassen found himself deeply at odds with virtually every other leader in the white power world. At issue were a number of factors, Klassen's own irascible personality, his long and rather tedious books that seemed to take delight in heaping scorn on virtually every leader and belief system in the milieu of the radical right, and his highly questionable judgment of people. It was in the end the latter that appeared to be most directly responsible for the eclipse of the COTC in its last days as Klassen first began to cast about for a successor as age and infirmity began to overtake him and as he tragically lost his wife and longtime helpmate, Henrie. The putative successors to the leadership of the COTC proved disastrous. Moreover, Klassen had little more luck in finding a "Hasta Primus" (literally "spearhead") to run the COTC's daily affairs and to help publish its newspaper, Racial Loyalty.[31]

But from the distance of Sweden, the COTC seemed to Tommy Rydén to be, at long last, the answer. Here was a racial religion which, unlike Identity, did not seek to contest with the Jews for the prophetic mantle of Old Testament. Rather, the COTC heartily agreed that Christianity was indeed built on the foundation of Judaism. That being the case, Klassen derisively dismissed Christians as dupes in an age-old Jewish plot to subvert the white man's glory, but reserved even greater contempt for the Identity Christian community who would seek to wrest from the Jews the poisonous fruits of this religious legacy.[32]

Tommy Rydén first heard of Ben Klassen and the Church of the Creator while he was still associated with the BSS:

> It was a member of the movement Keep Sweden Swedish, BSS, who
> sent me a cassette, an audio tape. He made one record, Ben Klassen,
> when he talked about his creed and this was a cassette from that same
> broadcast. So I had listened to that, so if I remember it right, he had also
> enclosed the address to Ben Klassen. So I wrote to him. I didn't know
> what guy it was. So that was my first contact. That was before my trip to
> South Africa. It was in 1980 something. '86.[33]

He wrote to Klassen in 1983, but little came of this correspondence. Rydén recalls of this time:

> I came back to Sweden, and I felt that I had to have something. You can't just be a Christian for many years and then just throw it in the litter and be without anything. One needs a faith, something to live [by] . . . some creed of some kind, so I got in touch with Ben Klassen once again I might say because the first contact I had with him was in 1983, but I was a Christian at that time so I was not interested in his message. But when I came back from South Africa I got in touch with the Church again and for some reasons, I began to correspond with him, and I began to realize that perhaps this might be the right thing for me. A platform, something to work from . . . Since that I have been working for the COTC in Sweden, and in 1991 I spent four, no, two months in jail for distributing *Racial Loyalty* and fliers without knocking anyone down or anything like that.[34]

Ben Klassen replied personally to this new round of questions:

> Dear Mr. Ryden:
>
> This will acknowledge receipt of your interesting letter of July 31. Evidently you have had a number of revealing and educational experiences since we last corresponded five years ago, and I detect that you have increased your learning considerably as far as our program of survival, expansion and advancement of the White Race. I am glad that among these is the realization about what a farce is the spooks in the sky swindle.
>
> Regarding some of your questions starting with No. 1, if you will explain to me what a "spirit" is, I might be able to answer your question about "spiritualism." As far as following the program in Salubrious Living, it is not mandatory to do so to become a member of our church. It is a helpful guide to better health, and the individual can take the advice and benefit from it.
>
> Do we ever have members in South Africa! One of the most flourishing church groups in our movement is under the leadership of Rev. Jan S. Smith, . . .
>
> We would be happy to hear from you again soon and have you as a member. In the meantime, RAHOWA!
>
> For a Whiter and Brighter World,
>
> Creatively Yours,
B. Klassen, P. M.[35]

Thus began Tommy Rydén's association with the Church of the Creator. The COTC would prove to be his longest lasting organizational commitment. He did not officially resign from the COTC until 1995.[36] The Swedish COTC period was eventful, exciting, but ultimately unsuccessful. The Church (Kreativistens Kyrka), despite the efforts of both Tommy Rydén and his wife Maud, was never able to attract more than a handful of adherents. Rydén offers his own brief history of the group:

> The Kreativistens Kyrka later changed its name to the Ben Klassen Academy and the Reorganized Kreativistens Kyrka due to conflicts with the leadership after Klassen's 1990 retirement. The Kreativistens Kyrka in all its forms always remained loyal to Klassen, whom they said "came as a light in the darkness." Ben Klassen in turn praised Rydén in his last book, *Trials, Tribulations and Triumphs.* The Kreativistens Kyrka was dissolved in 1995 due to a lack of members and problems related to the mother church in the USA, but some of its material is still sold through a project called the DeVries Institute, which is named after the author of the COTC book *Salubrious Living.*[37]

The Kreativistens Kyrka period however, meant for Rydén considerably more than such capsule prose would indicate. Of greatest import, he met his wife Maud during this period and they joined the COTC together. It was in connection with the COTC that Rydén was arrested for distributing the COTC paper, *Racial Loyalty,* and was sentenced to four months in prison in 1991.[38] And it was through his association with the COTC that Rydén would come into his most intensive contact with an American group. The results, in retrospect, were often less than edifying. While Rydén's respect for Ben Klassen remains very much intact, he nonetheless is candid in describing the man's shortcomings. Rydén is even more critical of the revolving "successors" to Klassen and the too often lazy, incompetent, or simply criminal parade of Hasta Primus title holders.

In reality, it could have been no other way. While Rydén argues today that Klassen's message was often misunderstood, or more precisely, read selectively by Creativity adherents, this would seem to be more a symptom than a cause of the underlying malady that slowly devoured the COTC. In truth, the COTC message, despite exhortations for white self-sufficiency and industriousness, for healthy living and mutual cooperation, was primarily negative. So much space in COTC texts and in *Racial Loyalty* was given to vicious polemical assaults on any and all potential allies that it is little wonder that the positive aspects of the message were overshadowed.[39] Indeed, few Creators bothered to follow the stringent dietary and healthy living prescription of the COTC. In this, Klassen himself hardly set an example. His autobiographical volumes, *Against the Evil Tide—An Autobiography* and *Trials, Tribulations and Triumphs* note in wearisome detail Klassen's fondness for an evening highball and American chain eateries, and are replete with his choice of cuisine on any particular night. Worse, the primitive racial animus in Klassen's writings (or in contemptuous movement parlance, the "nigger this and nigger that" syndrome) was hardly designed to attract stable families who would raise their children according to the Creativity creed. The message was, however, tailor made for attracting a clientele composed primarily of prisoners, skinheads and other alienated and rootless young men. No better authority for this state of affairs can be offered than the Pontifex Maximus himself:

> I was now 68, and I was desperately searching for a man whom I could not only trust to carry on the Creativity movement, but one that I felt could do a better job than I was doing in promoting the great new White Man's religion. What I was really looking for was another Adolf Hitler, a prospect not too likely to happen. In so doing, I approached just about anybody and everybody that I thought showed some kind of leadership in the racial movement, and believe me, I ran into a variety of strange and twisted characters, probably half of whom were Jewish stooges or government agents.[40]

If the potential leaders were "strange and twisted characters," one can well imagine the collection of "reverends" the COTC managed to attract! Nonetheless, the COTC was a truly transnational movement. It was centered in America, but had adherents scattered thinly throughout North America, Europe, and South Africa. While no authoritative demographic data is available on the COTC's membership, it is safe to assume that the movement was overwhelmingly composed of single white males aged twenty to thirty. Indeed, a lonelyhearts column in the COTC newspaper *Racial Loyalty* and a considerable amount of correspondence within the COTC world appears to have been aimed at finding mates for these young men. In 1989 for example, when Maud Rydén requested the names and addresses of other COTC women to correspond with, she was informed by the Hasta Primus of the moment that only one, an American, was available. However, while on the subject:

> ALONG THE SAME LINES AS ABOVE, I AM A YOUNG SINGLE MAN (22). IF YOU KNOW ANY ELIGIBLE GIRLS, I WOULD BE INTERESTED IN HEARING FROM THEM. I MAY BE REACHED HERE AT WORLD HEADQUARTERS, OTTO, NC, USA. I AM 6'1", 190, BROWN HAIR, BLUE EYES.[41]

The situation would get worse. In another letter to Rydén from COTC headquarters in Otto, North Carolina, the request is made to help a well-heeled contributor find a nice Swedish girl:

> I have given your address and phone # to one of our supporters who is coming to Sweden about the time you receive this (26th of March or thereabouts). His name is Prescott Rathbone. He is about 50, very wealthy, from New Orleans, Louisiana. He dabbled in Christian Identity, like yourself, for a couple of years. I think he still has some reservations

about the COTC. Anyway, he wants to find a bride while there. Help
bring him around to us a little more if you can.[42]

The question of the COTC's inability to attract women to its ranks concerned both Rydén and Ben Klassen himself. Rydén recalls:

I once asked Ben Klassen about that, and his—and my own—answer to
that is that it is natural for men to make war. Women are generally a
softer nature. This is the major reason.

But, like I said during our conversation, there could be far more
women in the movement if we had more of those [men] who not only
talk about it, but also act like men in their deeds. Strong, motivated and
well-behaved men would attract good women to our circles.[43]

Maud Rydén today notes that the situation is not as dire as these missives
would make it sound. For her own part, she notes that:

I have contacts with other women both in the USA and my own
country. But I also have female friends that do not share my point of
view. Our children play with the other kids . . .

[However] I think the women will always be in a minority [in the
movement]. How to reach more women? Well, maybe through change
in the way of presenting the message—so that women feel that it is
directed also to them.[44]

With this brief portrait of the COTC, it becomes immediately obvious that
Tommy and Maud Rydén were the exceptions in the movement. They formed
a stable family unit. Their racial activism was limited to organizing and propaganda, considering recourse to violence both futile and foolish, given the current balance of power between racialists and the state.[45]

So exceptional is a stable family unit in the small world of the COTC and
the wider world of the racialist right that the question of what would attract a
woman to the movement becomes particularly acute. Maud Rydén's experiences
are thus instructive. She, like Tommy, is well educated and articulate, although
she is far more reticent and she shuns the public spotlight. She, too, is well aware
of the outside world, and for family reasons lived briefly in Florida. Of herself,
she states:

My full name is Maud Wailith Rydén. Before I married Tommy my last
name was Ahlm. I was born in Söderköping. We only lived there for
another three years after I was born. Then we moved to Jönköping. My
father got the job he wanted. To work as an engineer. My mother was a
housewife all her life after she had married my father. After grundskolan
I went to gymnasiet[46] for two years and learned about distribution,
economics, English.

I worked in book shops, different kinds of shops as for example a small shop that was selling cosmetics. It was hard for a time to find jobs [which] I was educated [for], so I even worked as a teacher at different schools. I also worked as a receptionist at the communal dentist. I ended up . . . working at a workshop with a computerized weldrobot. But no, I did not have "political consciousness" before I met Tommy. But I have always felt a strong feeling against immigration of non-White people. I had [some] personal experience of that already in my early school years. I grew up in a "multicultural" neighborhood.[47]

As noted, Maud and Tommy Rydén joined the COTC at the same time. Her introduction into the world of racialist politics was however, through Tommy.[48] But her memories of the "multicultural neighborhood" of her youth were such that she was receptive to the racialist message, although she adopted the ideology slowly and with many questions:

The [COTC] books . . . inspired me. They made me understand more. Everything that I had thought about prior to this was verified in the books.[49]

Just as Tommy Rydén would go through a bridge-burning experience in the aftermath of his youthful attack on the home of the local gypsy family, Maud Rydén would go through such an experience with the alienation of her relatives, particularly after Tommy Rydén was tried and imprisoned for his COTC-related activities. Asked about this time, and about the prospects of her children in Swedish society as it is currently constituted, Maud Rydén reflects:

My relatives have had almost no contact with me since Tommy's trial in 1990–91 and the publicity surrounding it. They reacted negatively. For me Tommy and my family were much more important.

[As for the children] I believe they will do just fine. They will look at the society with open eyes and critical and intelligent minds. I teach my children to find out facts for themselves and not just believe what we or other people say.[50]

Tommy Rydén's break with the COTC was less than amicable. Today, he is somewhat ambivalent in his assessment of the group's impact:

TR: We (the Swedish COTC) have been a propaganda success—some of our ideas have been absorbed by the other groups. Like this thing with RAHOWA, Racial Holy War, the term and its implications. And perhaps even more healthy living, *Salubrious Living.* That's also something we introduced in the movement. But we haven't received such big interest when it comes to creating a proper organization.

But that has been a problem, unfortunately . . . I have to say that Ben Klassen from my point of view was a great man as an author, as a pen friend, as an inspiration, in fact Maud and my marriage was brought by the COTC. We joined the Church at the same time. We discussed these things and we could say that our marriage, our will to have children, etc., was built entirely on the Sixteen Commandments. Perhaps we are the only ones in the whole world who have actually practiced the COTC [laughter], do you suppose?[51]

    With Ben Klassen's suicide, however, the now tenuous connection with the American church fell apart entirely. Rick McCarty took over, rallied the faithful briefly, and then left, reportedly taking with him the COTC's treasury.[52] The Swedish branch did not long survive Klassen either. Rydén's own resignation from the movement is noted above. Today, Tommy Rydén is philosophical about the COTC period of his life. Reacting to Kaplan's criticisms of the movement, Rydén reflects:

You say that because of his attacks on other faiths, he attracted some bad people? I can agree with you that too much time and money was spent on attacking others, but not the rest. If you read the books, and not just the phrases about other races and religions, you will see that he constantly talks about "think and act positively," "honor the family unit," a "healthy lifestyle," "only a better people can build a better world," etc. This and much more can be found in the COTC books. Yet it seems like many members never read those parts, and I think that says more about the general white movement in the USA than it does about Ben Klassen. He was too intelligent for the American people. Irrespective of what you might have heard, I can *assure* you that *here* [in Sweden] we had men and women who were sober and decent.

    [You say he was a] poor judge of people. You are right about that I guess. But the *real* problem was that there was no charismatic David Koresh-type of leader[53] who could succeed Klassen and turn the organization into a truly religious movement!

    [You say that many around Klassen] "were more interested in their own pockets"; In TTT there are examples of that yes.

    You also mentioned the problems in North Carolina [COTC headquarters in Otto, NC]. However, I can't say that we had any problems—serious problems that is—as long as they stayed in NC. The trouble started when they moved to Wisconsin and Mark Wilson & CO took over! A **young British man** paid them a visit in Wisconsin. When he came home he wrote me a letter and informed me that Mark Wilson and the others had salaries but slept over every morning and achieved very little. He also told me that one Steve Thomas was openly negative about me! I think I know why. I was a dedicated Creator, but he was false. I was a parent and he was a criminal. So he hated me. How Klassen could turn everything over to them is beyond my understanding!

He [Klassen] told me about the change of leadership in a letter dated June 6, 1992 and adds: "I wish we had a million more fighters of your caliber."

The original COTC is dead. But his creed is alive in me and will in due time influence millions of people in one way or another.[54]

As noted, the COTC by 1997 appears to be making something of a comeback under the leadership of Matt Hale. A new Kreativistens Kyrka in Sweden has formed and has taken to the World Wide Web.[55] But Tommy Rydén has moved on to a variety of interests. In 1996–1997, Rydén adapted some of the old Ásatrú Free Assembly rituals created by Steve McNallen in the U.S. to perform an Ásatrú "baptism"; in an abortive move, he attempted to form a Cosmotheist church [Cosmotistkyrkan] modeled on that of the American National Socialist figure William Pierce; he translated Jost's Arya Kriya materials into Swedish for dissemination in Scandinavia; he put aside his distaste for skinheads and their "revolution by compact disk" to become associated with the music magazine *Nordland*; and he became part of a new political party that has had some localized success, the Hembygdspartiet.[56]

Home and Hearth

Along with these movement commitments, Rydén is a husband and father, and these responsibilities became acute in 1997. It would be an understatement to say that the Rydéns are no materialists, and they live on a minimal amount of money. Yet even under Sweden's once generous social welfare system, four small children and a wife who must remain in the home to care for them represents a considerable responsibility. For many years, Rydén was able to eke out an existence as a full-time activist thanks to the Swedish social support, supplemented by occasional contributions from family members and other activists. When these sources proved insufficient for a growing family, Tommy Rydén began to search for a job in earnest.

This is no easy task for a figure such as Tommy Rydén. His notoriety is such that there is a constant risk of antiracist activists finding his employer and seeking to get him fired—if that is, an employer could be found willing to give him a chance to work. This isolation represents a primary impediment to those seeking to leave the movement—the bridges have been burned making reintegration into society at best, problematic.[57] Rydén faced this frustration, but refused to give up and, in 1997, he found a job as a salesman. This opportunity to support his family like any other husband and father represented yet another life changing event for Tommy Rydén. Rydén's pride in this achievement is evident, and there is no better note on which to conclude this chapter:

> Let me first give you the good news that I now got employment as a salesman at a company! I found the job through my own hard work. Began to hunt for a job like never before, and booked job interviews (not bad at all, since most people do not even get that far!), but this job as a salesman was the one that I really wanted, and perhaps they could see that in my eyes!
>
> For years I have put the cause before my own wellbeing and our family's economy, but with this employment I have now decided to withdraw from the nationalist scene . . . no articles, no party leader, etc. No, I have not changed my views. But I must concentrate 100 percent on my family and see to it that my children get a decent future. No one else will do it for us.
>
> The projects I have been involved in will be taken over by other activists, or will disappear entirely.
>
> The big problem in Sweden is that the citizens have been so passivated by the state's Marxism—so they still sit there and expect "big brother" (the politicians) to save them. They do not support us who try to do something, no matter how you try to market it.
>
> And to this the sad fact that I am the only one in this whole nationalist movement here who has the guts to stand for my views with name and picture (even on the Internet), while so many others hide behind made-up names and protected identities.[58]
>
> So I will not waste the upcoming years on these lazy Swedes. It is more productive to invest time and money in family and friends—the only things of value in the Ragnarök that awaits us around the corner.
>
> As a poor man, I cannot fight the forces that we are up against, nor can I help others. So I am leaving the battle scene for a moment—everyone who has studied Sun-Tzu's writing on the art of war will understand me (the others will continue to listen to their compact disks and understand nothing).[59]

A New Order?

Is this the first step toward leaving the movement entirely? Undoubtedly not. Although in reaction to the suggestion that his hiatus from the movement is less than permanent, Rydén reflects:

> You say that you do not believe that I will totally disappear from the "movement." Maybe you are right about that. However, I do want to emphasize that it is my family's principle to associate with the very best of people we know. To get around winners and stay away from people

who are going nowhere with their lives—and therefore Maud and I no longer feel that we are, as you say, a part of this current "movement" because its membership is made up mostly of people who in fact are the very opposite to what they preach. If my children were teenagers today I would advise them to not join any of these racialist groups.[60]

Yet Tommy Rydén remains committed to his racialist and anti-Semitic weltanschaung.[61] Virtually every long time activist has dreamed of what it would be like to live a "normal" life, with wife and children and the respect of the community. In this, Tommy Rydén is no different. He, too, has toyed with such thoughts.[62] But weighed against such dreams are the years of contacts with distant activists, the notoriety that accrues to even the infamous in the form of television talk shows, newspaper articles, and indeed, having a chapter in an academic book dedicated to his ideas and actions. But perhaps of greatest import, there is the fact that after having lived so long as an outsider, as an object of curiosity and, indeed, of fear,[63] it is no easy task given the best of intentions to be allowed to act the part of the normal husband and father.

Yesterday I was at an information meeting for parents in the school our Ronja will attend in August. The school is nearby and the female teacher seems to be OK as a human being. There will be 14 in the class. 3 of them non-Whites, one is racemixed (Chinese/White, the mother is adopted from somewhere) and the two others from the Middle East with parents who can hardly speak Swedish at all. Their children will receive home language training (the only thing they never cut down on in our lovely country). We had preferred an all-Swedish class, but I guess the situation could have been worse. I could see that the Asiatic woman recognized me (tell me who does not!) and looked very uneasy. I would not be surprised at all if she demands that her kid is moved to another class! I am dangerous you know! Anyway, we teach our children to be proud in a positive way. To focus on positive things (11 against 3) and to become problem solvers. At the same time I realize, like Maud, that sooner or later we will have to stand up and fight for our children. Funny, at the parents meeting I was the only one who asked most of the questions—and will continue to do so.[64]

Conclusion	Fade to Black

Final Observations

In THE PRECEDING CHAPTERS we have called attention to the appearance of a Euro-American radical right movement. Our intention has not been to frighten or shock the reader by exaggerating the movement's threat to the Western democracies or their citizens. Instead, our purpose has been to identify and then analyze the emergence of a strongly antidemocratic movement, still quite limited in scale, whose political prospects seem uncertain but need not be a cause for great alarm at the moment. In bringing this volume to a conclusion we thought it would be helpful to restate briefly our principal observations and contentions.

Initially the movement belonged to the genre of émigré politics. During the 1920s and 1930s anti-Soviet Russian exiles along with some Italian and German immigrants to the United States became attracted to the European fascist and Nazi movements of that era. The visible successes of the Mussolini and Hitler dictatorships aided by subsidies from Italian and German sources encouraged the formation of such support organizations in the United States as the German-American Bund. The flow of ideas and material support was almost invariably from east to west, from Europe to America. America during the interwar period, the Depression era especially, did not lack for a homegrown radical right movement. Some of the central figures in this movement chose to become "native fascists," mimics of their European models.[1]

In the immediate postwar period and for relatively obvious reasons there was a hiatus in the development of the Euro-American radical right. Both the Italian and German dictatorships and the ideas with which they were identified were thoroughly discredited. But the subsequent cold war conflict between the United States and the Soviet Union provided the context for a revival of transatlantic radical right activism. To the extent that dormant (or a new generation) right-wing extremists could paint the communist menace in anti-Semitic terms they were back in business.

In the succeeding decades we have witnessed some very substantial changes in the contours of the Euro-American radical right. First, the flow of influence has shifted to a considerable extent. While at first America was the recipient of European ideas, in recent times the inspiration for the movement has tended to shift in the opposite direction, with the establishment of various American-based groups on European soil: White Aryan Resistance, KKK, and so on. Also, now it is often such American figures as William Pierce and Louis Beam who are called upon to address their European counterparts, rather than the other way around.

Next, the Euro-American movement is now a largely private undertaking, one largely financed, to the extent it is financed, by a handful of wealthy admirers on both sides of the Atlantic.[2] No longer are there fascist regimes to offer subventions and moral support. Fourth, Euro-American radical rightism is no longer a primarily émigré phenomenon. There are exceptions to be sure, Ernst Zundel and George Dietz for example, but by and large we are dealing with American neo-Nazis or Swedish-born followers of Identity or Creativity religious views. Concomitantly, the contemporary Euro-American movement is much more influenced by religious sentiments than was true in earlier decades.

The collapse of the communist enterprise and the disintegration of the Soviet Union itself did not bring the Euro-American movement to an end, far from it. If anything, radical right groups on both sides of the Atlantic have enjoyed a renaissance in the postcommunist era. Further, in our view the transatlantic links between them have grown and intensified. Why?

There is the general phenomenon of "globalization." These days it has become common for the leaders of various European and American parties and movements to confer with one another on a regular basis. Thus representatives of the New Labour party in Britain discuss electoral tactics with new Democrats in Washington. American campaign organizers are hired to help parties competing in Russian or Polish elections. Movement entrepreneurs interested in such causes as environmental protection, the elimination of land mines, finding a cure for AIDS, protecting the rights of women, and combating anti-Semitism have established transatlantic linkages. In this context it is hardly astonishing that right-wing extremists have done likewise.

The conditions promoting the current Euro-American radical right though require specification. We have no wish to simply recapitulate contentions drawn from earlier chapters. Here it should suffice to point out the growing similarity of economic and social conditions in Western Europe and the United States. The effect of this occurrence, the appearance of a multicultural and multiracial Western Europe and its consequent resemblance to the United States in particular, has promoted racial resentments. Some whites, defined as Aryans, Teutons, and so on, have become so alienated from their respective national societies they have become sympathetic to the formation of a racial folk community that is Euro-American in scope and indeed reaches out to include "kinsmen" in South Africa, Australia and New Zealand as well.

There is a certain irony in this. The idea of a racial folk community carries with it certain notions about traditional forms of human interaction, ideas that stress highly personal face-to-face encounters of people living in village or small-town settings.[3] Europe during the Middle Ages often furnishes an ideal, as do often idealized Viking "golden age" scenarios. As we discussed in chapters 6 and 7 especially, these communal dreams (e.g., the NS Kindred) sometimes take the form of tiny separatist enclaves, a Nordland, where the racially conscious can find refuge.

For those who worship the idea of community, the impersonal and technology dependent contemporary urban environment represents the opposite. Formal encounters between strangers playing different "roles" under the auspices of complex machines is the antitheses of community. For the Euro-American radical right movement, the irony is this: in order to pursue the idea of a racial folk community, one binding together Aryans on both sides of the Atlantic and beyond, they have had to make use of the most modern forms of computer technology. It remains to be seen whether a racial folk community formed in cyberspace can be achieved and what the social and political meaning of that achievement would be. But at a minimum we can say that the effort is now underway.

Notes

Introduction

1. A recent journalistic exception would be Martin Lee, *The Beast Reawakens* (Boston, MA: Little, Brown, 1997).
2. See, for example, Stein Larsen (ed.), *Modern Europe after Fascism* (New York: Columbia University Press, 1998).
3. See for example, Edward Shils, *The Torment of Secrecy* (Glencoe, IL: Free Press, 1956); and David Bennett, *The Party of Fear* (Chapel Hill: University of North Carolina Press, 1988).

Chapter 1 Overview

1. Terrence Petty, "Fake Klansmen, Cat Hunting: TV 'News' Producer Caught in Hoax," *San Jose Mercury News*, 2 February 1996, distributed as e-text.
2. Tore Bjørgo, "Extreme Nationalism and Violent Discourses in Scandinavia," in Tore Bjørgo, ed., *Terror from the Right* (London: Frank Cass, 1995), 182–220; Maurizio Blondet, *I nuovi barbari:gli skinheads parlono* (Milan: Effedieffe, 1993), 85–86; Ingo Hasselbach, "How Nazis Are Made," *The New Yorker*, 8 January1996, 36–56; Ingo Hasselbach with Tom Reiss, *Führer-Ex* (New York: Random House, 1996); Les Back, Michael Keith, and John Solomos, "Racism on the Internet: Mapping Neo-Fascist Subcultures in Cyberspace," in Jeffrey Kaplan and Tore Bjørgo, eds., *Nation and Race* (Boston, MA: Northeastern, 1998).
3. "Young Nazi Killers: The Skinhead Danger," *ADL Special Report* (1993), p. 5.
4. See for example, *White Patriot* 94 (1994), 1; NSV Report 12:1 (1994), 8; *Calling Our Nation* 73 (n.d.), 2. Cf. Michael Barkun, "Millenarian Aspects of 'White Supremacist' Movements," *Terrorism and Political Violence* 4 (October 1989).
5. John George and Laird Wilcox, *American Extremists, Supremacists, Klansmen, Communists and Others* (Buffalo, NY: Prometheus Books, 1996), 341. The original quote was published in *Calling Our Nation* 60 (1989), 4. See also for another example, the long open letter, Manfred Roeder, "Teutonic Unity," *Aryan Nations* 43 (July/August 1982), 1–3.
6. Umberto Eco, "Eternal Fascism," *UTNE Reader* 72 (November-December 1995), 57–59; Piero Ignazi, "The Extreme Right in Europe: A Survey," in Peter Merkl and

Leonard Weinberg, eds., *The Revival of Right-Wing Extremism in the 1990s* (London: Frank Cass & Co., forthcoming).

7. See for example *Klanwatch Intelligence Report* 77 (March 1995), 12–14; ADL, *Hate Groups in America: A Record of Bigotry and Violence* (New York: ADL, 1988).

8. See any copy of Ricky Cooper's *NSV Report, Resistance Magazine* (either in its music magazine form published by George Eric Hawthorne or in its National Socialist newsletter form published by Harold Covington), or any number of interviews with activists on both sides of the Atlantic.

9. See especially, Daniel Bell, ed., *The Radical Right* (New York: Doubleday & Co, 1963); for a commentary see William Hixon, Jr., *Search for The American Right-Wing* (Princeton, NJ: Princeton University Press, 1992), 3–26.

10. Franco Ferraresi, *La destra radicale* (Milan: Feltrinelli,1984).

11. *Parliamentary Affairs* 45:3 (July 1992), 327–344.

12. For discussions see Klaus von Beyme, "Right-Wing Extremism in Postwar Europe," *West European Politics* 11:2 (April 1988), 1–18; and Cas Mudde, "Right-Wing Extremism Analyzed," *European Journal of Political Research* 27 (1995), 204–223.

13. Seymour Lipset and Earl Raab, *The Politics of Unreason* (New York: Harper & Row, 1970), 3–24.

14. Richard Hofstadter, *The Paranoid Style in American Politics* (New York: Alfred A. Knopf, 1965), 14. Cf. for a taxonomy of twenty features applicable to contemporary political extremists, Laird Wilcox, "What is Political Extremism?" In *Guide to the American Right, 1995* (Olathe, KS: Editorial Research Service, 1995).

15. See for example, Pat Robertson, *The New World Order* (Dallas, TX: New Word Publishing,1991), 3–14. Cf. Militia of Montana, *The Blue Book* (Noxon, MT: MOM, n.d.).

16. For a lively discussion see, Roger Eatwell, "The Rise of 'Left-Right' Terminology: The Confusions of Social Science," in Roger Eatwell and Noel O'Sullivan, eds., *The Nature of the Right* (Boston, MA: Twayne Publishers,1990), 32–46.

17. Piero Ignazi, *L'Estrema destra in Europa* (Bologna: Il Mulino, 1994), 16–19.

18. Cas Mudde, "Right-Wing Extremism Analyzed," 210.

19. Michael Billig, "The Extreme Right: Continuities in Anti-Semitic Conspiracy Theory in Post-War Europe," in Eatwell and O'Sullivan, eds., 146–166; Mudde, 205–209; Hans-Georg Betz, *Radical Right-Wing Populism* (New York: St.Martin's, 1994), 69–106.

20. For an account of the rise of anti-Semitism in postcommunist Russia see Walter Laqueur, *Black Hundred* (New York: Harper Collins, 1993), 119–180. For an inside discussion of the crucial importance of Holocaust denial to the contemporary German radical right, see Ingo Hasselbach with Tom Reiss, *Führer-Ex.*

21. The classics include, Neil Smelser, *Theory of Collective Action* (New York: The Free Press,1962), and Charles Tilly, *From Mobilization to Revolution* (Reading, MA: Addison-Wesley,1978). For an exceedingly dry, but thorough, review of this literature as it pertains to revolutionary violence, see Ekhart Zimmerman, *Political Violence, Crises and Revolutions* (Cambridge, MA: Schenkmann Publishing Co., 1983).

22. Sidney Tarrow, *Power in Movement* (New York: Cambridge University Press,1994), 3–4.

23. Mark S. Hamm, *American Skinheads* (Westport, CT: Praeger, 1984), 26.

24. See for example, Russell Dalton, Manfred Kuechler, and Wilhelm Burklin, "The Challenge of New Movements," in Russell Dalton and Manfred Kuechler, eds., *Challenging the Political Order* (New York: Oxford University Press, 1990), 3–20.

25. Martin Baldwin-Edwards and Martin Schain, "The Politics of Immigration: Introduction," *West European Politics* 17:2 (1994), 9.

26. See for example, Tore Bjørgo and Rob Witte, eds., "Introduction," *Racist Violence in Europe* (New York: St. Martin's Press, 1993), 1–15.

27. See for example, "The Family: Home Sweet Home," *The Economist* (September 9–15, 1995), 25–29.

28. See for example, Raphael Ezekiel, *The Racist Mind* (New York: Viking, 1995) 149. Peter Merkl, "Rollerball or Neo-Nazi Violence," in Peter Merkl, ed., *Political Violence and Terror* (Berkeley and Los Angeles, University of California Press, 1986), 229–255; Heléne Lööw, "Racist Violence and Criminal Behaviour in Sweden: Myths and Reality," in Tore Bjørgo, ed., *Terror From the Extreme Right*, 130–140.

29. Robert Reich, *The Work of Nations* (New York: Alfred A. Knopf,1991), 171–184.

30. See for example, Patrick McCarthy, *The Crisis of the Italian State* (New York: St. Martin's Press, 1995), 139–165.

31. For the classic discussion of "working-class authoritarianism" see Seymour Lipset, *Political Man* (New York: Doubleday,1960), 97–130.

32. Seymour Martin Lipset, "The Western Allies 50 Years Later," *Journal of Democracy* 6:3 (1995), 5.

33. Ingo Hasselbach with Tom Reiss, *Führer-Ex*, 60–63; Walter Laqueur, *Black Hundred*, 157; Kaplan interview with the then head of Nordland Records Peter Milander, Stockholm, Sweden, 7 August 1995; Kaplan interview with Mark Parland, Helsinki, Finland, 10 August 1995.

34. Ignazi, *L'Estrema Destra in Europa*, 243–259.

35. Key texts in this regard that are dear to the hearts of movement people on both sides of the Atlantic include Oswald Spengler, *Decline of the West*, 2 vols., (New York: Random House, 1945, 1966); and Ulick Varange [Francis Parker Yockey], *Imperium* (Costa Mesa, CA: Noontide Press, 1962).

36. See for example, "Nationalsozialistische Deutsche Arbeiterpartei Auslandsund Aufbauorganisation," *Progress Report* 103 (June 1992). Kaplan interview with Nils Mandel, Stockholm, Sweden, 9 August 1995. It should be noted, however, that the increasing popularity of Rudolf Hess Day demonstrations remains as yet a largely European phenomenon, with little American participation.

37. David Irving, *Hitler's War* (New York: Viking, 1977), 390–362, 660, 718; Deborah Lipstadt, *Denying the Holocaust* (New York: The Free Press, 1993), 161–163.

38. Joe Pierce, *Screwdriver: The First Ten Years* (London: Screwdriver Services, 1987).

39. See for example, Bundesamt fur Verfassungsschutz, "NS-Propaganda aus dem Ausland," 17 (August 1994), 2–3; Ingo Hasselbach with Tom Reiss, *Führer-Ex*, 296.

40. See for example, Dennis Mahon, "We Want the Workers," *The Oklahoma Separatist* (1989), 1–2.

41. See for example, Laird Wilcox, *Guide to the American Right, 1996* (Olathe, KS: Editorial Research Service, 1995); Phillip Reese, *Biographical Dictionary of the Extreme Right* (New York: Simon and Schuster, 1990).

42. *Political Extremism and the Threat to Democracy in Europe* (London: European Centre for Research and Action on Racism and Anti-Semitism,1994).

43. See for example, Tony Judt, "Austria & the Ghost of the New Europe," *The New York Review of Books* 33:3 (February 15, 1996), 22–25.

44. On the Storm Network, see the Anti-Defamation League, *Web of Hate: Extremists Exploit the Internet* (New York: ADL, 1996). On the World Anti-Communist League, see Russ Bellant, *Old Nazis, the New Right and the Republican Party* (Boston, MA: Southend Press, 1991); and Scott Anderson and Jon Anderson, *Inside the League* (New York: Dodd, Mead, 1986). On the Swedish COTC, Kaplan interview with Tommy Rydén, head of the Swedish COTC and its successor organizations, the Ben Klassen Akademie and the DeVries Institute, 28 July 1995. On Rydén and the Swedish COTC, see chapter 8.

45. Our system of classification is loosely based upon James Rosenau, *Linkage Politics* (New York: The Free Press, 1969), 44–63.

46. For those interested in such dates there is now a white people's calendar available (The 1996 White Calendar) available on the Internet from Marc Lemire's Freedom Site, an address closely associated with Ernst Zundel and the Canadian Heritage Front.

47. On this subject see for example, Alan Cowell, "Neo-Nazis Now Network on Line and Underground," *The New York Times* (October 22,1995), 3.
48. *Political Extremism and the Threat to Democracy*, 117.
49. Dennis King, *Lyndon LaRouche and the New American Fascism* (New York: Doubleday, 1989), 166–167.

Chapter 2   The Euro-American Radical Right: A Brief History ˙

1. For histories see David Bennett, *The Party of Fear*, 80–237; and Seymour Lipset and Earl Raab, *The Politics of Unreason*, 72–109.
2. See for example, Kenneth T. Jackson, *The Ku Klux Klan in the City, 1915–1930* (Chicago, IL: Oxford University Press, 1967); and David Chalmers, *Hooded Americanism* (Chicago, IL: Quadrangle Books, 1965), 28–38.
3. Daniel Levitas, "Anti-Semitism and the Far Right," in Jerome Chanes, ed., *Anti-Semitism in America Today* (New York: Carol Publishing, 1995), 177.
4. Murray Levin, *Political Hysteria in America* (New York: Basic Books, 1971), 28–90.
5. Leonard Dinnerstein, *Anti-Semitism in America* (New York: Oxford University Press, 1994), 79–84.
6. "The International Jew" remains in circulation today as a four-volume set of texts that can be purchased from right-wing mail order houses and Afrocentric bookstores. The primary work, however, is *Dearborn Independent, The International Jew: The World's Foremost Problem* (Dearborn, MI: The Dearborn Publishing Co., 1920).
7. Adolf Hitler, *Mein Kampf*, trans. by Ralph Manheim, (Boston, MA: Houghton Mifflin Co., 1971), 639.
8. Walter Laqueur, *The Black Hundred* (New York: HarperCollins, 1993), 79–80; John Stephan, *The Russian Fascists* (New York: Harper & Row, 1978), 91–140; and Charles Higham, *American Swastika* (Garden City, NY: Doubleday, 1985), 121–133.
9. Gaetano Salvemini, *Italian Fascist Activities in the United States* (New York: Center for Migration Studies, 1977), 12.
10. Morris Schonbach, *Native American Fascism During the 1930s and 1940s* (New York: Garland Publishing, 1985), 82–83.
11. Ibid., 90.
12. Michael Ledeen, *Universal Fascism* (New York: Howard Fertig, 1972), 107.
13. See O. John Rogge, *The Official German Report* (New York: Thomas Yoselof, 1961), 173–218, and Lawrence Dennis and Maximillian St. George, *A Trial on Trial: The Great Sedition Trial of 1944* (Torrance, CA: Institute for Historical Review, 1945, 1984).
14. Leland Bell, *In Hitler's Shadow* (Port Washington, NY: Kennikat Press, 1973), 7–8.
15. Ibid., 15–16
16. O. John Rogge, *The Official German Report*, 240–241.
17. For a neo-Nazi perspective on this gathering see, S.S. Action Group, "An Unsung Day of Triumph for the German American Bund," (P.O. Box 67, Dearborn Hts., MI., April 20,1984), 1–2.
18. On the concept of mimetic fascist movements see Roger Griffin, *The Nature of Fascism* (London and New York: Routledge, 1991), 164–174.
19. David Bennett, *The Party of Fear*, 244.
20. James Burnham, *Congress & the American Tradition* (Chicago, IL: Regnery, 1959).
21. Paul Hollander, *Political Pilgrims* (New York: Oxford University Press, 1981).
22. O. John Rogge, *The Official German Report*, 240–241. For further details of Dilling and Pelley's adventures in Nazi Germany, see chapter 5.
23. Stefan Kuhl, *The Nazi Connection* (New York: Oxford University Press, 1994), 27–36.
24. David Wyman, *The Abandonment of the Jews* (New York: Pantheon Books, 1984), 9.

25. Leo Ribuffo, *The Old Christian Right* (Philadelphia, PA: Temple University Press, 1983), 80–127.

26. Gerald B. Winrod, *Adam Weishaupt: A Human Devil* (no publication data, c.1935).

27. Leo Ribuffo, *The Old Christian Right*, 114.

28. Gerald B. Winrod, *Hitler in Prophecy* (Wichita, KS: Defender Publishers, 1933). It should be noted that Winrod balanced these pro-Nazi sentiments with the oft-repeated observation that the German dictatorship could not be exported to the U.S. as Hitler's model of government was incompatible with American constitutional liberties. On these issues, see chapter 5.

29. On the Winrod-Swift connection, see Michael Barkun, *Religion and the Racist Right* (Chapel Hill: University of North Carolina Press, 1994), 62. For David Winrod's Alaskan odyssey, see the series of articles in the *Ketchikan Daily News* from April and May, 1991.

30. For varying views of Winrod and his ministry, see Clifford R. Hope, Jr., "Strident Voices in Kansas Between the Wars," in Martin E. Marty, ed., *Modern American Protestantism and its World, vol. 10: Fundamentalism and Evangelicalism* (Munich: K.G. Sauer, 1993), 144–169; Martin E. Marty, *Modern American Religion, Volume 2: The Noise and the Conflict 1919–1941* (Chicago, IL: University of Chicago Press, 1991), 265–267; J. Gordon Melton, *Religious Leaders of America* (Detroit, MI: Gale Research Inc., 1991); and anon, *Fire By Night and Cloud By Day: The Amazing History of the Defenders of the Christian Faith* (Wichita, KS: Mertmont Publishers, 1966).

31. William Dudley Pelley, *The Door to Revelation: An Intimate Biography* (Asheville, NC: Foundation Fellowship, 1935), quoted in Adam Parfrey, *Cult Rapture* (Portland, OR: Feral House, 1995), 366.

32. Leo Ribuffo, *The Old Christian Right*, 57. Pelley's life would be celebrated in the literature of the contemporary National Socialist movement through the pages of the *New Order*, the organ of Gary Lauck's NSDP/AO, which is currently available as e-text from the Stormfront web site.

33. *New Order*, 10. The more reliable figures can be found in Philip Reese, *Biographical Dictionary of the Extreme Right Since 1890*, 292; and John George and Laird Wilcox, *American Extremists*, 33.

34. Charles Stember et al., *Jews in the Mind of America* (New York: Basic Books, 1966), 48–170.

35. Alan Brinkley, *Voices of Protest* (New York: Alfred A. Knopf, 1982), 82–106.

36. For brief coverage of these encyclicals, as well for a useful biography of Father Coughlin, see Richard McBrien, ed., *Encyclopedia of Catholicism* (New York: Harper Collins, 1995), 370, 1074, 1106.

37. Martin E. Marty, *Modern American Religion*, Volume 2, 275–276.

38. Ibid., 277. Seymour Lipset, "Three Decades of the Radical Right," in Daniel Bell, ed., *The Radical Right*, 317–326.

39. Alan Brinkley, *Voices of Protest*, 269–283.

40. O. John Rogge, *The Official German Report*, 173–218. For a strong critique of these prosecutions see Leo Ribuffo, *The Old Christian Right*, 178–224. For a defendant's-eye view, see Dennis and St. George, *A Trial on Trial*.

41. See for example, Piero IgNazi, *Il Polo Escluso* (Bologna: Il Mulino, 1989), 15–52; and Rand Lewis, *A Nazi Legacy* (New York: Praeger, 1991), 27–62.

42. Arnold Forster, *A Measure of Freedom* (Garden City, NY: Doubleday, 1950), 222–229.

43. Michael Barkun, *Religion and the Racist Right*, 47–71.

44. Glen Jeansonne, *Gerald L. K. Smith: Minister of Hate* (New Haven, CT: Yale University Press, 1988).

45. See for example, Renzo de Felice, *Fascism: An Informal Introduction to Its Theory and Practice* (New Brunswick, NJ: Transaction Publishers, 1976), 97–101.

46. Giuseppe Gaddi, *Neofascismo in Europa* (Milan: La Pietra, 1974), 189–191; and Angelo Del Boca and Mario Giovana, *Fascism Today* (New York: Random House, 1969), 82–84.

47. Ernesto Cadena, *La Offensiva Neo-Fascista* (Barcelona: Acervo, 1978), 223–227.

48. For a discussion see Scott Anderson and Jon Anderson, *Inside the League*, xvi-xviii.

49. Vera Ebels-Dolanova, ed., *The Extreme Right in Europe and the United States* (Amsterdam: Anne Frank Foundation, 1985), 32–33.

50. Russ Bellant, *Old Nazis, the New Right and the Republican Party*, 2–57.

51. Charles Higham, *American Swastika*, 274–280.

52. Frederick Simonelli, *American Führer: George Lincoln Rockwell and the American Nazi Party* (Ph.D. dissertation, Department of History, University of Nevada, 1995), 150.

53. Ibid., 159.

54. Fredrick J., Simonelli, "The World Union of National Socialists and the Post-War Transatlantic Nazi Revival," in Jeffrey Kaplan and Tore Bjørgo, eds., *Nation and Race*.

55. Göran Assar Oredsson interview with Dr. Heléne Lööw, 1996. Oredsson adds in the same interview that the WUNS membership in Iceland, the homeland of Rockwell's ex-wife and a land where he himself resided for a time during his stint in the U.S. Navy, numbered an impressive 300. A brief English language history of Oredsson's NRP is provided in Göran Assar Oredsson, News of the NRP, undated pamphlet distributed by the NRP.

Chapter 3   The Politics of Right-Wing Extremism

1. Quoted in Michael Minkenberg, *The New Right in Comparative Perspective* (Ithaca, NY: Cornell Studies in International Affairs, 1993), 8,

2. See for example, John Finn, *Constitutions in Crisis. Political Violence and the Rule of Law* (New York: Oxford University Press,1991), et passim.

3. See for example, Richard Stoess, "The Problem of Right-Wing Extremism in West Germany," *West European Politics* (April 1988), 34–46.

4. Ekkart Zimmermann and Thomas Saalfeld, "The Three Waves of West German Right-Wing Extremism," in Peter Merkl and Leonard Weinberg, eds., *Encounters with the Contemporary Radical Right* (Boulder, CO: Westview Press, 1993), 50–74.

5. See for example, Harvey Simmons, *The French National Front* (Boulder, CO: Westview Press, 1996).

6. For a discussion see Peter Merkl, "Why Are They So Strong Now? Comparative Reflections on the Revival of the Radical Right in Europe," in Peter Merkl and Leonard Weinberg, eds., *The Revival of Right-Wing Extremism in the Nineties*, 17–46.

7. For a fuller account see Leonard Weinberg, "Conclusions," in *Revival of Right-Wing Extremism*, 273–277.

8. See especially, Hans-George Betz, *Radical Right-Wing Populism in Western Europe* (New York: St. Martin's Press, 1994); Herbert Kitschelt, *The Radical Right in Western Europe* (Ann Arbor: University of Michigan Press, 1995); Piero Ignazi, *L'Estrema Destra in Europa* (Bologna: Il Mulino,1994) and idem., "The Silent Counter-Revolution," *European Journal of Political Research* 22:1 (1992), 3–34.

9. See for example, Ingo Hasselbach, "How Nazis are Made," *The New Yorker* (January 8, 1946), 36–56.

10. See for example Ronald Inglehart, *The Silent Revolution* (Princeton, NJ: Princeton University Press, 1977).

11. For a discussion see for example, Charles Tilly, *From Mobilization to Revolution* (Reading, MA: Addison-Wesley,1978), 7–8.

12. See for example, Dietrich Thranhardt, "The Political Uses of Xenophobia in England, France and Germany," *Party Politics* 1:3 (1995), 323–345.

13. For an unusual angle on the Freedom Party see, Yossi Halevi and Vince Beiser, "Peter and the Wolves," *The Jerusalem Report*, November 28, 1996, 24–27.

14. Philip Gourevitch, "The Unthinkable: How Dangerous is Le Pen's National Front," *The New Yorker*, April 28-May 5,1997, 110–149.

15. See for example, Alessandro Caprettini, *La Nuova Destra* (Palermo: Arbor,1995), 231–255.

16. See, Duane Swank and Hans-George Betz, "Right-Wing Populism in Western Europe," paper presented at the 1995 Annual Meeting of the American Political Science Association, August 31–September 3, 1995, Chicago, IL.

17. Herbert Kitschelt, *The Radical Right in Western Europe*, 257–279.

18. See for example, *Verfassungsschutzbericht 1994* (Bonn: Bundesministerium des Innern, 1994).

19. William Eubank, Leonard Weinberg, and Allen Wilcox, "Reflections on Right-Wing Radicalism and Democratic Defense in Western Europe," paper presented at the CPS Interim World Congress/South African Sociological Association Joint Meeting, University of Natal, Durban, South Africa, July 7–11,1996, 9.

20. See for example, Maurizio Blondet, *I Nuovi Barbari: Gli Skinheads Parlano* (Milan: effedieffe,1993); and Giampaolo Cadalanu, *Skinheads: dalla Musica Giamaicana al Saluto Romano* (Lecce: ARGO,1994).

21. Helmut Willems, "Development, Patterns and Causes of Violence Against Foreigners in Germany," in Tore Bjørgo ed., *Terror from the Extreme Right*, 162–181.

22. Ingo Hasselbach, *Fuhrer-Ex*, 101–113.

23. Franco Ferraresi, *Minacce alla democrazia* (Milan: Feltrinelli,1995), 69–70.

24. See Joyce Mushaben, "The Rise of Femi-Nazis? Female Participation in Right-Extremist Movements in Unified Germany," paper presented at the Annual Meeting of the American Political Science Association, Chicago, August 31–September 3, 1995). On women in the Norwegian radical right, see Katrine Fangen, "Separate or Equal? The Emergence of an All-Female Group in Norway's Racist Underground," *Journal of Terrorism and Political Violence* 9:3 (Fall 1997).

25. *Extremism from the Atlantic to the Urals*, 97–99.

26. Ibid., 116.

27. For details of the Swedish Church of the Creator and the attraction of Christian Identity in Scandinavia, see chapter 8.

28. Weinberg interviews with Professor Nonna Mayer, *Maison de la science del'Homme*, Paris, July 27,1995; and Dr. Marco Tarchi, University of Florence, Florence, July 14, 1995.

29. See for example, Jim Keith, *Black Helicopters Over America* (Lilburn, GA: Illumnet Press, 1994); Gary Kah, *En Route to Global Occupation* (Lafayette, Louisiana: Huntington House, 1991). Cf. Michael Barkun, "Conspiracy Theories as Stigmatized Knowledge: The Basis for a New Age Racism?" in Jeffrey Kaplan and Tore Bjørgo, eds., *Nation and Race*.

30. See for example, Tore Bjørgo, "Militant Neo-Nazism in Sweden," *Terrorism and Political Violence* 4:3 (Autumn 1993), 28–57.

31. Weinberg interview with Professor Richard Stoess, Free University of Berlin, Berlin, July 25, 1995.

32. For an interesting discussion of the phenomenon see, Michael Billig, "The Extreme Right: Continuities in Anti-Semitic Conspiracy Theory in Post-War Europe," in Roger Eatwell and Noel O'Sullivan, eds., *The Nature of the Right* (Boston, MA: Twayne, 1989), 146–166.

33. See for example, Renzo de Felice an interview with Michael Ledeen, *Fascism: An Informal Introduction to its Theory and Practice* (New Brunswick, NJ: Transaction Publishers, 1976), 89–107.

34. See for example, Paul Hockenos, *Free to Hate* (New York and London: Routledge,1993).
35. See, Michael Minkenberg, "The Right in France and Germany," in Peter Merkl and Leonard Weinberg, eds., *The Revival of Right-Wing Extremism in the Nineties*, 71–90.
36. Franco Ferraresi, "Tradition, Reaction, and the Radical Right," *Archives Europennes de Sociologie* XXVIII (1987), 107–151.
37. For an interesting first hand account from the point of view of an outsider see, Yaron Svoray and Nick Taylor, *In Hitler's Shadow* (New York: Doubleday, 1994), 133–183.
38. Elisabeth Young-Bruehl, *The Anatomy of Prejudices* (Cambridge, MA: Harvard University Press, 1996), 216–217.
39. Ingo Hasselbach, *Fuhrer-Ex*, 21.
40. Ehud Sprinzak, " Right-Wing Terrorism in a Comparative Perspective: The Case of Split Delegitimization" in Tore Bjørgo, ed., *Terror from the Extreme Right*, 17–43.
41. Graeme Atkinson, "Germany: Nationalism, Nazism and Violence," *Racist Violence in Europe*, 154–166.
42. Jeffrey Kaplan, "Right-Wing Violence in North America," *Terror from the Extreme Right*, 45–46; idem., Radical Religion in America; and Michael Barkun, "Conspiracy Theories as Stigmatized Knowledge: The Basis for a New Age Racism?" in Jeffrey Kaplan and Tore Bjørgo, eds., *Nation and Race*.
43. See for example, David Capitanchik and Michael Whine, *The Governance of Cyberspace: Racism on the Internet* (London: Institute for Jewish Policy Research, 1996).
44. Jeffrey Kaplan, "Leaderless Resistance," *Terrorism and Political Violence* 9:3 (Fall 1997).
45. See for example, Franco Ferraresi, *La destra radicale* (Milan: Feltrinelli, 1984).
46. *This Week in Germany* (September 22,1994), p.1; *This Week in Germany* (March 3, 1995), 1.
47. See for example, "The Populist Party: The Politics of Right-Wing Extremism," *ADL FACTS* 30:2 (1985).
48. Dan Carter, *The Politics of Rage* (New York: Simon and Schuster,1995), 324–370.
49. Anti-Defamation League, *Danger: Extremism* (New York: ADL,1996), 198–199; idem., *The Church of the Creator: Creed of Hate* (New York: ADL, 1993), 1–4.
50. Russ Bellant, *Old Nazis, the New Right and the Republican Party*, 2–57.
51. See for example, Douglas Rose, ed., *The Emergence of David Duke* (Chapel Hill and London: University of North Carolina Press, 1992).
52. Morris Dees, *Gathering Storm* (New York: Harper,1997), 54–55.
53. See for example, Anti-Defamation League, *The Religious Right: The Assault on Tolerance and Pluralism in America* (New York: ADL, 1994); Michael Lind, *Up From Conservatism* (New York: The Free Press, 1996), 97–137; and Theodore Lowi, *The End of the Republican Era* (Norman and London: University of Oklahoma Press, 1996), 158–217.
54. For a recent discussion see, Seymour Lipset, *American Exceptionalism* (New York and London: W.W. Norton, 1996), 60–67; and Glenn H. Utter and John W. Story, *The Religious Right* (Santa Barbara, CA: ABC-CLIO, 1995), 77–93.
55. Fred Simonelli, *American Fuehrer: George Lincoln Rockwell and the American Nazi Party* (Champaign-Urbana; University of Illinois Press, forthcoming), 224–230. It should be noted, however, that this is a minority view in the field with such observers as Michael Barkun and others according less weight to Rockwell's efforts in the evolution of modern Identity Christianity.
56. See for example, Philip Lamy, *Millennium Rage* (New York: Plenum Press, 1996), 193–217; on the Order, Kevin Flynn and Gary Gerhardt, *The Silent Brotherhood*.
57. On the seditious conspiracy trial of 1988 see Raphael Ezekiel, *The Racist Mind*, 26–57. For an amusing day-by-day account of the event from the jaundiced eye of one of the defendants, the late Robert Miles, see the issues of his newsletter, *From the Mountain*, (March-April 1987–March-April 1988).

58. See Laird Wilcox, ed., *Guide to the American Right: Directory and Bibliography* (Olathe, KS; Editorial Research Service, 1995), 1–44.

59. John George and Laird Wilcox, *American Extremists*, 246–274. Wilcox is quick to point out that the guide merely lists addresses. It should not be taken as an indication of the number of far right groups or individuals in America. Some years he does a wholesale purge of the list and some years he simply adds a few listings and deletes a few others. It is intended as a resource for researchers and not any kind of statement about the composition of the political landscape. Email message from Wilcox to Kaplan, 2 July 1997.

60. *Klanwatch Intelligence Report* 1 (February 1996) 4–7.

61. See for example, James Coates, *Armed and Dangerous* (New York: Hill and Wang, 1987), 123–156.

62. For two thorough accounts see, Richard Abanes, *American Militias* (Downers Grove, IL: Inter-Varsity Press,1996); Kenneth Stern, *A Force Upon the Plain: The American Militia Movement and the Politics of Hate* (New York: Simon and Schuster,1996).

63. See for example, James Corcoran, *Bitter Harvest: Gordon Kahl and the Posse Comitatus* (New York: Penguin Books, 1990).

64. See for example, Anti-Defamation League, *Armed and Dangerous* (New York: ADL,1994), 17–19. Morris Dees, *Gathering Storm*, 89–90.

65. See, *Republic of Texas Finalizes Steps Under Law of Nations for International Recognition* Press Release (June 19,1996), Republic of Texas Web Site <www.flash.net/>.

66. Anti-Defamation League, *Beyond the Bombing: The Militia Menace Grows* (New York: ADL,1995), 1.

67. Anti-Defamation League, *Danger Extremism* (New York: ADL, 1996), 1–175; *False Patriots* (Montgomery, AL: Southern Poverty Law Center,1996), 48–57.

68. For a discussion of the fascinating interactions between African-Americans and white supremacists, see Mattias Gardell, "Black and White Unite in Fight? On the Inter-Action Between Black and White Radical Racialists," paper delivered to the conference "Rejected and Suppressed Knowledge: The Racist Right and the Cultic Milieu," Stockholm, Sweden, 13–17 February 1997.

69. Raphael Ezekiel, *The Racist Mind*, 122–146.

70. *The Shadow Government* (Constitution Society, 1994), 4.

71. Jack McLamb, *Operation Vampire Killer 2000* (Phoenix, AZ: mimeo, n.d.), 2–4.

72. *Mission Statement* (The United States Militia Association, Box 1300, Blackfoot, Idaho, n.d.), 1.

73. See for example, Jim Keith, *Black Helicopters Over America: Strikeforce for the New World Order*.

74. See for example, Richard Abanes, *American Militias*, 30–31.

75. See for example, Phillip Finch, *God, Guts and Guns: A Close Look at the Radical Right* (New York: Seaview/Putnam, 1983).

76. Maj. George Westmoreland, USMC Ret., *How to Start and Train a Militia Unit* (PM 8–94, 1994).

77. *Klanwatch Intelligence Report* 86 (Spring 1997), 8–9.

78. Ibid., 13–14.

79. James Brooke, "Freemen Farm Attracts the Fringe," *The New York Times* (April 28, 1996), 10.

80. For a discussion see, Stephan Talty, "The Method of a Neo-Nazi Mogul," *The New York Times Magazine* (February 25, 1996), 40–43. The origins of the term may be traced to the COTC, and in particular to the text *RaHoWa, The Planet is Ours!* by Ben Klassen.

81. Jeffrey Kaplan, "Leaderless Resistance."

82. Quoted in Gary Lee Yarborough, "Alert Update and Advisory" (Spring 1993), p.6.

83. See for example, Walter Laqueur, *The Age of Terrorism* (Boston, MA: Little, Brown, 1987), 24–71.

Chapter 4 The Ties that Bind: The Euro-American Radical Right's "Special Relationship"

1. On the theme of anti-Americanism see Michele Brambilla, *Interrogatorio alle Destre* (Milan: Rizzoli,1995); Walter Laqueur, *Fascism: Past, Present, Future* (New York: Oxford University Press, 1996), 94, 99; and Weinberg interviews with Marco Tarchi, Florence, July 1995, Richard Stoess, Berlin, July 1995, and Nonna Mayer, Paris, July 1995.

2. See especially, Michael Ledeen, *Universal Fascism*, 103–155.

3. See for example, Erik Jensen, "International Nazi Cooperation: A Terrorist Oriented Network," in Tore Bjørgo and Rob Witte, eds., *Racist Violence in Europe*, 80–95.

4. Weinberg interview with Mike Whine, staff director Jewish Board of Deputies, London, July 1996.

5. Quoted in Kevin Flynn and Gary Gerhardt, *The Silent Brotherhood*, 422–423; Stephen Singular, *Talked to Death* (New York: William Morrow, 1987), 251–252; Jeffrey Kaplan, *Radical Religion in America*, 65–66.

6. Sidney Tarrow, *Power in Movement* (New York: Cambridge University Press, 1994), 33.

7. Jonathan Marcus, "Advance or Consolidation? The French National Front and the 1995 Elections," *West European Politics* 19:2 (1996), 307.

8. See for example, Tadeusz Piotrowski, *Ukrainian Integral Nationalism* (Toronto: Polish Educational Foundation of North America, 1997), 56–84; Bohdan Nahaylo, "Ukraine," *Radio Free Europe/Radio Liberty Research Report* 3:16 (1994), 42–49; Mikolaj Terles, *Ethnic Cleansing of Poles in Volhynia and Eastern Galicia 1942–1946* (Toronto: Alliance of the Polish Eastern Provinces, 1993); Wiktor Polisszuk, *Legal and Political Assessment of the OUN and UPA* (Toronto, author's self publication, 1997)

9. German authorities are inclined to think of their American counterparts as a bit hypocritical. As they see it, there is American pressure to crackdown on neo-Nazi activities while at the same time the U.S. Justice Department stresses First Amendment protections, thus making it more difficult for the Germans to prosecute individuals like Schmidt. Weinberg interview with Klaus Jensen, Federal Criminal Police, Mechenheim Germany, July 1995.

10. On Schmidt and Dietz see, Anti-Defamation League of the B'nai B'rith, *Extremism on the Right: A Handbook* (New York: ADL, 1988), 80–81, 154–155; idem., *Hitler's Apologists* (New York: ADL,1993), 30–32; idem., *Danger: Extremism*, 32–33, 135–137.

11. On the contemporary Canadian radical right, see Warren Kinsella, *Web of Hate: Inside Canada's Far Right Network* (Toronto: Harper Collins, 1994). Cf. Stanley R. Barrett, *Is God a Racist?* (Toronto: University of Toronto Press, 1987).

12. *The Canadian Encyclopedia*, vol. II (Edmonton: Hurtig,1985), 943–945.

13. Irving Abella and Franklin Bialystok, "Canada" in David Wyman, ed., *The World Reacts to the Holocaust* (Baltimore and London: The Johns Hopkins University Press, 1996), 773.

14. Van Pelt's remarks to Weinberg, Auschwitz, Poland, July 1997.

15. *NS-Propaganda aus dem Ausland—Bundesamt fur Verfassungsschutz*, n. 17 (Cologne; August 1994), 3–4; Weinberg interview with Dr. Heinrich Sipple, Federal Office for the Protection of the Constitution, Korweiler, Germany, July 1995.

16. *GANPAC BRIEF: New and Views by Hans Schmidt* 152 (June, 1995), 6.

17. NS Kindred, *Solution-Oriented for Family, Folk and the Future!* (NSJ, CA: NS Kindred, n.d..).

18. *Calling Our Nation*, 73 (1994), 20–21.

19. See for example, Ronald King, "On Particulars, Universals, and Neat Tricks," in Douglas Rose, ed., *The Emergence of David Duke*, 246–247; William Mayer, "The Presidential Nominations," in Gerald Pomper, ed., *The Election of 1996* (Chatham, NJ:

Chatham House, 1997), 52–55; Hans George Betz, *Radical Right-Wing Populism* (New York: St. Martin's Press,1994), 141–168.

20. For a discussion see, Tore Bjørgo, ed., "Introduction," in *Terror from the Extreme Right*, 8–13; Peter Merkl, "Why are They so Strong Now?" in Peter Merkl and Leonard Weinberg, eds., *The Revival of Right-Wing Extremism in the Nineties*, 17–46.

21. *Thule* 1:1 (1996), p.1.

22. Ingo Hasselbach, *Fuhrer-Ex*, 49–63.

23. One page flyer, "Introduction to the Volksfront."

24. "We Want the Workers," *The Oklahoma Separatist* 11–12 (1989), 1–2.

25. Flyer, "About, 'The European Liberation Front,' A Bulwark Against 'The Outer Forces'" (November, 1985).

26. Kevin Flynn and Gary Gerhardt, *The Silent Brotherhood*, 84–85.

27. On the history of the leaderless resistance concept in the American radical right, see Jeffrey Kaplan, "Leaderless Resistance."

28. *Danger Extremism*, 27.

29. McCalden soon broke with the IHR and became until his death a bitter enemy of IHR founder Willis Carto. McCalden's correspondence with such movement figures as Harold Covington offer chapter and verse of the alleged misdeeds of his former patron.

30. These accounts were drawn from Weinberg's interviews with Mike Whine, Board of Deputies of British Jews, London, July 1996, Professor Roger Eatwell, University of Bath, July 1996, Dr. Heinrich Sipple, Federal Office for the Protection of the Constitution, Korweiler, Germany, July 1995, Inspector Klaus Jensen, Federal Criminal Police, Mechenheim, Germany, July 1995, and Criminal Inspector Peter Haeberer of the Berlin Criminal Police, July 1995.

31. Jacob Heilbrunn, "Heil Harvard," *The New Republic* (September 1,1997), 15–17.

32. On Earl Jones and his ongoing explorations of conspiratorial historiography, see any issue of his publication, *Christian Crusade for Truth Newsletter*. Cf. Jeffrey Kaplan, *Radical Religion in America*, 121–122.

33. Pastor Earl F. Jones, "One World (Dis) Order Still Going Strong," *Candour* XLIX:1 (January 1996), 1–7.

34. "Newsletter from Poland," *Candour* (April 1992), 6–8.

35. *NSV Report* 12:3 (July/September, 1994), 4–5.

36. "World News Briefs" *ANP Newsletter* (December/January 1995), 5–7.

37. *The 1996 White Calendar* (Marc Lemire <freedom@pathcom.com>).

38. David Capitanchik and Michael Whine, "The Governance of Cyberspace: Racism on the Internet," 9.

39. Alan Cowell, "Neo-Nazis Now Network on Line and Underground," *The New York Times*, October 22, 1995, 3.

40. Capitanchik and Whine, 12.

41. See for example, Anti-Defamation League, *The Web of Hate*, 33–35.

42. See for example, Anti-Defamation League, *Neo-Nazi Skinheads: A 1990 Status Report* (New York: ADL,1990); Maurizio Blondet, *I Nuovi Barbari: Gli Skinheads Parlano*, 47–51; Anti-Defamation League, *The Skinhead International* (New York:ADL,1995), 56–58.

43. Raphael Ezekiel, *The Racist Mind*, 149–191.

44. *Calling Our Nation* 74 (1995), 2.

45. For a paradigmatic example of this phenomenon, see William Pierce's description of George Lincoln Rockwell's early candlelit altar to the Führer in William Pierce, *Lincoln Rockwell: A National Socialist Life* (Arlington, VA: NS Publications, 1969), 15–16.

46. For accounts see, James Aho, *The Politics of Righteousness* (Seattle and London: University of Washington Press,1990); and Michael Barkun, *Religion and the Racist Right*.

47. See for example, Heléne Lööw, "Racist Violence and Criminal Behavior in Sweden," in Bjørgo ed., *Terror from the Extreme Right*, 122–124.

48. For summaries see, Jeffrey Kaplan, "Right-Wing Violence in North America" in Bjørgo, ed., *Terror from the Extreme Right*, 59–67; Brad Whitsel, "Aryan Visions for the Future in the West Virginia Mountains," *Terrorism and Political Violence* 7:4 (1995), 117–139.

49. On Odinism, see Jeffrey Kaplan, *Radical Religion in America*, ch. 3; and idem., "The Reconstruction of the Ásatrú and Odinist Traditions," in James R. Lewis, ed., *Magical Religions and Modern Witchcraft* (Albany, NY: SUNY Press, 1996).

50. For a summary see, Anti-Defamation League, *The Church of the Creator: Creed of Hate*. For a view from the perspective of the Creators themselves, see the chapter "Tommy Rydén: A National Socialist Life," below.

51. Anti-Defamation League, *The Skinhead International*, 5. See also, Klaus Wasmund, "Neo-Nazi Attitudes and Violent Behavior among German Youth, " paper prepared for presentation at the World Congress of the International Political Science Association, Seoul, South Korea, August 17–21,1997; and Mark S. Hamm, *American Skinheads*.

52. Stephan Talty, "The Method of a Neo-Nazi Mogul," *The New York Times Magazine*, February 25, 1996, 40.

53. Ibid.

54. *Political Extremism and the Threat to Democracy in Europe*, 33; For a commentary about the German situation see for example, Martin Jay, "Postmodern Fascism?" *Tikkun* 8:6 (November/December 1993), 38–41.

55. Barry Mehler, "In Genes We Trust: When Science Bows to Racism," *Reform Judaism* 23:2 (Winter 1994), 11–14, 77–79.

56. On Holocaust denial see especially, Gill Seidel, *The Holocaust Denial* (Leeds, UK: Beyond the Pale Press,1986); Deborah Lipstadt, *Denying the Holocaust*; and Kenneth Stern, *Holocaust Denial* (New York: American Jewish Committee, 1993).

57. Clerkin has been in the NS scene for a number of years. In 1976, he formed the Euro-American Alliance in Milwaukee and began publishing *The Talon*, a 4-page monthly "newsletter" consisting of a short political essay and a few sentences of "Alliance Notes." For slightly longer expositions, Clerkin publishes the *Euro-American Quarterly*.

58. *Danger Extremism*, 72–74, 216–217.

59. Maj. D.V. Clerkin, "Who We Really Are," *Talon* (1989), 2–3.

60. See James Rosenau, *Linkage Politics* (New York: The Free Press, 1969), 44–63.

61. *Klanwatch Intelligence Report* 85 (Winter 1997), 19–22. While Klanwatch figures have proven considerably less than reliable in the past, we will note here only that the American community of adherents to explicitly National Socialist movements is exceedingly small, and that many "groups" are in reality merely post office boxes emblazoned with formidable sounding organizational monikers but which can boast of no actual members beyond the box owner. "Major" Clerkin's impressive sounding Euro-American Alliance noted above is a case in point.

62. Roger Eatwell points out there is an English printer (Tony Hancock) who comes close to earning his living by printing Holocaust denial writings for foreign consumption (Weinberg interview June, 1996). On the post-Hancock distribution network of these materials, see Kaplan interview with the ebullient Finnish Nazi, Nils Mandel, 9 August 1995. Mandel, currently resident in Sweden, makes an annual motor pilgrimage to London to pick up Hancock's material, all of which is printed in a variety of languages, and then delivers it to customers throughout continental Europe. Scandinavia. Eastern Europe (especially Poland and Hungary) is a growth market for these arcane items. It should be noted that Hancock's output is not limited to

Holocaust material, but includes a variety of stickers and pamphlets as well from a wide range of racist and anti-Semitic ideologies.

63. Leonard Zeskind, "Money Matters," *Klanwatch Intelligence Report* 87 (Summer 1997), 10–13. Indeed, the IHR was born of the financial largesse of Willis Carto.

64. *Political Extremism and the Threat to Democracy in Europe*, 3.

65. Vera Ebels-Dolanova, ed., *The Extreme Right in Europe and the United States* (Amsterdam: Anne Frank Institute, 1985), 21–22.

66. Gill Seidel, *The Holocaust Denial*, 41.

67. Here the reader might consult, Rand Lewis, *A Nazi Legacy* (New York: Praeger, 1991) 152–155; Erik Jensen, "International Nazi Cooperation: A Terrorist Oriented Network," in Tore Bjørgo and Rob Witte, eds., *Racist Violence in Europe* , 80–95.

68. See especially, Bundesamt fur Verfassungsschutz, *Aktuelle Entwicklungen und Tendenzen in Rechtsextremismus/ terrorismus* (April 30, 1995), 11–13.

69. See, Ingo Hasselbach, *Fuhrer-Ex*, 163.

70. Tore Bjørgo, " Militant neo-Nazism in Sweden," 28–57.

71. Anti-Defamation League, *The Skinhead International*, 1–4.

72. For accounts see Yaron Svoray and Nick Taylor, *In Hitler's Shadow*, 39–40, 59–60.

73. Eduardo Damaso, "Portugal," in *Extremism from the Urals to the Atlantic* , 209.

74. *The Skinhead International*, 1.

75. Cited in Gill Seidel, *The Holocaust Denial*, 42–43.

76. See Russ Bellant, *Old Nazis, the New Right and the Republican Party*, 2–57; Scott Anderson, *Inside the League*.

77. See for example, Anthony Smith, *National Identity* (Reno: University of Nevada Press, 1993), 19–42.

78. See for example, Dominique Schnapper, "The European Debate on Citizenship," *Daedalus* 126:3 (1997), 199–222.

79. Mattei Dogan, "Comparing the Decline Of Nationalisms In Western Europe: The Generational Dynamic," *International Social Science Review* 136 (1993), 177–198.

80. See for example, Leon Poliakov, *The Aryan Myth* (New York: Barnes and Noble, 1971), 183–254.

Chapter 5   **The Postwar Years Through the 1970s: An Internal History**

1. *Nordisk Kamp* 10 (26 August 1967). This was a memorial issue dedicated to George Lincoln Rockwell. Translated by Dr. Heléne Lööw.

2. Frederick Simonelli, *American Führer*; cf. A. M. Rosenthal and Arthur Gelb, *One More Victim: The Life and Death of a Jewish Nazi* (New York: New American Library, 1967), and for a movement perspective, Rick Cooper, "A Brief History of the White Nationalist Movement."

3. For a discussion on spatiality and religion, see Jonathan Z. Smith, *To Take Place: Toward a Theory of Ritual* (Chicago, IL: University of Chicago, 1987). For a discussion of spatiality and violence, see David C. Rapoport, "The Importance of Space in Violent Ethno-Religious Strife," Policy Paper #21, University of California Institute on Global Conflict and Cooperation, January 1996.

4. Russ Bellant, *Old Nazis, the New Right and the Republican Party*.

5. For an idyllic description of these times, see Jost, "Aryan Destiny Back to the Land," undated e-text distributed by the National Socialist Kindred. For an alarmist account from the watchdog perspective, see Kenneth S. Stern, *A Force Upon The Plain*.

6. A journalistic source for these rural redoubts is Phillip Finch, *God, Guts and Guns: A Close Look at the Radical Right*. For a brilliant analysis of the comforts, as well as the hypernomian nature of the culture of the religious enclave, see Emmanuel Sivan,

"The Enclave Culture," in Martin E. Marty and R. Scott Appleby, eds., *Fundamentalisms Comprehended* (Chicago, IL: University of Chicago, 1995).

7. As seriously as these training sessions seem to movement activists—especially in Germany—and as much alarm as these adventures engender among authorities and watchdog groups, one is reminded of a Bulgarian political joke of ancient vintage. In a mordant comment on the much mythologized battles between communist partisans and fascist forces, a partisan diary is found in the forest which describes a series of epic skirmishes in which first one side and then the other is expelled by its opposite number from the forest. This series of tit for tat battles ends when, tiring of the disturbance, the local forest ranger appears to order both sides out of the forest! Such is the comic opera nature of these sessions. For an entertaining record of these frolics, see such video recordings as the hilarious "Three Hours With SD," or the Viking-flavored romp in the forest hosted by Tom Metzger titled "Aryan Fest '90." The latter features the memorable Viking burning swastika dance. That Europe holds no redoubts safe from widespread public awareness of the presence of race activists was brought home in Kaplan interview with Tommy Rydén, 28 July 1995, and Kaplan interview with Väinö Kuisma, Lati, Finland, 12 August 1995.

8. Robert Welch, *The Neutralizers* (Belmont, MA: The John Birch Society, 1963).

9. Seymour Lipset and Earl Raab, *The Politics of Unreason*, 265–267; John George and Laird Wilcox, *American Extremists*, 186–196; and for the movement's own 'bible', Robert Welch, *The Blue Book of the John Birch Society* (Belmont, MA: The John Birch Society, 1961). A good, brief summary of the Birch Society's beliefs and aspirations can be found in Robert Welch, "A Brief Introduction to the John Birch Society" (a transcript of a speech delivered during the spring months of 1962 before the Commonwealth Club of San Francisco, the Executive Club of Chicago, and Other Audiences).

10. John George and Laird Wilcox, *American Extremists*, 208–210.

11. William L. Pierce, *Lincoln Rockwell: A National Socialist Life*, 23. A less enlightening document emerged in the late 1970s purporting to be from the ELF as well. This however, was a simple, rather incoherent, anti-Semitic screed. See "About, 'The European Liberation Front' A Bulwark Against 'The Outer Forces,'" undated mimeographed communiqué from the ELF. The document is notable only for its claims of direct descent from Yockey and that the group is forced to live a semi-clandestine life in London.

12. Carto is currently locked in battle with the board of directors that he himself appointed for control of the Institute for Historical Review. See Doreen Carvahal, "Extremist Institute Mired in Power Struggle; Courts: Staff Members Oust Founder of Holocaust Denial Center," *Los Angeles Times*, 15 May 1994. An inveterate litigant, Carto's latest courtroom duel is with Linda Thompson, the militia figure who heads the American Justice Federation over Carto's refusal to pay for copies of Thompson's Waco expose videos, "Waco: The Big Lie, Parts I & II." The full 50+ page court documents are archived by the Nizkor Project at: <http://www.nizkor.org/ftp.cgi?people/c/carto.willis/thompson-vrs-c>.

13. Kaplan interview with Else Christensen, 27 November 1992. The Yockey series can be found in "Our View of History," *The Odinist* 10 (December 1973); "The Structure of History," *The Odinist* 11 (March 1974); and "More Yockey," *The Odinist* 12 (June 1974).

14. House Committee on Un-American Activities, *Preliminary Report on Neo-Fascist and Hate Groups*, 17 December 1954, 1–2.

15. "James Hartung Madole: Father of Post-War Fascism," *Nexus* (November 1995). Madole's utopian vision of a Völkisch National Socialist America was serialized in his *National Renaissance Bulletin* throughout the mid-1970s as "The New Atlantis: A Blueprint for the Aryan 'Garden of Eden' in North America." Cf. Rick Cooper, "A

Brief History of the White Nationalist Movement."

16. James H. Madole, "The Program of the National Renaissance Party," *National Renaissance Bulletin*, (October 1953), 3–4. The document is reproduced in House Committee on Un-American Activities, *Preliminary Report on Neo-Fascist and Hate Groups*, Exhibit 2, 21–22.

17. "James Hartung Madole: Father of Post-War Fascism," *Nexus*, 23.

18. For a fascinating treatise on the subject, see Joel Carmichael, *The Satanizing of the Jews: Origin and Development of Mystical Anti-Semitism* (New York: Fromm, 1992).

19. This controversial fact has been noted by a bare handful of researchers. For a erudite exposition, see Nicholas Godrick-Clarke, *The Occult Roots of Nazism* (New York: New York University Press, 1985,1992), 1, who states that "fantasies can achieve a causal status once they have been institutionalized in beliefs, values and social groups. Fantasies are also an important symptom of impending cultural changes and political action." The same observation has been made in conversation with Kaplan by longtime observer Laird Wilcox.

20. The 1954 HUAC report estimates "anywhere from 200 to 700 persons," although even in this source the numbers were seen as sharply declining after 1954. House Committee on Un-American Activities, *Preliminary Report on Neo-Fascist and Hate Groups*, 10. The more realistic lower figure is from Gordon Hall, a contemporary observer of the scene. Hall is quoted in John George and Laird Wilcox, *American Extremists*, 325.

21. Rick Cooper claims that Koehl was never a member of the NRP, but rather of the National States' Rights Party. Whether a member or not, Koehl was certainly very close to the NRP, and to be a leader of the uniformed guard would seem to require membership. For his contrary view, see Rick Cooper, "A Brief History of the White Nationalist Movement."

22. On Burros, see A. M. Rosenthal and Arthur Gelb, *One More Victim: The Life and Death of a Jewish Nazi*. NRP members and associates are noted in John George and Laird Wilcox, *American Extremists*; House Committee on Un-American Activities, *Preliminary Report on Neo-Fascist and Hate Groups*; "James Hartung Madole: Father of Post-War Fascism," *Nexus*; and especially in the pages of the long running *National Renaissance Bulletin*.

23. John George and Laird Wilcox, *American Extremists*, 324–325. According to this text, many believe the highly eccentric (even by the standards of this milieu) Trujillo was an informant for, among others, the Anti-Defamation League of the B'nai B'rith.

24. House Committee on Un-American Activities, *Preliminary Report on Neo-Fascist and Hate Groups*, 5.

25. On Åberg's early career, see Heléne Lööw, "'Wir Sind Wieder Da'- From National Socialism to Militant Racial Ideology—The Swedish Racist Underground In An Historical Context," in *Strommar i tiden*, Mohamed Chaib, ed., (Göborg: Diadalos Forlag, 1995). For the claims to the title of the first Holocaust deniers on behalf of Bardéche and Rassiner, see Deborah Lipstadt, *Denying the Holocaust*, 50–51. Åberg and Bardéche were both delegates to the 1951 Malmö meeting which founded the European Social Movement.

26. Heléne Lööw, "'Wir Sind Wieder Da.'" For a capsule biography of Leese, see Phillip Reese, *Biographical Dictionary of the Extreme Right*, 227–228. Leese's work is kept alive in the world of the far right publishing houses and in the pages of such journals as *Jew Watch*, the vehicle of Der Freikorps, a small group of Texas Hitler cultists, whose title was chosen as a parody of Morris Dees's Klanwatch. *Jew Watch* intermixes translations of Nazi-era anti-Semitic propaganda with current news. In August, 1992 Der Freikorps began a new publication which purports to be the revival of the Nazi-era German newspaper, *Der Stürmer*, which Der Freikorps describes as "a kind of German *National Inquirer*."

27. E-mail message from Stephane Bruchfeld. Bruchfeld recalls that the artist may have regretted the missed opportunity to punch Åberg, as he later struck another anti-Semitic agitator and was rewarded with a two-month sentence in prison for his trouble.

28. Heléne Lööw, "Swedish National Socialism and Right-Wing Extremism After 1945," in Stein Larsen, ed., *Modern Europe After Fascism.*

29. Heléne Lööw, *Kampen som livsform; en studie av nationalsocialism och rasideologi efter 1945* [Struggle as a Way of life; National Socialism and Militant Racialism After 1945] (Stockholm: Ordfront Publishing House, forthcoming).

30. Heléne Lööw, "Swedish National Socialism and Right-Wing Extremism After 1945."

31. Abbie Hoffman, *Steal This Book: Twenty-Fifth Anniversary Edition* (New York: Four Walls Eight Windows, 1995).

32. Heléne Lööw, "'Wir Sind Wieder Da,'" 2.

33. Heléne Lööw, *Kampen som livsform.*

34. Ibid.

35. Heléne Lööw, "Swedish National Socialism and Right-Wing Extremism After 1945," 20–21.

36. Ibid., 19–21; Kaplan interview with Deitlieb Felderer, 26 July 1995.

37. Heléne Lööw, "'Wir Sind Wieder Da,'" 3.

38. The obituary was published in *Nordisk Kamp* and is quoted in Heléne Lööw, *Kampen som livsform.*

39. Fax from Tommy Rydén, 23 August 1996. It is possible too that the family simply didn't want to stir up further controversy and preferred not to discuss the subject with Rydén.

40. We are not alone in this view. See Michael Aquino, *The Church of Satan*, third edition (San Francisco, CA: Michael Aquino, 1993), 272, for a similarly critical view.

41. James H. Madole, "'The New Atlantis' A Blueprint for an Aryan 'Garden of Eden' in North America! (Part VIII)," *National Renaissance Bulletin* 7 and 8 (July and August 1975), 5.

42. James H. Madole, "'The New Atlantis' A Blueprint for an Aryan 'Garden of Eden' in North America! (Part XI)," *National Renaissance Bulletin* 3 and 4 (March and April 1976), 4.

43. See for example, A. Rud Mills, *The Odinist Religion: Overcoming Jewish Christianity* (Melbourne, Australia: self published, c. 1930).

44. "James Hartung Madole: Father of Post-War Fascism," *Nexus*, 25–26. The events are described by Madole himself in the *National Renaissance Bulletin*, March and April 1974. A sample of Madole's early recruiting pitch to Church of Satan adherents is preserved in a letter to COS member Stuart Levine: "I am trying to find a small group of people [and] utilize their services in breaking some of our NRP officers and men into the more advanced concepts of occult philosophy." Letter from James Madole to Stuart Levine, 17 September 1974, quoted in Michael Aquino, *The Church of Satan*, 272.

45. "A Brief History of Satanism in Detroit," *An Introduction to the Order of the Black Ram* (Warren, MI: Order of the Black Ram, n.d.), 1–2.

46. Letter from Anton LaVey to Michael Aquino, 24 June 1974, quoted in Michael Aquino, *The Church of Satan*, 270.

47. Michael Aquino, *The Church of Satan*, 269–270. On the Western Guard and other far right wing movements in Canada, see Stanley R. Barrett, *Is God a Racist?* .

48. Michael Aquino, *The Church of Satan*, 271.

49. Ibid.

50. Ibid. Dr. Heléne Lööw confirms this sentiment, recalling that in one of her many interviews with Swedish movement figures, an activist who in an insightful moment noted: "Well, we know that had we lived in Hitler's Germany, we would have been

the first to go up in the chimneys." Private communication, Lööw to Kaplan, October 1996.

51. Letter from LaVey to Aquino, 5 July 1974, in Michael Aquino, *The Church of Satan*, 271–272.

52. "James Hartung Madole: Father of Post-War Fascism," *Nexus*, 26.

53. Fredrick J. Simonelli, "The American Nazi Party, 1958–1967," *The Historian* 57 (Spring 1995), 554–557.

54. George Lincoln Rockwell, *This Time the World!* (Arlington, VA: Parliament House, 1963).

55. Letter from George Lincoln Rockwell to Einar Åberg, 17 December 1958. The letter is currently in the possession of Tommy Rydén.

56. For coverage of the internal debate along these lines within NS circles, see Jeffrey Kaplan, "Religiosity and the Radical Right: Toward the Creation of a New Ethnic Identity," in Jeffrey Kaplan and Tore Bjørgo, eds., *Nation and Race*.

57. This account is primarily based on three sources, George Lincoln Rockwell, *This Time the World!*; William L. Pierce, *Lincoln Rockwell: A National Socialist Life*; and New Order, *The Religion of Lincoln Rockwell* (Milwaukee, WI: New Order, n.d.).

58. William L. Pierce, *Lincoln Rockwell: A National Socialist Life*, 12.

59. Ibid., 15–16. Pierce dates these dreams as occurring in 1957–1958.

60. New Order, *The Religion of Lincoln Rockwell*, 5.

61. William L. Pierce, *Lincoln Rockwell: A National Socialist Life*, 18.

62. How deeply religious is revealed in the 1994 General Social Survey conducted by the National Opinion Research Center. According to this data, fully 94 percent of Americans report some belief in a higher power while only 2 percent evince no belief at all. By far the largest cluster of respondents, 64 percent state that they "believe without doubts." The next largest cluster, 16 percent, "believe with doubts." Glenn H. Utter and John W. Story, *The Religious Right*, 78.

63. Klaus Scholder, *The Churches and the Third Reich*, 2 vols., second edition, (Philadelphia, PA: Fortress Press, 1988).

64. Letter from George Lincoln Rockwell to Bruno Ludke, 11 February 1963, in Frederick J. Simonelli, *American Führer*, 223. Much of the religiously oriented material contained in *American Führer* is reprised in Frederick J. Simonelli, "Preaching Hate with the Voice of God: American Neo-Nazis and Christian Identity," *Patterns of Prejudice* 30 (April 1996): 43–54.

65. Ibid. The 1957 discussions took place with Emory Burke, an anti-Semite later charged but not convicted in the 1958 bombing of an Atlanta synagogue.

66. Letter from Bruno Ludke to Rockwell, 15 May 1962, in Frederick J. Simonelli, *American Führer*, 220.

67. Ibid., 220–225. On Jordan's more recent writings, see the ongoing "The Way Ahead" series in the 1995–1996 issues of *Gothic Ripples*. The series in fact is strongly reminiscent of many of the ideas broached by James Madole in the 1970s era "New Atlantis" series.

68. Kenneth T. Jackson, *The Ku Klux Klan in the City, 1915–1930*, 145.

69. Daniel Levitas, "Antisemitism and the Far Right: 'Hate' Groups, White Supremacy and the Neo-Nazi Movement," in Jerome Chanes, ed., *Antisemitism in America Today* (New York: Birch Lane Press, 1995), 177.

70. Heléne Lööw, *Kampen som livsform*.

71. The quote is credited to the Canadian Intelligence Service of Flesherton, Ontario, Canada, with editing credit to Einar Åberg in a 1958 tract entitled "Whose Is the Hidden Hand?"

72. On Dilys, see Jeffrey Kaplan, *Radical Religion In America*. Dilys has been a fixture on the street corners of Chicago for the last forty years. Like Åberg, Dilys' primary forte is a tireless worldwide correspondence with anyone who shares his anti-Semitic

zeitgeist, a penchant for marching around with sandwich signs denouncing the Jews and a seeming indifference to the frequent beatings he has suffered for his troubles. Dilys, a Lithuanian immigrant with a high school education, like Åberg came to adopt his own trademark motto. Eschewing the highbrow appeal of Burke, however, Dilys' signature quote is: "The synagogue is an embassy of Hell. Every Rabbi is an ambassador of Lucifer."

73. "Einar Aberg," *The Cross and the Flag* (January 1962), 8.

Chapter 6 *The Transatlantic Race Movement Today: At the Vanguard*

1. Reacting to an early draft of this chapter, James Mason, a longtime American National Socialist of whom much will be said below, takes the proposition further to argue that, not only is the movement's situation today analogous to the prewar Zionists, but: "I would take it further and say that we have an exact parallel with Egypt circa 1500 B.C. The twist is, as the Christian Identists would have it, that we were then and are now the Israelites." Kaplan interview with James Mason, 28 November 1996.

2. Letter to Kaplan from Varg Quisling Vigernes, 10 September 1996.

3. Kaplan interview with Nils Mandel, Stockholm, 19 August 1995. In 1996, the Belgians grew tired of hosting this chaotic event and it was moved to Trollhattan, Sweden, where violent clashes took place between skinheads and anti-racist activists. The highlight of the celebration, however, was the appearance of a group of naked anarchists who painted themselves blue to illustrate "the naked truth about fascism." "Swedish Neo-Nazi March Ends in Violence," *Reuters Wire Service* 17 August 1996. The report was downloaded and made available to the movement by the ANA e-mail news service.

4. "American Neo-Nazi Gets Four Years in Germany," *Boston Globe*, 22 August 1996. The article was gleefully uploaded and disseminated to the antiracist community via the Internet by the *Antifa Info Bulletin* on the same day that the article appeared. Lauck's NSDP/AO in Lincoln, Nebraska, predictably took a dimmer view of events. See in particular "Free Gerhard!," *New Order* 116 (May/June 1995), 1, and in particular "Free Gerhard!: Gerhard's Case Goes to the Danish Supreme Court," *New Order* 117 (July/August 1995), 1, for the NSDP/AO's reaction to the Danish arrest; "Gerhard Jailed!," *New Order* 118 (September/October 1995), 1, for coverage of Lauck's extradition to Germany; and "Fifteen Years for Free Speech!," *New Order* 123 (July/August 1996), 1, for commentary on the German trial.

5. On the importance of this material in Germany and throughout Europe, see Ingo Hasselbach with Tom Reiss, *Führer-Ex*. Cf. "Traitor!," *New Order* 120 (January/February 1996), 1, for Lauck's rebuttal to Ingo Hasselbach's charges as previewed in "How Nazis are Made," 8 January 1996. Of particular interest in Lauck's response is the rhetorical question: "Think about it—the enemy claims that we move 'TONS' of materials into Germany—for an organization of only 80 people? Ridiculous!"

6. The primary source of Mason's history is M. M. Jenkins's introduction to James Mason, *Siege!* (Denver, CO: Storm Books, 1992). Storm is the publishing house of Michael Moynahan, a writer and artist whose *Blood Axis* CD is arguably the best musical work to date to emerge from the occult current of National Socialism. For a revealing insight into Mason's early life, see "James Mason," *No Longer a Fanzine* 5 (n.d.), 11–16.

7. Mason notes that his impression not only of blacks, but of Jews as well, was on the whole rather positive in his early years. "James Mason," 11–12.

8. Kaplan interview with James Mason, 28 November 1996.

9. As one striking example, Sweden's Tommy Rydén who will serve as an in-depth case study of transatlantic activism in chapter 8 recalls from his own small town boyhood

reading a newspaper account at the age of eleven of the American Ku Klux Klan. Putting together scraps of information from a number of sources, Rydén was able to obtain the address of American Klan leader Bill Wilkinson. Interview with Tommy Rydén, Linköping, Sweden, 28 July 1995. In a not atypical denouement to this story, Wilkinson, who was most helpful to Rydén's early endeavors, turned out to be a long-time FBI informant. On Wilkinson, see John George and Laird Wilcox, *American Extremists*, 373–374.

10. John Carpenter, *Extremism U.S.A.* (Phoenix, AZ: Extremism USA, 1964). The photograph Mason refers to is on 137. The book actually says remarkably little about right-wing extremists, saving greater vitriol for the left. In both cases, the text is an exercise in middle-of-the-road "Americanism" of little historical value. The class-mate soon became disillusioned and dropped out of the movement. He committed suicide in 1992 or 1993. Kaplan interview with James Mason, 28 November 1996. Cf. "James Mason," 13.

11. Kaplan interview with James Mason, 28 November 1996.

12. This point is confirmed by Mason, and was particularly important to the West Coast faction of the movement which splintered under Koehl's leadership, driving some of the younger and more daring adherents into the camp of Joseph Tommasi and the violent revolutionary appeal of the National Socialist Liberation Front. Letter from Mason to Kaplan, 17 December 1996.

13. For a brief discussion of the mass vs. revolutionary action theory, see Jeffrey Kaplan, "Right Wing Violence in North America," 57.

14. The conflict was irreconcilable and Pierce left for the National Youth Alliance, a front group formed by Willis Carto that grew out of the 1968 George Wallace presidential campaign. The ideological point of contention centered around Pierce's charge that Koehl was a "cultist," but at a deeper level, Pierce had already begun his shift from the movement's typical conservatism to an embrace of revolutionary violence. Kaplan interview with James Mason, 28 November 1996.

15. James Mason, *Siege!* XI, no. 5, (May 1982).

16. Joseph Tommasi, "Building the Revolutionary Party," in James Mason, *Siege!*, 383.

17. Kaplan interview with James Mason, 28 November 1996. On the fragmentation of the Koehl-era party and the expulsion of Tommasi, see Jeffrey Kaplan, "Right Wing Violence in North America," 57.

18. Kaplan interview with James Mason, 28 November 1996.

19. Kaplan interview with Rick Cooper, 2 September 1997; letter to Kaplan from Dan Stewart, 12 September 1997. Given the common perception in movement circles of Koehl's homosexuality, one suspects that it was more the girls than the illegal substances which brought the ire of the NSWPP down on Tommasi's head. Whatever the source of this rivalry, it would cost Tommasi his life. In 1975, he was shot by an adherent of the NSWPP. On the movement perception of Koehl's sexual orientation, see Rick Cooper, "Brief History of the White Nationalist Movement." Indeed, the widespread rumors of Koehl's homosexuality so disturbed Rockwell that at one point the Commander imported an attractive and devoted female party member whose mission was to seduce Koehl and thus put to rest any suspicions regarding his virility. The mission was a fiasco. See Frederick Simonelli, *American Fuehrer*, 145. On Tommasi's death, see John George and Laird Wilcox, *American Extremists*, 337. The ADL weighs in on the subject in Anti-Defamation League of the B'nai B'rith, *Extremism on the Right*, 43. James Mason recalls that a lesser known charge of financial improprieties was lodged against Tommasi by California Koehl loyalists. Kaplan interview with James Mason, 28 November 1996.

20. Joseph Tommasi, "Building the Revolutionary Party," in James Mason, *Siege!*, 381. The original NSLF poster is reproduced in idem., 19.

21. James Mason, *Siege!*, 5.

22. Joseph Tommasi, "Strategy for Revolution," in James Mason, *Siege!*, 378–380. "Blows Against the Empire" was the title of an early 1970s Jefferson Starship album which held a certain vogue in right as well as left-wing circles of the day. Kaplan e-mail conversation with former national spokesman of the Minutemen, R. N. Taylor. Tommasi and the NSLF took the same playful approach to hippie culture, for example "Big Brother and the Holding Company," *Siege!* 2 (1974), 5. The article concerns an attack on the "law and order" preoccupation of the right wing, picturing police in contemporary leftist terms as pigs paid to enforce the American status quo. Big Brother and the Holding Company was also the name of Janis Joplin's first band.

23. Joseph Tommasi, "Strategy for Revolution," in James Mason, *Siege!*, 379.

24. Kaplan interview with James Mason, 28 November 1996. On founding Order member David Lane's revolutionary theories, see David Lane, "Wotan Is Coming," *WAR* (April 1993).

25. James Mason letter to Kaplan, 16 December 1996. Mason was responding to Kaplan's suggestion that this core/peripheral membership was at the root of differing claims by Tommasi of the level of NSLF support which was either more than forty or only four.

26. James Mason, *Siege!*, 104. Kaplan interview with James Mason, 28 November 1996.

27. For a view of the truth of this axiom holding the masses to be essentially feminine, see Leni Riefenstahl, *Leni Riefenstahl: A Memoir* (New York: St. Martin's Press, 1992). For a theoretical view, see Julius Evola, *Revolt Against the Modern World* (Rochester, VT: Inner Traditions International, 1995), 157–166.

28. John George and Laird Wilcox, *American Extremists*, 338.

29. Kaplan interview with James Mason, 28 November 1996.

30. For the ultimate example of this wish fulfillment, see Richard Kelly Hoskins, *Vigilantes of Christendom* (Lynchburg, VA.: Virginia Publishing Co., 1990). For a discussion of the importance of this text to the world of the radical right, see Kaplan's review in *Syzygy* 1:3 (Summer 1992).

31. Kaplan interview with James Mason, 28 November 1996. The "Pray for victory" quotation is borrowed by Mason from Tommasi's "Building the Revolutionary Party."

32. James Mason, *Siege!* XI, no. 5, (May 1982). It was in any case seen primarily as a personal vehicle for Mason's views. Mason notes that this was very much in keeping with the one man outfits common to the NS scene. Kaplan interview with James Mason, 28 November 1996.

33. This peaceful parting of the ways is so atypical of the fractious NS milieu that today Mason calls it: "one of the most decent and honorable things anyone has ever done within the movement." Kaplan interview with James Mason, 28 November 1996.

34. James Mason, *Siege!*, 87. For a discussion of the religionist/anti-religionist split in NS ranks, see Jeffrey Kaplan, "Religiosity and the Radical Right: Toward the Creation of a New Ethnic Identity," in Jeffrey Kaplan and Tore Bjørgo, eds., *Nation and Race*. Today, Mason notes that he found that religion is after all of key importance during his present incarceration, and he observes that the current situation in the world matches almost precisely the scenario of the Book of Revelations. Kaplan interview with James Mason, 28 November 1996.

35. James Mason, *Siege!*, 362. Today, Mason states that while he continues to admire Church of Satan founder Anton LaVey, he remains convinced that Satan "couldn't care less" about our doings, and if he did, he would most likely appear as "a three-piece suited, Ivy league politician" wanting your vote to move into "The Brave New World. Or the New World Order." Kaplan interview with James Mason, 28 November 1996.

36. Mason took his case for Manson, whom he credits with coining the term "Universal Order," to the skinhead and White Power rock world in James Mason, "Charles Manson: Illusion vs. Reality," *Resistance* 4 (Spring 1995), 20–22.

37. "The Manson Debate: Two of Our Readers Take their Sides," *Resistance* 5 (Fall 1995), 31–33.
38. Kaplan interview with Michael Moynahan, 19 December 1996. Indeed, Manson's recorded musings can be hypnotic, seemingly touched at one moment by crazed genius and at another as so purposefully obscure as to be incomprehensible, or even mad. James Mason notes in this regard that he once sent a CD of Manson talking to a psychiatrist of his acquaintance who wrote back that Manson "demonstrated a lot of 'Free Association' commonly connected with schizophrenia. But that immediately gave way to other considerations like simply being under-socialized, no social skills, or perhaps genius." James Mason letter to Kaplan, 16 December 1996.
39. Stoddard Martin, *Art, Messianism and Crime: A Study of Antinomianism in Modern Literature and Lives* (New York: St. Martin's Press, 1986).
40. Ibid., 3.
41. Kaplan interview with Michael Moynahan, 19 December 1996.
42. Manson CDs are available from White Devil Records and Storm Books. The most fascinating of these is the double CD *Manson Speaks* on White Devil Records. Zines featuring Manson articles are too numerous to mention. Some of the more interesting Manson books to return to the market include the "lost classic," John Gilmore and Ron Kenner, *The Garbage People* (Los Angeles: Amok, 1995); Nuel Emmons, *Manson in His Own Words* (New York: Grove Press, 1986); Nikolas Schreck, *The Manson File* (Los Angeles: Amok, 1988); and of course, the old warhorse has returned in book and tape versions, Vincent Bugliosi with Curt Gentry, *Helter Skelter* (New York: W. W. Norton, 1974). In addition, Manson family members and alumni such as Susan Atkins, Charles "Tex" Watson, and Lynette "Squeaky" Fromme have reappeared. See Tex Watson and Chaplain Ray, *Will You Die for Me?* (Old Tappen, NJ: Fleming H. Revell Company, 1978); and Susan Atkins and Bob Slosser, *Child of Satan, Child of God* (Plainfield, NJ: Logos International, 1974); and Jess Bravin, *Squeaky: The Life and Times of Lynette Alice Fromme* (New York: Buzz Books, 1997). Manson for his part in *Manson Speaks* states that *Manson in His Own Words* has little to do with anything he said and even the semi-legendary *The Garbage People* is garbage, having nothing to do with Manson, despite Manson's nearly eighteen-year-long relationship with the author.
43. This CD is of considerable relevance in that, like the CD from the skinhead band Rahowa, *Cult of the Holy War*, the quality of *The Gospel of Inhumanity* is such that it has the potential to break out of the underground genre of the Satanist and National Socialist music scene and to cross over to a wider audience. The influence of the Blood Axis CD is such that Rahowa lead singer and entrepreneur of Resistance Records George Eric Hawthorne has expressed a desire to work with Moynahan based on his admiration for *The Gospel of Inhumanity*. See the interview with Hawthorne in the French zine *Raven Chats*: "RAHOWA Racial Holy War," *Raven Chats* 7 (n.d.). For Moynahan's noncommittal reply, see idem., "Blood Axis." *Raven Chats* neither dates its issues nor provides page numbers. On the importance of Rahowa and *Cult of the Holy War*, see Heléne Lööw, "White Power Rock 'n' Roll—A Growing Industry," and for a discussion of *The Gospel of Inhumanity*, see Jeffrey Kaplan, "Religiosity and the Radical Right: Toward the Creation of a New Ethnic Identity," both in Jeffrey Kaplan and Tore Bjørgo, eds., *Nation and Race*.
44. Blood Axis, "Herr, nun laß in Frieden," from the CD *The Gospel of Inhumanity*. It should be noted that a virtually identical scene takes place in the novel *All Quiet on the Western Front* by Erich Maria Remarque.
45. Blood Axis, "Herr, nun laß in Frieden," from the CD *The Gospel of Inhumanity*.
46. James William Gibson, *Warrior Dream: Violence and Manhood in Post-Vietnam America* (New York: Hill and Wang, 1994).
47. James Mason, *Siege!*, 345–346. This dearth of women in a movement which sees the

race as on the verge of extinction is perhaps the most vexing problem facing movement activists on both sides of the Atlantic. It is a problem to which much thought
has been given, and few answers found. Milton Kleim, e-mail message to Kaplan, 2
October 1996. In the same message, Kleim notes that: "The Manson thing made me
want to lash out in disgust."

48. Kaplan interview with James Mason, 28 November 1996.

49. James Mason, *Siege!*, 328.

50. James Mason, "Charles Manson: Illusion vs. Reality," *Resistance* 4 (Spring 1995), 21.
For a discussion of the ATWA concept, see Charles Manson, "THOUGHT," e-text
available at the official Manson web site <http://www.atwa.com/thought.htm>.

51. James Mason, "Charles Manson: Illusion vs. Reality," 22.

52. Pastor Gayman's history and theology may be found in Jeffrey Kaplan, "Context of
American Millenarian Revolutionary Theology: The Case of the 'Identity Christian'
Church of Israel," *Terrorism and Political Violence* 5:1 (Spring 1993). Updated information on Pastor Gayman's church is included in idem., *Radical Religion in America*,
9–10.

53. Kaplan interview with Dan Gayman, 9–11 December 1991.

54. Church of Israel publications in 1996 include the *Watchman*, which has been pub-
lished for the last nineteen years, and the *Vision*, which began publication in 1996.
In addition, a number of pamphlets and booklets have been produced by the Church.
Of these, one of the most illuminating from the perspective of Identity Christianity
as a millenarian religion is Dan Gayman, *A Biblical World Vision for the Last Days*
(Schell City, MO: Church of Israel, 1993).

55. Kaplan conversation with pastor Dan Gayman, 30 October 1996.

56. In a letter dated 29 February 1988, Dan Gayman wrote: "Tommy, please share these
tapes with other Israelites [in South Africa] if you will." He did and pastor Gayman's
South African flock is the result. Letter to Kaplan from Tommy Rydén, 23 September 1995. In a fax to Kaplan dated 14 November 1995 Tommy Rydén notes that
most South African Identity believers now follow the more militant teachings of Pete
Peters.

57. Kaplan conversation with pastor Dan Gayman, 30 October 1996. Pastor Gayman
notes too that the tape ministry is not exported to Europe because of cost considerations.

58. Pastor Peters's experiments with technology as a form of mission outreach is documented in Jeffrey Kaplan, *Radical Religion In America*, 7. It should be noted that among
the more effective of pastor Peters's evangelizing endeavors is his annual Scriptures
for America Bible camp which is held in the Colorado mountains.

59. "Identity Minister's Church and Property Seized," *Klanwatch Intelligence Report* (April
1993), 4. Cf., "The LaPorte Church of Christ," undated e-text from the Scriptures
for America web site.

60. As this book was going to press, this situation had begun to change in Sweden. There,
the lucrative Swedish market for white power music has provided the skinheads associated with the Nordland label and eponymous glossy magazine with the funds to
buy some farmland and experiment with communal living. The reaction of the state
and the militant antiracist organizations when this fact becomes more widely known
will be an interesting test of this thesis.

61. See for example, David Myatt, "Reichsfolk—Toward a New Elite," unpublished but
widely distributed text provided to Kaplan by David Myatt. This new elite is to be
dubbed, according to this document, the Legion of Adolf Hitler. Other Reichsfolk
titles include "The Arts of Civilisation: Aryan Culture and the Importance of Honour,
Curiosity and Conquest," and "National Socialism and the Occult," to name but a
few. Cf. Kaplan interview with David Myatt, 29 April 1996.

62. The Order of the Nine Angles have, among their other accomplishments, succeeded

in frightening a number of people. For a somewhat humorous example, see the unnerving adventures of the Reverend Kevin Logan who, having arranged for the protection and surveillance of the local constabulary, braves the dark and lonely moors of central England to conduct an interview with Christos Beest. Kevin Logan, *Satanism and the Occult: Today's Dark Revolution* (Eastbourne: Kingsway Publications, 1994), 129–137. Reverend Logan managed to survive the ordeal, and Beest, queried about the book by Kaplan, wrote a pointed letter to "Rev. Kev" about the numerous distortions he found in the text. Reverend Logan did not respond to Beest's missive.

63. Letter to Kaplan from Christos Beest 16 September 1996. Mr. Beest also notes that another closely associated organization, the Order of Balder, are in the process of putting together their own communal experiment, the Jomsberg Community, which is seen as a cultural and community center. All three groups share a web site.

64. Letter to Kaplan from Christos Beest 16 September 1996. Letter to Kaplan from Vidharr Von Herske, 22 August 1996. Typical recruiting appeals of the Bolton-era Black Order are "Black Order," and "Dualism and the Cycles of Time," all available as e-text from Kerry Bolton. Each Bolton-era Black Order essay would end with the credo: "The Black Order is an esoteric body of men and women established to presence the 'dark' or 'Shadow' side of the European unconscious."

65. The premier issue of the American Black Order's publication, the *Abyss* appeared in the summer of 1996. Since then, the group has had a falling out with members of the New Zealand branch of the Black Order over the latter's acceptance of homosexuals. As a result, the American Branch is considering a name change to the White Order and have approached R. N. Taylor as a possible leader. On the Black/White Order's change of direction, e-mail messages to Kaplan from R. N. Taylor, 22 October 1996 and 26 October 1996.

66. For details of the Swedish Black Order, see Jeffrey Kaplan, "Religiosity and the Radical Right," in Jeffrey Kaplan and Tore Bjørgo, eds., *Nation and Race*. In 1996, the Swedish Black Order was again in the headlines with the arrest of several of its adherents for the ritual sexual abuse of young girls, which included the drinking of their blood in a vampire-inspired ceremony. E-mail message to Kaplan from Heléne Lööw, 18 November 1996. Yet another murder of a homosexual followed this incident, landing Gullwang and company back in trouble. As Gullwang's Gothenburg-based mentor, the old Nazi fighter Hans Carling put it with some exasperation: "[I hoped that the boys would] stop killing people—they never get anywhere killing [a] faggot here and there—but they can't help it, the temptation is so big!" E-mail message to Kaplan from Heléne Lööw, 14 October 1997.

Chapter 7 **The Communal Dream**

1. A journalistic source for the rural American compound phenomena is James Coates, *Armed and Dangerous*, 123–156. On the Freemen, see Catherine Wessinger, "The Montana Freemen," in idem. ed., *How the Millennium Comes Violently* (Syracuse, NY: Syracuse University Press, forthcoming).

2. The best available insider description of these urban communes is Ingo Hasselbach with Tom Reiss, *Führer-Ex*. Cf. Katrina Fangen, "Living out our Ethnic Instincts: Ideological Beliefs Among Right-Wing Activists in Norway," in Jeffrey Kaplan and Tore Bjørgo, eds., *Nation and Race*.

3. Phillip Weiss, "They've had Enough," *New York Times Magazine*, 8 January 1995. Cf. Richard Abanes, *American Militias*, 184–185. For an amusing account of Gritz's ill-starred presidential campaign, see Adam Parfrey, "Guns, Gold, Groceries, Guts 'n' Gritz," in idem., *Cult Rapture*, 249–266. Parfrey's account is particularly notable for the not to be missed saga of Gritz's desert meeting with an alien from a UFO!

4. A number of sources are available for Richard Butler and the Aryan Nations. See

for example James A. Aho, *The Politics of Righteousness*; and Michael Barkun, *Religion and the Racist Right* for good academic introductions. For an insider perspective of the Order by the man whose betrayal would cost Robert Mathews his life and for an excellent journalistic treatment of the Order, see respectively Thomas Martinez with John Gunther, *Brotherhood of Murder* (New York: Pocket Books, 1990) and Kevin Flynn and Gary Gerhardt, *The Silent Brotherhood*. In a book otherwise notable for its treacly heart-on-sleeve sentimentality, a good portrait of the isolation of the latter-day Richard Butler may be found in Raphael Ezekial, *The Racist Mind*, 122–142. For the best available coverage of the Randy Weaver imbroglio and the role of the Aryan Nations in that incident, see Jess Walter, *Every Knee Shall Bow: The Truth and Tragedy of Ruby Ridge and Randy Weaver Family* (New York: ReganBooks, 1995).

5. Details of the global publicity and the interest and involvement of race activists from around the world may be found in "Aryan Nations Progress Report 1," Aryan Nations e-text (1994); and in most issues of the Aryan Nations' publication *Calling Our Nation*.

6. James A. Aho, *The Politics of Righteousness*, 59. Cf. Thor, "1,000 Political Prisoners in West Germany," *Aryan Nations* 43 (c. 1982), 1–3. Thor is identified in a footnote as: "The pen name of a former officer of the Wehrmacht during the Third Reich. He is a noted historian, an expert linguist (six languages) and one of the most knowledgeable [people] in the world of [sic] existing conditions in Germany."

7. "The Aryan Warrior's Stand," *Aryan Nations*, Foundation Edition, (1979).

8. The Aryan Nations would over the years become increasingly radical over the question of miscegenation. In 1981, the Aryan Nations issued a flier with a picture of a particular interracial couple which has been much republished throughout the white supremacist milieu titled "Death of the White Race" which admonished the faithful that "YOUR FIRST LOYALTY MUST BE TO YOUR RACE WHICH IS YOUR NATION!" The flier is reproduced in James Ridgeway, *Blood in the Face* (New York: Thunder Mouth Press, 1990), 90. By the late 1980s however, much in line with the more draconian prescriptions of the *Turner Diary's* infamous "day of the rope," the "revolutionary government of the Aryan Nations" issued a second flier titled "Race Traitors," which decreed that blacks in interracial relationships would be shot on sight and that "White persons consorting with blacks will be dealt with according to the Miscegenation Section of the Revolutionary Ethic." Undated Aryan Nations flier.

9. "The Aryan Warrior's Stand."

10. Ibid.

11. Ibid.

12. Thomas Martinez with John Gunther, *Brotherhood of Murder*, 270–271.

13. "From Aryan Nations to Anti-Hate: Floyd Cochrane Talks About the White Supremacist Movement and the Reasons He Left It," *Klanwatch Intelligence Report* (October 1993).

14. Anti-Defamation League, *Hate Groups in America*, 54.

15. Marilee Strong, "Inside the Mind of a Racist," e-text downloaded from the Public Good home page. Withrow later left the movement, and in retaliation, was literally crucified to a board and his throat was cut by his former mates.

16. For details, see Heléne Lööw, "White Power Rock 'n' Roll—A Growing Industry," and idem., "Racist Violence and Criminal Behaviour in Sweden: Myths and Reality," 123.

17. Snell's most important death row work is the book-length Richard Wayne Snell, *The Shadow of Death! (Is There Life After Death?)* (self published and privately distributed, c. 1986). For an in-depth account of Snell's often moving death row writings, see Jeffrey Kaplan, *Radical Religion in America*, 59–61. Cf. Richard Lacayo, "The State Versus McVeigh," *Time Magazine On-line edition*, vol. 147, no. 16 (15 April 1996); and Anti-Defamation League, *Paranoia as Patriotism: Far Right Influences in the Mili-*

tia Movement (New York: ADL, 1996), 17–18.

18. William F. Jasper, "More Pieces to the OKC Puzzle," *New American,* vol. 12, no. 13 (June 24, 1996), 4–11. This welcome may be credited to the fact that James Ellison is married to Robert Millar's granddaughter. Whether Ellison continues to practice polygamy at Elohim City is unreported, however.

19. Mark S. Hamm, *Apocalypse in Oklahoma: Waco and Ruby Ridge Revenged* (Boston, MA: Northeastern University Press), 172–173.

20. Alijandra Mogilner, The McVeigh-Kohl Connection," e-text article available on web sites as diverse as Nazi Alert on the left and the Jewish Defense League Home page (!) on the right.

21. William F. Jasper, "More Pieces to the OKC Puzzle." Richard Lacayo, "The State Versus McVeigh."

22. One such was Gustav Niebuhr of the *New York Times.* Kaplan conversation with Gustav Niebuhr, December 1995. The best academic paper on Elohim City to emerge so far is Somer Shook, Wesley Delano, and Robert W. Balch, "Elohim City: A Participant-Observation Study of a Christian Identity Community," paper presented to the Communal Studies Association, Tacoma, Washington, 11 October 1997.

23. "Three Arrested in Alleged Bomb Plot," *CNN News Briefs,* 13 November 1995.

24. Dirk Johnson, "Lost in Freemen Standoff: First a Father, Now a Farm," *New York Times,* 10 June 1996; James Brooke, "Armed Group in Montana Has Sown Hate and Fear," *New York Times,* 31 March 1996. On the Republic of Texas, see Sam Howe Verhovek, "Before Armed Standoff, Texan Waged War on Neighbors," *New York Times,* 2 May 1997. For the reaction of the Republic of Texas itself, see "McLaren's Lawless Actions Condemned!!," Republic of Texas, 28 April 1997, e-text from Republic of Texas homepage.

25. Experience has taught Butler that the skinheads and the more staid, family-oriented regulars at the Aryan Nations' Annual Congress do not mix well. Thus, a special day for the skinheads is held on 20 April to celebrate Hitler's birthday.

26. Jost left the National Socialist movement at the end of his life, and out of respect to his wife who is loath to speak of this time, his real name will not be used.

27. James A. Aho, *The Politics of Righteousness,* 57.

28. *NSV Report,* vol. 2, no.3 (Jul/Sep 1984). Cooper today states that the Wolfstadt dream is officially dormant—a victim of a lack of funds and the dearth of individuals in the NS community with whom he (or for that matter, almost anyone else) would care to live in close proximity. Kaplan interview with Rick Cooper, 2 September 1997.

29. News of Jost's death spread quickly throughout the movement's jungle telegraph, and was publicized most widely through the medium of the Resistance Records electronic mail newsletter. See the *Resistance Records Electronic Newsletter,* vol. 2, no. 31 (14 October 1996). Cf. *NSV Report* 14:4 (October/December 1997), 8.

30. Undated fax to Kaplan from Tommy Rydén. Rydén is doing the translation and, although he notes that there are some aspects that he does not agree with, he and his family have become practitioners of Arya Kriya techniques.

31. This transition/alliance relationship between hippie and neo-Nazi culture is hardly unique to America. For a precisely analogous evolution in East Germany, see Ingo Hasselbach with Tom Reiss, *Führer-Ex.* For younger adherents, a similar process sees movement from essentially left-wing and anarchist punk culture to skinhead culture—often of the neo-Nazi variety. Kaplan interview with *Nordland* editor Peter Milander, and with Nitton, lead singer of Midgårds Söner, 7 August 1995, Stockholm, Sweden. Cf. Mark S. Hamm, *American Skinheads.*

32. Jost, "Aryan Destiny: Back To The Land," undated e-text distributed by the National Socialist Kindred.

33. See for example, Manfred Roeder, "South Africa is not Lost," *Folkish Observations* (1993), e-text from the National Socialist Kindred; Colin Jordan, "National

Socialism: Then And Now: A Philosophical Appraisal," *National Socialist Kindred* (n.d.); and David Lane Wodensson, "Divided Loyalties," *National Socialist Kindred* (n.d.).

34. Kaplan interview with Steve McNallen, 1 May 1996; Kaplan interview with Larry White, 29 April 1996; e-mail message to Kaplan from R.N. Taylor, 5 November 1996. On the American Ásatrú community, see Stephen E. Flowers, "Revival of Germanic Religion in Contemporary Anglo-American Culture," *The Mankind Quarterly*, vol. XXI, no. 3 (Spring 1981); Jeffrey Kaplan, "The Reconstruction of the Ásatrú and Odinist Traditions," in James Lewis, ed., *Magical Religions and Modern Witchcraft* (Albany, NY: SUNY Press, 1996); or idem., *Radical Religion in America*.

35. Jost, *The Essentials of Mein Kampf* (Volksberg, CA: NS Kindred, 1988).

36. Jost, "Love: An Eternal law of Nature and first Tenet of National Socialism," undated flyer from the National Socialist Kindred.

37. Jost, "ARYAN DESTINY: Why Hitler had to be Overcome," pamphlet from the National Socialist Kindred (1989).

38. Letter from Jost to Tommy Rydén, 10 May 1996.

39. "Arya Kriya: Vetenskapen om påskyndad evolution," undated poster issued by the DeVries Institute (c. 1996); fax to Kaplan from Tommy Rydén, 21 October 1996. The DeVries Institute is a survivor from the period in which Rydén led the Swedish Church of the Creator and is named for Arno DeVries, the author of *Salubrious Living*, the only COTC book not written by Ben Klassen.

40. For an academic overview of these questions, see Les Back, Michael Keith and John Solomos, "Racism on the Internet: Mapping Neo-Fascist Subcultures in Cyberspace," in Jeffrey Kaplan and Tore Bjørgo, eds., *Nation and Race*.

41. This argument is based on Colin Campbell's early 1970s theoretical work with the cultic milieu. Further references were suggested in the introduction to this book. For a still unsurpassed movement view of the phenomenon, see Louis Beam, *The Seditionist* 1 (Winter 1988). Utilizing the ZOG discourse, Beam states that, for the movement, "the tenets of the 1940's, '50s, '60s, and '70s will some day seem as quaint and strange as former belief in the flatness of the earth does now." Beam, ever the visionary, foresaw the cornerstones of movement ideology which would emerge as including white separatism, the widespread acceptance of some elements of Christian Identity doctrine, and an acceptance of the models offered by the Third World (i.e., nonwhite) liberation struggles of colonized peoples from around the world.

42. For a dry rendition of these events, see "Beam Captured," *Klanwatch Intelligence Report*, no. 35 (December 1987), 1, 3.

43. Anti-Defamation League, *Computerized Networks of Hate* (New York: ADL, 1985). The second BBS was run by the Pennsylvania-based neo-Nazi George Dietz, whose Liberty Bell publications offers one of the larger selections of movement books and World War II Nazi artifacts available. In the case of Beam's Aryan Net, the BBS consisted of a number of files freely available to all, and a smaller menu of "secret" files supposedly open only to those with a password. As the charges against Beam for the internal system's contents at Fort Smith indicate, neither the government nor the watchdogs had much difficulty obtaining the requisite passwords.

44. On the Fifth Era Klan, see the series of essays Beam co-authored with John C. Calhoun, "The Perfected Order of the Klan," in the *Inter-Klan Newsletter and Survival Alert* (c. 1984). For a concise review of Beam's career from the watchdog perspective, see Anti-Defamation League, *Extremism on the Right*, 66–67. The vision of Beam as an armed psychopath is drawn from Bill Stanton, *Klanwatch: Bringing the Klan to Justice* (New York: Grove Weidenfeld, 1991).

45. "Computers and Patriots," *The Seditionist* 10 (Summer 1991), 8.

46. Louis Beam, "Computers and the American Patriot," *Inter-Klan Newsletter and Survival Alert* (c. 1984). It should be noted that during its short lifetime, the *Inter-Klan*

Newsletter and Survival Alert did not see fit to aid future scholars by providing such data as numbered issues, dates, or even page numbers.

47. "Computers and Patriots," *The Seditionist* 10, 8–10.
48. Sources here are many and varied. The watchdog perspective is summed up in Anti-Defamation League, *The Web of Hate: Extremists Exploit the Internet.* A good scholarly source which includes some technical explanations and a concise history of the technology is offered by David Capitanick and Michael Whine, *The Governance of Cyberspace: The Far Right on the Internet.* A concise insider account is provided by Milton John Kleim, Jr., "Internet-Recruiting," in Jeffrey Kaplan, *Encyclopedia of White Power* (Golleta, CA: ABC-CLIO, forthcoming). For Don Black's view, see Lori Rozsa, "High-tech Hate: Ex KKK Member Goes On Line," *Knight-Ridder-Washington,* 17 March 1995.
49. Kleim, "Internet-Recruiting."
50. Milton John Kleim e-mail message to Kaplan, 15 December 1996. In late 1997, the ANA list disappeared following its Internet provider's decision to cancel their account.
51. This service was interrupted in as a result of Hawthorn's incarceration on assault charges and the April 1997 raid by Canadian and American authorities on Resistance Records. In 1998, Hawthorn quietly left the movement. The *Resistance* magazine and email list is thus defunct. The Swedish Nordland music label sent several people to the U.S. to keep the Resistance Records label in operation.
52. Anti-Defamation League, *The Web of Hate,* 13.
53. Milton John Kleim, Jr., "On Strategy and Tactics for Usenet." The full e-text version was at one time archived at a racist site, but this soon vanished. E-mail message from Kleim to Kaplan, 24 December 1996. This mercurial aspect of information is typical of the virtual realm. A short version remains available from the NIZKOR archives <http://www.nizkor.org/>. Cf. Anti-Defamation League, *Hate Group Recruitment on the Internet* (New York: ADL, 1995). Ironically, two of the three individuals most heavily featured in the ADL report, Kleim and Ronald C. Schoedel III, have left the movement, and according to Kleim, Schoedel is "like me, more interested in women [than the movement] now." E-mail message from Kleim to Kaplan, 15 November 1996.
54. Milton John Kleim, Jr., "On Strategy and Tactics for Usenet." The history of this document gives remarkable insight into the closed world of the cyberspace war between racist and antiracists. Kleim originally wrote the essay as an "eyes-only" document intended for top-level activists. It was sent out only to the most trusted subscribers of Kleim's ANA list. It quickly fell into the hands of Ken McVay of the Nizkor Project which groups together net watchdogs. McVay lost no time in posting it in the Nizkor archives. Kleim was decidedly "NOT pleased" and so he wrote an expanded version which was widely distributed. Milton Kleim email message to Kaplan, 18 December 1996.
55. Kleim, "Internet-Recruiting."
56. The story of the effort to provide the subscribers to alt.support.lonliness with a friendly racist to talk to may be found in "A Campaign to Limit the Voices of White Supremacists on the Internet Has Defenders of the First Amendment Worried," *Time Magazine Electronic Edition,* vol. 147, no. 4, 22 January 1996.
57. E-mail messages from Milton Kleim to Kaplan, 2 October 1996 and 15 November 1996.
58. Milton John Kleim, Jr., "Duty," e-text briefly available from Kleim homepage.
59. One of the most notable of these is Greg Withrow whose speech to the Aryan Nations' congress was noted above. See Marilee Strong, "Inside the Mind of a Racist." E-mail message from Kleim to Kaplan, 2 October 1996. For further reflections on this question, see the following chapter's discussion with Tommy Rydén.

60. This evolution may be noted in a series of e-mail exchanges between Kleim and Kaplan in October and November, 1996.
61. Milton J. Kleim, Jr., "Duty."
62. Kaplan interview with Ken McVay, 5 July 1997; Kaplan interview with John Drobniki, 1 July 1997.
63. The NIZKOR address is <http://www.nizkor.org>. A good view of the various approaches taken by the watchdog groups to the "web of hate" is provided by Pamela Mendels, "Monitoring the Growing Web of Hate," *New York Times Electronic Edition,* 12 November 1996. For an academic view, see David Capitanick and Michael Wine, *The Governance of Cyberspace.*
64. A fairly comprehensive listing, *sans* addresses, may be found in the Anti-Defamation League, *The Web of Hate.* At this time, the most exhaustive set of links to the newest racialist homepages (with useful links to Holocaust-denial sites, militia sites, conspiracy organizations and such oddities as the Satanist site, the Alter of Unholy Blasphemy, is available from the Bizarre Webpage which is run by an antiracist who finds the proliferation of racism on the net so appalling that he wishes to direct everyone's attention to it. His view, probably correct in our judgment, is that for most people to see these sites will result in precisely the opposite of the intended effect— it will repel rather than serve as an attractive medium for recruitment. The Bizarre Webpage may be accessed at <http://www.tcac.com/%7Esteveb/bizarre.html>.
65. George Lincoln Rockwell, *This Time the World,* 193.
66. Marcus Kabel, "Computer Links Strengthen German neo-Nazis," *Reuters,* 15 December 1993; "Cyber Nazis Baffle German Police," *Calgary Herald,* 2 February 1994; and Elizabeth Neuffer, "Neo-Nazis Spreading Hate With High Tech: Global Networking Aids German Cells," *Boston Globe,* 12 June 1994. An interesting journalistic exposé of the German movements is provided by Michael Schmidt, *The New Reich: Violent Extremism in Unified Germany and Beyond* (New York: Pantheon, 1993).
67. Chris Cobb, "Censoring Internet Can't Stop Zundel," *Calgary Herald,* 6 February 1996; and David Capitanick and Michael Wine, *The Governance of Cyberspace.* For a movement view of the implications of net censorship, see Louis R. Beam, "Conspiracy to Erect an Electronic Iron Curtain," e-text available from both the Stormfront and Aryan Crusaders' Library websites.
68. "Germany Drafts Multimedia Law Regulating Internet," *Yahoo!-Reuters News,* 11 November 1996. The Germans are nothing if not dogged, however. In December 1996 they redrafted the law yet again. "Bonn Cracks Down of Internet," *Yahoo!-Reuters News,* 12 December 1996.

Chapter 8   *Tommy Rydén: A National Socialist Life*

1. For example, Herbert Hillary Booker, an American Nazi Party veteran who is blessed with what he cheerfully admits to be an at best slight artistic gift found in the 1980s a link with Michael McLaughlin's British Nationalist and Socialist Movement which was stronger than any he could find in the U.S.
2. This strictly vegetarian, caffeine- and alcohol-free regimen is described in the Church of the Creator text *Salubrious Living.*
3. Kaplan interview with Tommy Rydén, 28 July 1995.
4. Kaplan interview with Tommy Rydén, 22 February 1997.
5. Kaplan interview with Tommy Rydén, 22 February 1997.
6. Kaplan interview with Tommy Rydén, 28 July 1995. In other interviews, Rydén places the age at which he contacted the Klan at closer to thirteen. The younger age is more likely as when the incident involving the Gypsies occurred when he turned fifteen, he was already in contact with Wilkinson.
7. Kaplan interview with Tommy Rydén, 22 February 1997.

8. Anti-Defamation League, *Extremism on the Right*, 27–28.
9. "Some of the Best of Bill Wilkinson and the Invisible Empire of the KKK," cassette tape distributed by the Invisible Empire (n.d.).
10. John George and Laird Wilcox, *American Extremists*, 43.
11. Kaplan interview with Tommy Rydén, 22 February 1997.
12. This sense of the superior effectiveness of the American movement was noted previously in these pages with regard to the Swedish National Socialist leader Göran Assar Oredsson's over-estimation of the size and strength of Rockwell's American Nazi Party.
13. Kaplan interview with Tommy Rydén, 22 February 1997.
14. Kaplan interview with Tommy Rydén, 22 February 1997.
15. Ron Michaelson is an American National Socialist whose letters and materials have appeared in a variety of NS publications over the years. Recently married, Mr. Michaelson was kind enough to provide Kaplan with a videotape of his wedding which integrated elements of National Socialism into the ceremony.
16. Heléne Lööw interview with anonymous adherent. In Heléne Lööw, "Racist Youth Culture in Sweden: Ideology, Mythology and Lifestyle," unpublished paper.
17. Among younger National Socialists, this view is becoming increasingly prevalent, and is a tenet of faith within the skinhead music subculture. No better encapsulation of this view could be offered than the recent anthology CD containing tracks from white noise bands from Poland, Spain, Portugal, Great Britain, Italy, Germany, the Czech Republic, Slovakia, Italy, and Sweden evocatively titled "No More Brother Wars." The CD is distributed by Di-Al Records.
18. Heléne Lööw interview with Tommy Rydén, 17 July 1991. In Heléne Lööw, "Swedish National Socialism and Right Wing Extremism After 1945."
19. Heléne Lööw, "'Wir Sind Wieder Da.'"
20. In these years, Rydén made some quixotic attempts to form organizations of his own. Three of these, Konservativt Forum, Motståndsrörelsen and Imperium were merely self-described "paper tigers . . . newsletters not organizations." On the eve of his departure for South Africa, a more serious organizational venture, Västerländska Motståndsrörelsen, intended as "some kind of John Birch Society," had more serious intent, but was quickly subsumed in the excitement of the imminent move. E-mail message to Kaplan, 17 June 1997.
21. Kaplan conversation with Tommy Rydén, 28 July 1995; e-mail message to Kaplan from Tommy Rydén 6 July 1997. Rydén adds in this context: "For me, the White woman symbolizes the beauty in this world."
22. Kaplan interview with Tommy Rydén, 28 July 1995.
23. Eugene TerreBlanche was sentenced to six years in prison in 1997 for beating one of his black workers who was caught eating on the job. "Neo-Nazi Chief Gets Jail Term in South Africa," *New York Times*, 18 June 1997.
24. That activist was Torulf Magnussen. Magnussen, a young friend and admirer of Tommy Rydén, is today associated with the white power band Svastika for whom he writes Odinist-inspired lyrics, and with the Swedish music magazine *Nordland*. Magnussen's South African experience was less idyllic than Rydén's. He too recalls the meeting which the two expatriate Swedish racialists unbeknownst to each other attended. His other experiences however, were not as sanguine. Although he can laugh about it today, Magnussen's South African adventure was probably more typical of the lives of young European racialists in Southern Africa. Promised a job and a place to stay if he moved to South Africa, Magnussen eagerly jumped at the opportunity for the same reasons as did Tommy Rydén. However, work was not so easily found and the virulently racist Magnussen eventually found himself working for very little pay in a factory in which he was the only white in a sea of black African laborers! Things went downhill from there, and Magnussen soon returned to his

native Linköping. Kaplan interview with Torulf Magnussen, Linköping, Sweden, 19 February 1997.

25. Letter from Tommy Rydén, 23 September 1995. All emphasis as in original.
26. Kaplan interview with Tommy Rydén, 28 July 1995.
27. Letter to Kaplan, 23 September 1995; fax to Kaplan, 14 November 1995.
28. For just such a "death of the COTC" analysis, replete with a mocking epitaph from Harold Covington, see Jeffrey Kaplan, *Radical Religion in America*, 41–42. For Hale's decision to assume the leadership of the remnants of the post-Klassen COTC, see "My Hopes for Unification," *The Struggle* VI (December 1995), 1. This issue includes the eight point self-defense program of the reconstituted COTC.
29. Ben Klassen, *Trials, Tribulations and Triumphs* (East Peoria, IL: COTC, 1993), 1.
30. For an analysis of the sixteen Commandments, see Jeffrey Kaplan, "Right Wing Violence in North America," in Tore Bjørgo, ed., *Terror from the Extreme Right*, 64–66. The original sixteen Commandments can be seen in Ben Klassen, *The White Man's Bible* (Otto, NC: Church of the Creator, 1981), 408–409.
31. Chapter and verse on these problems is chronicled in Ben Klassen, *Trials, Tribulations and Triumphs*.
32. These ideas are expounded at remarkable length in Ben Klassen, *Nature's Eternal Religion*; idem., *The White Man's Bible*; idem., *Expanding Creativity*; idem., *Building a Whiter and Brighter World*; and idem., *Rahowa! The Planet is Ours*. All are COTC publications.
33. Kaplan interview with Tommy Rydén, 22 February 1997.
34. Kaplan interview with Tommy Rydén, 28 July 1995.
35. Letter to Rydén, 24 August 1988.
36. The official resignation, published under the imprimatur of the De Vries-Institutet's July-August 1995 newsletter, decried in particular the increasing negativity of the post-Klassen COTC.
37. Tommy Rydén, "Kreativistens Kyrka," in Jeffrey Kaplan, *Encyclopedia of White Power*.
38. Rydén describes this experience in stark terms in an open letter to his fellow Creators in the August 1991 issue of *Racial Loyalty* (p. 4). Rydén was originally given only a fine. The jail sentence was tacked on after he appealed the conviction.
39. Rydén humorously notes this problem in retrospect: "Yes, I think too much time was spent on criticizing people. And too much money was spent on printing books and newspapers, [there] should have been a different marketing plan for the COTC." Kaplan interview with Tommy Rydén, 22 February 1997.
40. Ben Klassen, *Trials, Tribulations and Triumphs*, 128.
41. Letter from a COTC Reverend [name withheld] to Tommy Rydén, 20 August 1989. The capitalization as in original.
42. Letter from Hasta Primus Will Williams to Tommy Rydén, 19 March 1989. The same letter congratulates Tommy and Maud on their engagement.
43. Letter from Rydén to Kaplan, March 1997 (the day had inadvertently been omitted from the letter).
44. Kaplan interview with Maud Rydén, 28 June 1997.
45. It must be noted here that the propaganda aspect of Rydén's COTC activities constituted a violation of the Swedish law forbidding incitement to racial hatred and would ultimately cost Tommy Rydén a prison sentence. It must be noted too that the same activity—distributing *Racial Loyalty*—would be considered protected speech in the U.S. under the provisions of the First Amendment.
46. Grundskolan in Sweden is equivalent to elementary school. Gymnasiet is for students aged 17 to 18 and functions as a sort of cross between a junior college and a high school.
47. Kaplan interview with Maud Rydén, 28 June 1997.
48. Kaplan interview with Tommy Rydén, 22 February 1997. Rydén notes that a young

racialist can make no greater error than to try to hide or "finesse" his views when getting to know a woman. There is simply no way to compartmentalize this part of the activist's life, and not being completely honest from the outset will invariably doom the relationship. On the other hand, as a practical matter, it is better not to be overly vociferous at the outset, lest the potential mate be frightened away. With Maud, Tommy Rydén recalls having perhaps in retrospect "pushed the envelope" a bit in their early meetings.

49. Kaplan interview with Maud Rydén, 28 June 1997. The books referred to are *Nature's Eternal Religion* and the *White Man's Bible*.

50. Kaplan interview with Maud Rydén, 28 June 1997.

51. Kaplan interview with Tommy Rydén, 28 July 1995.

52. Klassen's death was announced to the Creativity faithful in "Letter to all Creators from Dr. Rick McCarty," 12 August 1993. Word of McCarty's disappearance with the group's funds was disseminated in a number of ways, including a plea for funds in a document titled "Northeast Director's Report," 11 April 1994. Tommy Rydén apprised the Swedish movement of the news in an undated flyer, "Judas Rick McCarty Upplöser COTC."

53. David Koresh and the Branch Davidians did not fail to capture Rydén's attention, and he lost no time in getting in touch with one of the surviving Davidians in the U.S., from whom he obtained copies of tapes made during the Waco siege. Indeed, Rydén's curiosity is insatiable, leading him to seek to contact individuals and groups as disparate as the Jewish Third Temple movement and the former president of the Bosnian Serb Republic (and indicted war criminal) Dr. Radovan Karadzic, who was moved to opine: "I must tell you I was deeply touched reading your words of support. Your letter was the proof that our fight for our ancestors' land was understood properly after all. We are always happy to know that not all the world is against us, and that the ordinary people like yourself understand our aims and are with us." Letter to Tommy Rydén from Dr. Radovan Karadzic, 8 November 1996.

54. Letter to Kaplan from Tommy Rydén, 13 October 1995.

55. Rydén notes that the fledgling group did not contact him so as to learn from past mistakes. E-mail message from Tommy Rydén, 17 June 1997.

56. On the baptism, letter to Kaplan from Tommy Rydén, 3 May 1996. On the Kosmostheist Church, letter to Kaplan from Tommy Rydén, 3 December 1996, and on the failure of that endeavor, e-mail message to Kaplan 6 July 1997, in which Rydén notes "People in the movement are consumers, not activists"; on Arya Kriya, letter to Kaplan from Tommy Rydén, 5 July 1996; and on the Hembygdspartiet, Tommy Rydén, "Hembygdspartiet," in Jeffrey Kaplan, *Encyclopedia of White Power*. The *Nordland* association is kept somewhat quiet due to the fact that anyone found editing the magazine is subject to a jail term under Swedish laws dealing with incitement to racial hatred. Peter Millander (neé Rindell) was the last to receive this perk of office.

57. Tore Bjørgo, "Entry, Bridge-Burning and Exit Options: What Happens to Young People Who Join Racist Groups—And Want to Leave?," in Jeffrey Kaplan and Tore Bjørgo, eds., *Nation and Race*.

58. In Sweden, not only does the state in effect subsidize antistate activists from a bewildering variety of causes, but through the use of "protected identities," the government hides and protects activists from reprisals by opposing activists (and occasionally from the local police investigating crimes committed by those with protected identities).

59. Fax from Tommy Rydén to Kaplan, 13 April 1997.

60. E-mail message to Kaplan, 6 July 1997.

61. Rydén takes some exception to the anti-Semitic label, noting that it is not a precise fit for his more nuanced view of Jews. Rydén's description of his refusal to condemn

Jews *in toto* was noted above. In this regard, he notes as well that in *Nordland* (nos. 7–8, 50), he had positive comments regarding the late Jewish militant, Rabbi Meir Kahane (the only Jewish figure against which the ADL felt obliged to issue an oppositional tract). Moreover, "Tzvi Katzover, the Jewish mayor in the Kiryat Arba community [in Hebron] in Israel wrote a friendly letter to me in May this year [1997] after . . . I had written a letter to his settlers where I stated that although I was reluctant to choose side[s] in the Middle East conflict I nevertheless had to admit that they appeared to be much smarter and [more] dedicated than the Arabs. So no, I do not hate those Jews who fight for their own people down there. But I do hate those who try to blackmail Swiss banks and who try to force their exaggerated war stories upon our children." E-mail to Kaplan from Tommy Rydén, 6 July 1997.

62. Kaplan interview with Tommy Rydén, 22 February 1997.
63. This element of fear is important. Maud Rydén notes that even people who visit the Rydén home for one reason or another are clearly afraid. This was brought home to Kaplan in particularly graphic form in Linköping, Sweden, in 1997. While interviewing skinhead activist Torulf Magnusson in a coffee shop—and even more while walking with him through the streets—it became apparent that a number of people would turn and stare with genuine fear as he passed. Asked about this, Magnusson was clearly embarrassed. To be a local object of dread does wonders for a teenager's ego, but with age, the situation can become very uncomfortable for all concerned.
64. Letter to Kaplan from Tommy Rydén, 21 May 1996.

Conclusion

1. Roger Griffin, *The Nature of Fascism*, 164–165.
2. While we realize that the movement has seen some "creative" approaches to fund raising in the recent past—from the short term capital acquisition of the Order's armored car robberies on the American side and a wave of European imitators in the 1980s to the more secure base of the taxable profits generated by such "white noise" music labels as Resistance in the United States and Nordland and Ragnörok in Sweden—it is too early to be certain what if any impact this will have on the movement's traditional penury.
3. See, Robert Nisbet, *The Sociological Imagination* (New York: Basic Books, 1966), 47–106.

Index

About the Authors

JEFFREY KAPLAN is an assistant professor of history at Ilisagvik College in Barrow, Alaska. He is the author of *Radical Religion in America: Millenarian Movements From the Far Right to the Children of Noah* (Syracuse, NY: Syracuse University Press, 1997); and has co-edited several volumes on the transatlantic radical right including Jeffrey Kaplan and Tore Bjørgo, *Nation and Race: The Developing Euro-American Racist Subculture* (Boston, MA: Northeastern University Press, 1998); and Jeffrey Kaplan and Heléne Lööw, *Rejected and Suppressed Knowledge: The Racist Right and the Cultic Milieu* (Stockholm: Swedish National Council of Crime Prevention, forthcoming 1998). His articles on the radical right and on religious violence have appeared in such publications as *Terrorism and Political Violence*, *Christian Century*, *Syzygy*, and *Nova Religio*, for which he serves as book review editor. With Leonard Weinberg, he was awarded a Harry Frank Guggenheim Foundation Research Grant in 1995. In 1997, Kaplan was awarded the Fulbright Bicentennial Chair in American Studies at the University of Helsinki for the 1998–1999 academic year.

LEONARD WEINBERG is Foundation Professor of Political Science at the University of Nevada, Reno. He has also been a visiting professor at the University of Florence (1992) and was a Fulbright Senior Research Fellow for Italy in 1984. His recent books include *The Revival of Right Wing Extremism in the Nineties*, *Encounters with the Contemporary Radical Right* (both edited with Peter Merkl), and *The Transformation of Italian Communism*. Weinberg's articles have appeared in the *British Journal of Political Science*, *Comparative Politics*, *Party Politics*, the *Journal of Terrorism of Political Violence* and other professional journals.